Best Rail Trails
PACIFIC NORTHWEST

Help Us Keep This Guide Up to Date

Every effort has been made by the author and editors to make this guide as accurate and useful as possible. However, many things can change after a guide is published—trails are rerouted, regulations change, facilities come under new management, and so forth.

We would love to hear from you concerning your experiences with this guide and how you feel it could be improved and kept up to date. While we may not be able to respond to all comments and suggestions, we'll take them to heart, and we'll also make certain to share them with the author. Please send your comments and suggestions to the following email address: falconeditorial@rowman.com.

Thanks for your input, and happy trails!

Best Rail Trails
PACIFIC NORTHWEST

MORE THAN 60 RAIL TRAILS IN WASHINGTON, OREGON, AND IDAHO

THIRD EDITION

NATALIE L. BARTLEY

FALCONGUIDES

Essex, Connecticut

FALCONGUIDES®

An imprint of Globe Pequot, the trade division of The Rowman & Littlefield Publishing Group, Inc.
4501 Forbes Blvd., Ste. 200
Lanham, MD 20706
www.rowman.com

Falcon and FalconGuides are registered trademarks and Make Adventure Your Story is a trademark of The Rowman & Littlefield Publishing Group, Inc.

Distributed by NATIONAL BOOK NETWORK

Photos by Natalie L. Bartley unless otherwise noted
Maps by Melissa Baker and The Rowman & Littlefield Publishing Group, Inc.

British Library Cataloguing in Publication Information available

Library of Congress Cataloging-in-Publication Data

Names: Bartley, Natalie L., author.
Title: Best rail trails. Pacific Northwest: more than 60 rail trails in Washington, Oregon, and Idaho / Natalie L. Bartley.
Other titles: Pacific Northwest
Description: Third edition. | Essex, Connecticut: Falcon Guides, [2023]
Identifiers: LCCN 2022046363 (print) | LCCN 2022046364 (ebook) | ISBN 9781493065042 (paperback) | ISBN 9781493065059 (epub)
Subjects: LCSH: Rail-trails—Northwest, Pacific—Guidebooks. | Outdoor recreation—Northwest, Pacific—Guidebooks. | Northwest, Pacific—Guidebooks.
Classification: LCC GV191.42.N75 B37 2023 (print) | LCC GV191.42.N75 (ebook) | DDC 917.9704/44—dc23/eng/20220928
LC record available at https://lccn.loc.gov/2022046363
LC ebook record available at https://lccn.loc.gov/2022046364

♾️™ The paper used in this publication meets the minimum requirements of American National Standard for Information Sciences—Permanence of Paper for Printed Library Materials, ANSI/NISO Z39.48-1992.

CONTENTS

IDAHO

ACKNOWLEDGMENTS

My heartfelt thanks go to dozens of people who willingly gave their time to bring this book's updated version to reality. Trail managers in all three states unselfishly agreed to discuss and review details regarding their trails, putting aside their own deadlines to do so. For example, professionals such as Kevin Lease, ranger at Wallace Falls State Park, Cody Swander, assistant parks and recreation director for City of Nampa, and Matt Sawyer, marketing director for the Route of the Hiawatha, all contributed in-depth reviews of trails. Managers and advisors such as Robert Foxworthy, King County Parks and Recreation regional trail coordinator, Jared Bowman, North Zone recreation manager with the Malheur National Forest, and Ben Mayberry, Snoqualmie recreation maintenance and use manager with the Washington State Department of Natural Resources, filled me in on trail details. Various bike shops throughout the region provided further insight about trends, trail conditions, and accessibility. Information experts from chambers of commerce / visitor centers and governmental agency staffers such as Michael Wentworth, visitor information volunteer at the Astoria-Warrenton Visitors Center, Penny Wagner, public affairs specialist with the Olympic National Park, and Katijo Maher, visitor information specialist at the Snoqualmie National Forest expanded on trail features. To all the other trail consultants, please forgive me if I have not included you; you are in my thoughts, and I offer you gratitude for your time and interest regarding this project.

Love, light, and laughter go to my family and friends, including Dave Lindsay, Carol Peterson, Piper Lee, Katja Burmester, and Julie Stutts. A big thank-you is due to David Legere, editorial editor at Globe Pequot/FalconGuides, for his understanding and support during the book preparation process. I'd also like to thank production editor, Felicity Tucker; copyeditor, Melissa Hayes; and cartographer, Melissa Baker. Lastly, kudos to Mia Barbera, the author of an early edition regarding rail trails in Washington and Oregon. It's been my pleasure to rebuild and update three more editions by retracing her prior work, adding Idaho trails, and updating information for this edition regarding the ever-expanding network of rail trails in the Pacific Northwest.

INTRODUCTION

The rail trails of Washington, Oregon, and Idaho provide scenic refuge, education, history, play, and physical adventure. Pick your trails and enjoy the surrounding cities, towns, and landscapes.

Trails described in these pages range from a 12-foot-wide paved path to a narrow, rugged, dirt singletrack. You'll look out over an unobstructed view of the Columbia River, up to surrounding desert canyon walls, ahead through dense evergreen forest, or down upon neighborhood homes. Skaters, bicyclists, equestrians, anglers, walkers, runners, skiers, snowshoers, and strollers join together to get fit, get relaxed, or get to work in these linear parks. The trails skirt wineries, dams, cultural centers, waterfalls, old mines, rivers, lakes, fine dining, breweries, and the ocean.

The region is graced with waterfalls such as Snoqualmie Falls in Washington, accessible from rail trails.

Dave Lindsay

A Bit of Pacific Northwest Rail History

The Pacific Northwest is separated east from west by the Cascade Mountains. Agriculture built the east, where you'll find distinct seasons and striking rock formations. Logging dominated the temperate western side, which features lush forests and interesting urban centers.

Before the railroad reached them, Washington, Oregon, and Idaho were islands, their geographic isolation restricting trade. The story of how the railroad got here fills volumes. Territorial and financial politics, bankruptcy, buyouts, personal glory, personal breakdown, and financial maneuvering paint as chaotic and colorful a picture as you'll find in any chunk of history.

Simply getting to the mountain passes in winter to scope out a railroad route left engineers fighting for their lives. Even after the tracks were built, traveling over passes, below rock cliffs, above rivers, and through tunnels put rail passengers at risk of smoke asphyxiation and avalanches of snow and rock. In fact, the worst disaster in railroad history played out on Stevens Pass in 1910. A heavy snowstorm stopped one train on the tracks. After the frightened passengers watched rockslides and collapsing

A bridge passes over an inlet on Crescent Lake along the Spruce Railroad Trail in Washington.
Dave Lindsay

trees for eight days, an avalanche shoved the railcars off the track into the valley below. Ninety-six people lost their lives.

In 1850 railroads were experimental; few lines in the country were more than 150 miles long. In 1851 the first tracks were set down in the Pacific Northwest—a crude 6-mile portage line built alongside the Cascades Rapids on the Washington side of the Columbia River. The train was not powered by an engine; instead, the flatcars were hauled by mules. The first steam train arrived in 1862. By 1863, 19 miles of track had been laid in Oregon and 6 in Washington, all beside the Columbia River. Because the rapids were impassable by steamboats on this important inland water route, railroad portages picked up each load and dropped it off at a ship on the other side of the turbulent waters. The next set of tracks was built over the following decade to serve the agricultural Willamette Valley in Oregon.

Meanwhile, in Idaho railroad service first arrived in 1874 in the southeastern part of the state. Another boost to service in the Pacific Northwest was the completion of the Oregon Short Line across southern Idaho in 1884. Known as an outlet for the Union Pacific Railroad, it went through the Snake River Valley in Idaho and on to Portland, Oregon.

Finally, in 1883 the first tracks reached the Pacific Northwest from the East; however, the dream of reaching the Pacific Coast had started decades earlier. In 1864 the US Congress authorized the largest land grant in American history: A 60-million-acre swath the size of New England, extending from Lake Superior to the Pacific Ocean, was given to the Northern Pacific Railway. Even when you subtract the land that the company forfeited by failing to meet deadlines, Northern Pacific netted 39 million acres from this deal—twice the size of any other railroad grant. As a result, when many railroads consolidated into the Burlington Northern Railroad in 1970, this company became one of the largest private landholders in the country.

Northern Pacific's land grant provided it with timber to build tracks and cash from land sales. Land sales adjacent to the railroad path served another purpose. While Eastern railroads were built between existing towns and transportation centers, this line would—in the words of one cynic—"have to generate passengers and freight revenue by running from nowhere in particular to nowhere at all, through thousands of miles of rugged and lightly populated country." The railroads of the West, in other words, would have to foster development. The area had no investors or capital; only the federal government could finance this project. The railroad would have to build the need for trains.

Due to financial problems, the Oregon Railway and Navigation Company (ORN) reached Portland from the East before the Northern Pacific route to Tacoma became a reality. In 1883 the owner of the ORN, Henry Villard, purchased the Northern Pacific to extend the ORN tracks east from the Columbia Gorge. He consolidated the two railroad companies to build the first railroad to connect the Midwest with the Pacific Northwest. Northern Pacific tracks had reached Tacoma from Portland years before, completing a route to Washington State. Only when threatened by a Seattle businessman's plan to build a line to the lucrative agricultural valleys of the Palouse and Walla Walla did Henry Villard extend his railroad up through the Yakima Valley, over Stampede Pass, and into Tacoma. In 1893 the Northern Pacific went bankrupt, and in January of that year the next transcontinental line reached over Stevens Pass and into Seattle.

The railroad did build the need for trains. Wherever a depot sprouted, so did a post office and a population. Between 1887 and 1889, 95,000 newcomers arrived in Washington, a number of people equal to the residents of the territory in 1880. Seattle's population grew from 3,533 in 1880 to 42,837 in 1890. Tacoma went from 1,098 to 36,006. Many towns along the railroad line in rural Washington had a larger population than they have today.

In northern Idaho, mining and timber communities benefited from the full-scale effort ultimately known as the Milwaukee Road. About 2,300 miles of railroad went through five significant mountain ranges, including Idaho's Bitterroot Range and the Pacific Northwest's Cascade Range. The rails were built in an unusually rapid time span—just three years. Construction began in 1906, with the route open for passenger service the entire way to Seattle by 1909.

The Milwaukee Road, known in 1909 as the Chicago, Milwaukee, St. Paul & Pacific Railroad, was the third set of tracks to hit Seattle. It did not make instant railroad history when it arrived in the Pacific Northwest, as the first two lines had. A more significant event came in 1917, however, when the Milwaukee Road became the first electrified transcontinental railroad and the nation's longest electrified train. Travel became easier, faster, cheaper, and safer. Not only did the electrical system help clear smoke from railway tunnels, but trains braking while heading downhill regenerated power back into the overhead catenary wires—thereby powering the uphill trains. The electric railroad was so well designed that it operated from 1917 into the 1970s with few problems.

Trains of the Pacific Northwest carried passengers to a weekend at the shore or on an elegant ride from town to town. The Union Pacific Railroad established the Sun Valley Resort in Idaho in 1936, creating the first ski lift–assisted resort in the world that still serves as a famous, internationally known full-season resort. Trains carried skiers from California to Idaho for ski holidays. Trains laden with logs climbed switchbacks to reach the mills or ships departing for the Orient. Coal cars ran to the bunkers on Puget Sound to ship their load to San Francisco. Produce from the fertile soils of the Palouse, Walla Walla, and Willamette Valleys, as well as southeastern King County, rolled through farmland to warehouses and on to the cities.

Today these same railbeds allow you to journey for days through neighborhoods and on isolated pathways, resting at hotels, bed-and-breakfasts, or campsites. You'll see the farmland, the mines, and the trees that built the Pacific Northwest once the rail lines freed the area from its unique geographic isolation. The trails now enable us to see our communities, our industries, and our neighbors' way of life– traveling from town to town, desert to mountains, city to sea; beside huge rivers, forest streams, urban lakes, Puget Sound, and the Pacific Ocean. Stay the weekend or spend a week on these trails, enjoying the culture, beauty, and variety of the Pacific Northwest.

Benefits of Rail Trails

Railbeds are an ideal location for trails. They come in all sizes, surfaces, and gradients. The paths of main lines are quite flat with wide, rounded turns, allowing them to safely accommodate equestrians, beginner skaters and bicyclists, cross-country skiers, snowshoers, and families. Main lines rarely exceed a 2 percent grade, even on mountain switchbacks. Logging and mining lines occasionally offer steeper grades for a challenging mountain bike ride or a great workout on foot.

Rail trails provide an ideal transportation corridor for commuters. Many lie in the path of local industry or run from rural areas to city centers. They often link to bus routes and highways. Get creative. Take a bus

Berry picking is a popular pursuit along the region's rail trails, such as the Interurban Trail North: Snohomish County in Washington.
Dave Lindsay

halfway to work and ride or walk the rest of the route, or bus to work and bicycle home.

Much like the logging roads of the Pacific Northwest, however, rail trails also frequently abandon streets and highways for a more remote experience. They're parks that go somewhere. They expose us to our neighbors, to diverse lifestyles and commercial areas, to rural diners and waterfront restaurants, and, of course, past many espresso stands. They bring our communities closer together and provide the best of tourist opportunities.

Try a rail trail during the American Hiking Society's National Trails Day held annually in June, or during your state's or city's trail or fitness promotion days. As a bonus, get healthy, build friendships, and see the sights.

One of the great joys of train travel lies in the route—one moment you're in the middle of the city, and the next you're in a remote region of beauty. That we now enjoy such experiences on a rail trail is nothing less than a gift from the railroad companies and our cities, counties, states, the federal government, community advocates, and the RailstoTrails Conservancy.

You can view Port Angeles, Washington, from the trail along Ediz Hook.
Dave Lindsay

The History of the Rails-to-Trails Conservancy

As road construction and increased reliance on cars forced railroads to the sidelines, the question arose: What's to be done with all the abandoned tracks that crisscross the states?

Enter the Rails-to-Trails Conservancy (RTC). Based in Washington, DC, this nonprofit organization strives to create a national network of trails from former rail lines. Regional offices support the organization's efforts to connect community corridors and develop healthy places and people. Since 1986 the conservancy has campaigned to convert the railroad tracks to nature paths through advocacy, education, and advice to local trail developers.

The beauty of RTC is that by converting the railroad rights-of-way to public use, it preserved a part of our nation's history and allowed a variety of outdoor enthusiasts to enjoy the paths and trails.

Bicyclists, in-line skaters, nature lovers, hikers, equestrians, snowshoers, and cross-country skiers can enjoy rail trails, as can railroad history buffs. There is truly something for everyone on these trails, many of which are also wheelchair-accessible.

The concept of preserving these valuable corridors and converting them into multiuse public trails began in the Midwest, where railroad abandonments were most widespread. Once the tracks were removed, people started using the corridors for walking and hiking while exploring the railroad relics that were left along the railbeds, including train stations, mills, trestles, bridges, and tunnels.

Although it was easy to convince people that the rails-to-trails concept was worthwhile, the reality of actually converting abandoned railroad corridors into public trails proved a great challenge. From the late 1960s until the early 1980s, many rail trail efforts failed as corridors were lost to development, sold to the highest bidder, or broken into many pieces.

In 1983 Congress enacted an amendment to the National Trails System Act, directing the Interstate Commerce Commission to allow about-to-be-abandoned railroad lines to be "railbanked," or set aside for future transportation use while being used as trails in the interim. In essence this law preempts rail corridor abandonment, keeping the corridors intact as trails or for other transportation uses into the future.

This powerful new piece of legislation made it easier for public and private agencies and organizations to acquire rail corridors for trails, but many projects still failed because of short deadlines, lack of information, and local opposition.

In 1986 the Rails-to-Trails Conservancy was formed to provide a national voice for the creation of rail trails. RTC quickly developed a strategy that was designed to preserve the largest amount of rail corridor in the shortest period of time. A national advocacy program was formed to defend the new railbanking law in the courts and in Congress; this was coupled with a direct project-assistance program to help public agencies and local rail trail groups overcome the challenges of converting a rail into a trail.

The strategy is working. In 1986 RTC knew of less than 200 rail trails in the United States. Now, RTC states, there are greater than 24,000 miles of rail trails, with more than 8,000 potential miles of rail trails anticipating development. The RTC vision of creating an interconnected network of trails across America is becoming a reality for a wide range of users. People across the country are experiencing and valuing the incredible benefits of the rail trails. Pacific Northwest rail trails are also an integral part of the RTC's developing Great American Rail-Trail project. The route of this 3,700-mile cross-continental trail consists of interconnected rail trails, greenways, and other multiuse paths stretching from Washington, DC, to Washington State. As of 2022, the cross-country linkage of the preferred route is over 55 percent completed, sporting 2,025 existing trail miles. Several of the longer Northwest rail trails serve as part of the 150 "host trails."

In recognition of the crème de la crème of the rail trails, RTC developed the Rail-Trail Hall of Fame in 2007, of which 4 of the 39 listed in 2022 are located in the Pacific Northwest. See the Burke-Gilman Trail (Trail 1) in Washington, the Springwater Corridor (Trail 29) in Oregon, the Trail of the Coeur d'Alenes (Trail 34) in Idaho, and the Route of the Hiawatha (Trail 35), also in Idaho. RTC states that inductees were selected based "on merits such as scenic value, high use, trail and trailside amenities, historical significance, excellence in management and maintenance of facility, community connections and geographic distribution." Look for the special signage along these famous trails and read about them and the Great American Rail-Trail in *Rails to Trails* magazine or on the RTC's website at www.railstotrails.org.

How to Get Involved

If you really enjoy rail trails, there are opportunities to join the movement to save abandoned rail corridors and to create more trails. Donating even a small amount of your time, expertise, or money can help get more trails up and going. Here are some ways you can help the effort:

- Write a letter or e-mail to your city, county, or state elected official in favor of pro trail legislation. You can also contact the editor of your local newspaper, highlighting a trail or trail project.

- Attend a public hearing to voice support for a local trail.

- Volunteer to plant flowers or trees along an existing trail or to spend several hours helping a cleanup crew on a nearby rail trail project.

- Lead a hike along an abandoned corridor with your friends or a community group.

- Become an active member of the Rails-to-Trails Conservancy and support trail efforts in your area. Many groups host trail events; undertake

Signs at trailheads alert users to trail etiquette.

fund-raising campaigns; publish brochures, blogs, and newsletters; and carry out other activities to promote a trail or project. Virtually all of these efforts are organized and staffed by volunteers, and there is always room for more helping hands.

- Whatever your time allows, get involved. The success of a community's rail trail depends on the level of citizen participation. The Rails-to-Trails Conservancy enjoys local and national support. By joining RTC you receive discounts on all of its publications and merchandise, updates on trail challenges, and access to expert help while supporting this progressive and active national trail organization.

How to Use Rail Trails

By design, rail trails accommodate a variety of trail users. While this is generally one of the many benefits of rail trails, it also can lead to occasional conflicts among trail users. Everyone should take responsibility to ensure trail safety by following a few simple trail etiquette guidelines.

One of the most basic etiquette rules is "Wheels yield to heels." The "Trail Courtesy" photograph below indicates the correct protocol for yielding right-of-way. Bicyclists (and in-line skaters) yield to other users; pedestrians yield to equestrians.

Generally this means that you need to warn the users to whom you are yielding of your presence. If, as a bicyclist, you fail to warn a walker that you are about to pass, the walker could step in front of you, causing an accident that easily could be prevented. Similarly, it is best to slow down and warn an equestrian of your presence. A horse can be startled by a bicycle, so make verbal contact with the rider and be sure it is safe to pass.

Here are some other guidelines to follow to promote trail safety:

- Obey all trail rules posted at trailheads.

- Stay to the right except when passing.

- Pass slower traffic on the left; yield to oncoming traffic when passing.

- Give a clear warning signal when passing.

- Always look ahead and behind when passing.

- Travel at a responsible speed and not faster than the posted speed.

- Keep pets on a leash.

- Do not trespass on private property.

- Move off the trail surface when stopped to allow other users to pass.

- Yield to other trail users when entering and crossing the trail.

- Do not disturb the wildlife.

- Do not swim in areas not designated for swimming.

- Watch out for traffic when crossing the street.

- Obey all traffic signals.

- Take only pictures and memories.

- Pack out your trash if trash receptacles are not available.

How to Use This Guide

For this book, Washington, Oregon, and Idaho's top rail trails were chosen based on their length, historical or aesthetic features, access, and location. Some trails have a more detailed description and are identified by a number and name, starting in Washington with Trail 1, the Burke-Gilman Trail. Additional trails are listed with an alphabet letter under More Rail Trails, following the numbered trails for each state, providing you with a teaser and the basics to get you on the trail to make your own discoveries.

At the beginning of each chapter, you will find a map showing the location of the rail trails within that region. The main rail trails featured in this book include basic maps for your convenience. A feature in this edition is the inclusion of Global Positioning System (GPS) coordinates to guide you to the trail. The GPS coordinates indicate the turn into the trailhead, the trailhead parking lot, or the start of the trail for the described route. In some cases, the satellites that collect data lined up perfectly and the GPS reading provided is right on target. In other cases, the GPS will get you to the general location of the trailhead. Use the written instructions, the map, and the GPS to guide you to the starting point of the trails described.

It is recommended, however, that you also use street maps, topographic maps such as US Geological Survey (USGS) quads, a state atlas, and trail website maps to supplement the maps in this book.

In terms of indicated length, mileages may differ from distances indicated along the trail or in other printed sources. Trails are in constant flux, with many trail improvements occurring throughout the region, including trail extensions. Various sources may differ regarding exact distances. As you bicycle, hike, run, skate, or horseback-ride the trails, be aware that trails may have been rerouted, landmarks may have disappeared, or other changes may have occurred to the terrain. Some services, such as information kiosks, water, and restrooms, may have closed or been added. Mileage may vary a bit depending on the device you use on the trail, such as your GPS, bike computer, phone, pedometer, or other mileage tracker. In summary, be flexible, be prepared, and be ready for a great adventure no matter what you find along the trail.

The Northwest Timber Trail in Tiger Mountain State Forest: East Tiger Mountain Trail System features wooded scenery.

The text description of every trail begins with the following information:

- **Trail name:** The official name of the rail trail.

- **Activities:** A list of icons tells you what kinds of activities are appropriate for each trail.

- **Location:** The areas through which the trail passes.

- **Length:** The length of the described trail in miles (one way) and additional described side tour miles.

- **Surface:** The materials that make up the rail trail vary from trail to trail. This section describes each trail's surface. Materials range from asphalt and crushed stone to the significantly more rugged original railroad ballast.

- **Wheelchair access:** Some of the rail trails are wheelchair-accessible. This allows physically challenged individuals the opportunity to explore the rail trails.

- **Difficulty:** The rail trails range from very easy to hard, depending on the grade of the trail and its general condition.

- **Food:** Names of the towns near the rail trails in which restaurants and fast-food shops are located.

- **Restrooms:** If a restroom, vault toilet, or temporary portable toilet is available near the trail, its location is noted and indicated on the map.

- **Seasons:** Most of these trails are open year-round, but special circumstances, such as severe winter rains or localized flooding, may preclude the use of certain routes during some seasons. Other trails may be inaccessible due to heavy winter snow that remains into the late spring. Check the trail's suggested website for trail updates.

- **Rentals:** Some of the rail trails have bicycle shops or other trail-related outdoor gear stores nearby. This will help you locate rentals, or a shop in which you can have repairs made if you have problems with your equipment. Check out appendix A for a summary of rental information.

- **Contacts:** The name and contact information for each trail management agency is listed. The selected contacts are generally responsible for managing the trail and can provide information about the trail and its condition. Additional information sources are also listed for each trail. See appendix B for organizations for advocacy, education, and information.

- **Bus routes:** Bus routes listed provide an alternate return route for individuals traveling the trails one way. Some extend the entire length of the trail; others cover only a portion. Contact carriers directly for more detailed and up-to-date information.

- **Access and parking:** The book provides directions to each rail trail and describes parking availability at one or several sites. A GPS coordinate is provided for the trail description start point. It is either the location of the trailhead parking, a trail entry point, or both, also indicated as "Start" on the trail map, which may or may not be the trail's official terminus.

- **Description:** The numbered rail trails include an overview of the trail and its history, followed by a detailed description, allowing you to anticipate the experience of the trail. Alphabet-lettered rail trails follow

Autumn is a colorful time to visit Cowiche Canyon Trail near Yakima, Washington.

the numbered trails in each state and include a brief description of the trail and the above details to get you started.

Information in this book was confirmed via exploration of the trails, discussions with managers, and ongoing research, and is correct to the author's knowledge prior to press time. Given that rail trails are often in a state of change—hopefully enhancements and lengthening of trails— trail users may want to contact the local resources prior to a visit to obtain current information. Rockslides, flooding, fires, and heavy snowpack in the mountains can close trails, increase the difficulty of accessing them, or make trail use challenging. In metropolitan areas such as Seattle, Spokane, Portland, and Boise, road and population expansions impact trail access, parking, and potential trail growth. Be sure to check for an update on trail conditions before you start on a trail. If you discover changes along a trail, or that a store or restaurant has gone out of business, please contact us so that corrections can be made in future editions.

Legend

Local Roads	═══ 4N01 ═══
State Roads	═══ (151) ═══
US Highway	═══ (101) ═══
Interstate	═══ (5) ═══
Main Route	▬ ▬ ▬ ▬ ▬ ▬ ▬
Other Trail	‑ ‑ ‑ ‑ ‑ ‑ ‑
Railroad	┼┼┼┼┼┼┼┼
County Line	‑ ‑ ‑ ‑ ‑ ‑ ‑
State Line	▬▬▬▬▬▬▬
Country Line	▬ ▪ ▬ ▪ ▬ ▪ ▬
Creeks/Rivers	‑ ‑ ‑ ‑ ‑ ‑
Park/Open Space	▭
Tunnel/Bridge	)(
Picnic	🎪
Rentals	**R**
Parking	**P**
Camping	**▲**
Restrooms	🚻
Information Center	**I**
Mountain/Peak	▲
Point of Interest	■
Start/End	**START** **END**

Key to Activities Icons

	Backpacking		Horseback Riding		Running
	Bird Watching		In-line Skating		Swimming
	Camping		Mountain Biking		Walking/Day Hiking
	Cross-Country Skiing		Paddle Sports		Wildlife Viewing
	Fishing		Biking		Snowshoeing
	Historic Sites				

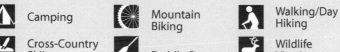

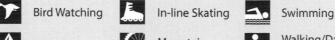

Boulevard Park, along the South Bay Trail, offers views of Bellingham Bay.

Washington

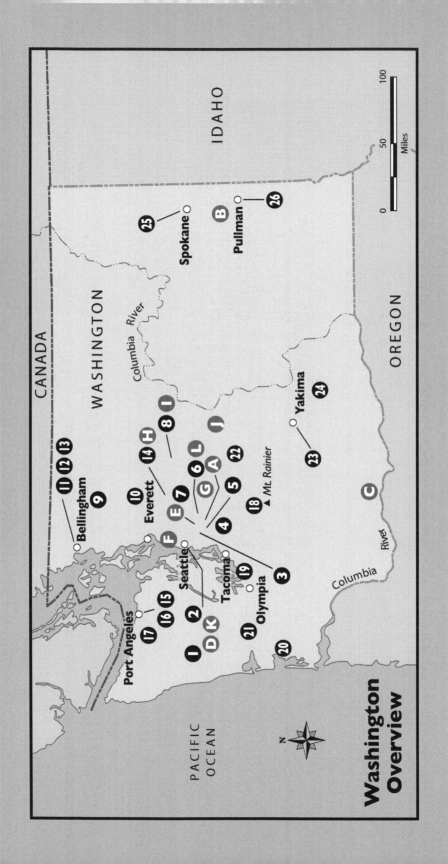

Washington
Overview

Washington

Puget Sound

1. Burke-Gilman Trail
2. Elliott Bay Trail
3. Coal Creek Trail
4. King County Interurban Trail (South)
5. Cedar River Trail and Green-to-Cedar Rivers Trail
6. Preston–Snoqualmie Trail
7. Snoqualmie Valley Trail

Northwestern Washington

8. Iron Goat Trail
9. Cascade Trail
10. Snohomish County Centennial Trail
11. Whatcom County and Bellingham Interurban Trail
12. South Bay Trail
13. Railroad Trail
14. Wallace Falls State Park: Old Railroad Grade Trail
15. Olympic Discovery Trail: Deer Park Scenic Gateway Center to Sequim
16. Olympic Discovery Trail: Port Angeles Waterfront
17. Olympic Discovery Trail: Spruce Railroad Trail

Southwestern Washington

18. Foothills Trail
19. Chehalis Western Trail
20. Willapa Hills Trail: Raymond to South Bend Riverfront Trail
21. Lake Sylvia State Park

Eastern Washington

22. Palouse to Cascades State Park Trail
23. Cowiche Canyon Trail
24. Lower Yakima Valley Pathway
25. Spokane River Centennial Trail
26. Bill Chipman Palouse Trail: Pullman, Washington

More Washington Rail Trails

A. Tiger Mountain State Forest: East Tiger Mountain Trail System
B. Colfax Trail
C. Dry Creek Trail
D. Alki Trail
E. Issaquah–Preston Trail
F. Interurban Trail North: Snohomish County Segment
G. Middle Fork Trail
H. Necklace Valley Trail
I. Pacific Crest National Scenic Trail: Stevens Pass Right-of-Way Section
J. Rainier Trail
K. South Ship Canal Trail
L. Snoqualmie Centennial Trail–Corridor Trail

Washington State, its cities, towns, and citizen groups deserve mountains of praise for their hard work in overcoming the financial, political, and social obstacles in their way as they developed these paths to fitness, sensible transportation, and joy. This section describes thirty-eight of the numerous Washington trails.

The trails of Puget Sound run on main lines that once carried timber, coal, and passengers; logging lines that headed into the hills; and elegant interurban trolleys. Of the many trails, the Burke-Gilman Trail receives heavy use. Commuters, bicyclists, skaters, children, and walkers have discovered that there's no better route for exploring the north-side neighborhoods of Seattle. Take yourself to breakfast, lunch, and dinner on this route. Sip cappuccino on the South Ship Canal; watch floatplanes land while you enjoy happy hour beside Lake Washington; view kites soaring over Lake Union; ride, walk, or skate through the U-district at the University of Washington; and finish with a meal in Fremont. Daniel Burke and Judge Thomas Gilman, founding fathers of Seattle, built the Seattle, Lake Shore & Eastern Railway on this route.

The Elliott Bay Trail carves a corridor through Seattle's waterfront and through parks, ending at Smith Cove Park and Marina, former site of coal bunkers.

Meanwhile, the King County Interurban Trail (South) heads through the industrial regions and neighborhoods of South King County, passes the racetrack and a huge mall, and continues to the tiny towns of Algona and Pacific. Commute, shop, have a day at the races, tour the cities along the way, or just enjoy a great workout while on this wide, paved trail. Urban trails also head north from Lynnwood to Everett along the old trolley line.

The trails east of Seattle offer some screaming mountain bike rides in Tiger Mountain State Forest, a great commuter trail along the Cedar River, and a 31-mile trail through the Snoqualmie Valley. Cedar River Trail starts in the city of Renton on Lake Washington and ends in a wooded setting. The Snoqualmie Valley Trail traverses the rolling terrain of a rural area showing the signs of development. Local antiques shops and eateries remain while Starbucks, grocery chains, and fast foods encroach. This pretty valley takes you near Snoqualmie Falls, with the luxurious Salish Lodge at its lip. The nearby Snoqualmie Centennial Trail–Corridor Trail begins at the Northwest Railroad Museum and continues alongside the old tracks, where trail users pass beside retired engines from the past. The Snoqualmie Valley Trail presently connects to the Palouse to Cascades State Park Trail.

Rail trails in northwestern Washington pass by farms, through forests, beside waterfalls, through the college town of Bellingham, and out to the Olympic Peninsula. Contemplate the calm waters of Lake Crescent and the views of distant peaks from the Olympic Discovery Trail: Spruce Railroad Trail. Enjoy the oceanfront city of Port Angeles and the forest bouquets of wildflowers on the Olympic Discovery Trail. For a good look at a logging route ascended by the "steam donkey" trains, along with dramatic waterfalls, follow the Wallace Falls State Park Old Railroad Grade Trail as it climbs through the forest. The Iron Goat Trail near Stevens Pass is an impressive interpretive hiking trail that transports you back to the difficulties and disasters the Great Northern Railway experienced as it made its way through this rugged territory.

Southwestern Washington offers several rural rail trails. To the east you'll find the Foothills Trail, in the shadow of Mount Rainier; to the west is the Willapa Hills Trail on the Willapa River. Follow the trail to Raymond from South Bend, discovering this prior Oyster Capital of the World. There's the easily accessible Woodard Bay conservation area just off I-5 near the state capital of Olympia (Chehalis Western Trail) and rugged dirt trails in Lake Sylvia State Park.

Head to eastern Washington for sunshine and hot, dry desert. East of the Cascades you'll discover Yakima wine country, the pretty Cowiche Canyon, and a trail through the city of Spokane to the Idaho border. Turbulent dams, museums, and an equestrian area accent the 40-mile Spokane River Centennial Trail. Follow 250 miles of the path of the *Olympian-Hiawatha* passenger train that once rolled from Seattle to Chicago on the Milwaukee Road. Travel through changes in terrain, climate, and scenery; along rivers; through towns and tunnels; and over the Columbia River on the Palouse to Cascades State Park Trail. Adventurous travelers can continue east past the Columbia River to the border of Idaho on the less-developed portion of the trail.

Seattle and many of this region's areas have a serious traffic problem. Commuting on a rail trail is as sensible as commuting on the trains that once ran these routes—and just as pleasant. Hop a bus one way or for part of your route, and take your bike, skates, or your feet the rest of the way. Get fit and lean, meet people, protect the environment, and live longer.

Men and women in their eighties and nineties haul groceries on primitive bikes in countries like India, Cuba, and China. We can likewise use our modern bikes and ride to work in comfort as we age, staying healthy and feisty. Check the bus schedules, talk to your coworkers, and make a plan. Join your local bicycle club's trail work day or ride-to-work event this year. (See appendix B for contact information.) The trail planners have ambitious plans and trails are changing frequently. For example, in King County, Washington, the urban trails program is improving the network by building out the trail system and filling in gaps. Wherever or however you start your tour, don't miss the chance to see, play, study, commute, or simply wander Washington's wonderful rail trails.

1 BURKE-GILMAN TRAIL

Seattle's Burke-Gilman Trail invites you on a tour of funky Fremont, Lake Union and the Ship Canal, the University District, Lake Washington, and north-end neighborhoods. You'll pass above the old Sand Point naval base and along the busy, commercial Lake City Way. Several parks dot this Rails-to-Trails Conservancy's Hall of Fame trail.

Activities:

Location: North Seattle to Lake Forest Park, Kenmore, and Bothell

Length: 18.8 miles, in Seattle and King County

Surface: Paved

Wheelchair access: The entire trail is wheelchair-accessible.

Difficulty: Easy

Food: In the town of Fremont and along Lake City Way, you'll find every-thing from breweries and grocery stores to fast food and gourmet dining.

Restrooms: You'll find restroom facilities at Golden Gardens Park, Gas Works Park, Burke-Gilman Place Park, Matthews Beach Park, and Tracy Owen Station at Log Boom Park.

Seasons: The trail can be used year-round.

Rentals: See appendix A for rental options.

Contacts: View information and/or maps at King County Parks and Recre-ation Division www.kingcounty.gov/recreation/parks/trails; Seattle Parks and Recreation Department, (206) 684-4075, https://www.seattle.gov/

parks/find/hiking-and-trails; Seattle Department of Transportation map, www.seattle.gov/transportation; Cascade Bicycle Club, (206) 522-3222, www.cascade.org; Washington Bikes, (206) 522-3222, www.wabikes.org.

Bus routes: For more information, call Metro Transit at (206) 553-3000, or visit www.kingcounty.gov.

Access and parking: You can access the trail from many points. This trail description avoids an approximately 1-mile disruption in the trail near its southern area by starting a few blocks from the east end of the disruption. Begin at 8th Avenue Northwest and Northwest 43rd Street just off Leary Way and head eastwardly. You can park on the street and hop on the trail near the Ballard Fred Meyer. GPS: N47 39.56' / W122 21.98'

This trail description ends after 14 miles at the Tracy Owen Station at Log Boom Park near the trail's northern terminus. Log Boom Park offers convenient parking, picnicking, fishing, and boating opportunities. The park is located on 61st Avenue Northeast and Northeast Bothell Way in Kenmore. It is possible to stay on the trail eastward from Log Boom Park to Blyth Park in Bothell.

|||||||||||||||||||||||||||||||||||||||||||||||||||||||||||||||||||||||||||||||||||||||

What a train ride this must have been! In 1885 Judge Thomas Burke and Daniel Gilman, two of Seattle's city fathers, set out to establish the Seattle, Lake Shore & Eastern Railway. Originally planned to connect with the Canadian Transcontinental at Sumas, the rail line made it only to Arlington. Still, it became a major regional line serving Puget Sound logging areas. Northern Pacific purchased the line in 1913, used it heavily until 1963, and finally abandoned it in 1971. A cooperative effort by King County, Seattle, and the University of Washington then led to the right-of-way's development as a trail, dedicated in 1978.

Now a popular recreation and commuter pathway, the Burke-Gilman Trail takes you past boats, bridges, and breweries. You can stop at cafes, parks, and bookstores. Take time to marvel at the University of Washington's Gothic architecture and the shiny, square buildings. Be alert, cautious, and considerate while sharing this busy trail.

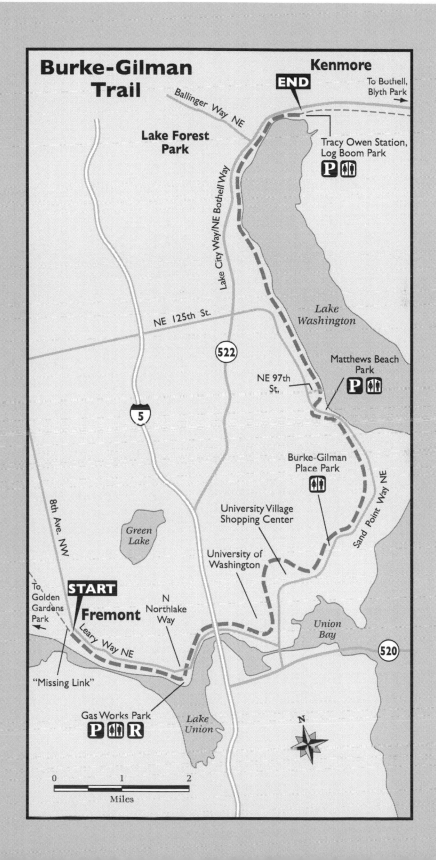

A bicycle club rides toward Tracy Owen Station at Log Boom Park at the northern portion of the trail.

The official southwestern terminus of the Burke-Gilman Trail is at Golden Gardens Park. A 1.8-mile section of the trail heads south from the park. The trail runs past the Ballard Locks, adjacent to Hiram Chittenden Locks, and then continues between 32nd Avenue Northwest and 28th Avenue Northwest. There's an approximately 1-mile break in trail continuity, known as the "Missing Link," ahead. Plans are to improve this section. Presently, trail users are rerouted onto roads in the area. The trail segment described next is a 14-mile section that starts near the Fred Meyer store, located about 3.3 miles from the southwest terminus at Golden Gardens Park, and continues to a northern trailhead at Tracy Owen Station at Log Boom Park. You can access the trail from many points along the way.

To follow this description, access the trail at a street corner in a busy area by the Fred Meyer. Fremont Canal Park lies about 0.5 mile ahead. The trail then leaves Fremont city center to dip down to the edge of Lake Union. You can take a side trip here to enjoy Fremont's street art and food. The trail passes Gas Works Park at mile 1.8; there's an uphill grade here. Stop for great views of the city, Mount Rainier, and Lake Union. You'll cross several roads over the next approximately 5 miles. As you pass University of Washington Medical Center, the south campus, and Husky Stadium at 3.6 miles, you might notice you are also on the Cheshiahud Lake Union Loop (a 6-mile multiuse urban trail linking parks and lake access). You are on the northern section of this loop. Arrive at 25th Avenue Northeast and the University Village Shopping Center at 5.0 miles. Discover lots of treats and espresso drinks here.

The trail northward is easy; it's especially good for beginner skaters and bikers. You'll find just a bit of grade and mostly small street crossings. At 40th Avenue Northeast you'll pass Burke-Gilman Place Park and then enter a forested area. Maples, dogwoods, and hedges frame lake views north of Northeast 77th Street (mile 8.0). There's a slight grade and frequent small road crossings. A bridge crosses Sand Point Way to Matthews Beach Park at 9.0 miles. This lakeside park offers picnicking and swimming. North of Northeast 97th Street the character of the trail changes, with views of waterfront homes. Pass Lakeside Place Northeast at 10.6 miles. The trail reaches Lake City Way at Northeast Ballinger Way (mile 13.5).

There are many coffee and fast-food spots on the main drag ahead. The Burke-Gilman Trail passes through Tracy Owen Station at Log Boom Park in Kenmore, which offers a convenient starting or ending point. You can continue approximately another 3 miles on the Burke-Gilman Trail to the Blyth Park in Bothell. From there access the Sammamish River Trail to Redmond.

Alternately, if you are ready to turn around, hop a bus to return to your starting point and check out the western terminus at Golden Gardens Park.

2 ELLIOTT BAY TRAIL

The Elliott Bay Trail provides a picturesque tour of Seattle's vibrant downtown waterfront and travels through various bay-side parks. At the southern end of the trail beyond Olympic Sculpture Park you'll find the beautifully updated and modernized downtown waterfront promenade. You can fill your day with a visit to the Seattle Aquarium, a boat tour, a seafood meal, and a Ferris wheel ride. Other visitors simply relax at eateries along the waterfront.

Activities:

Location: Downtown Seattle, in King County

Length: 3.45 miles

Surface: Paved

Wheelchair access: The entire trail is wheelchair-accessible.

Difficulty: Mostly easy, although the pavement may be bumpy for novice skaters. There are a few little hills.

Food: Numerous restaurants along Alaskan Way and the downtown Waterfront promenade near the Olympic Sculpture Park and at Smith Cove Marina.

Restrooms: There are restrooms at Myrtle Edwards Park, Smith Cove Park, and the Fishing Pier at Centennial Park Pier 86.

Seasons: The trail can be used year-round. Smith Cove Park is open year-round but closed at night.

Rentals: See appendix A for a list of bike rentals in the Puget Sound area.

Contacts: View information and/or maps at Cascade Bicycle Club, www.cascade.org, (206) 522-3222; Washington Bikes www.wabikes.org; Washington Trails Association, www.wta.org; Seattle Department of Transportation, www.seattle.gov/transportation; Seattle Office of the Waterfront and Civic Projects, www.waterfrontseattle.org.

Bus routes: Call County Metro Transit at (206) 553-3000, or visit www.king-county.gov.

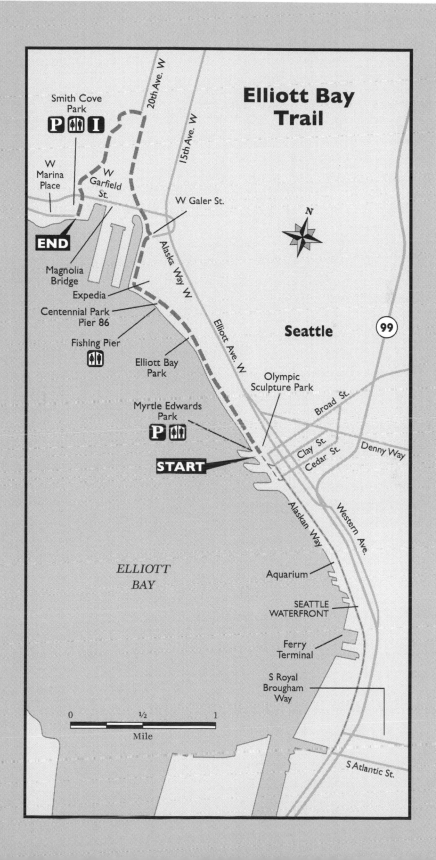

Access and parking: To reach the Elliott Bay Trail, head west from I-5 to Edgar Martinez Drive, which turns into Alaskan Way. You can park along Alaskan Way or near Broad Street at this trail's southern terminus at the Olympic Sculpture Park. GPS: N47 36.91' / W122 21.30'

Find parking at the northern end at Smith Cove Park.

|||||||||||||||||||||||||||||||||||||||||||||||||||||||||||||||||||||||||||||||||||||||||||||||

The Elliott Bay Trail winds through parks as it passes between the waterfront and the active Burlington Northern Santa Fe Railway line. The trail can be accessed from many points along the way; this description begins at Olympic Sculpture and Myrtle Edwards Parks, and then continues north through Centennial Park to Smith Cove Park. At Myrtle Edwards Park the trail separates into different sections for wheels and for pedestrians.

Sunsets can be spectacular along the trail. At mile 1.0 you may want to stop by the Fishing Pier at Centennial Park for the restrooms. Cross in front of the entrance to Terminal 91 and follow the trail signs. After the park you'll encounter the Expedia property and the updated trail section with excellent views of Elliott Bay.

As it leaves the waterfront beyond Galer Street, the trail crosses old railroad tracks, quickly and briefly becomes very narrow, then climbs and descends a steep overpass. Be cautious here. Beyond this overpass, the trail is flat and wide.

Several popular road bike routes take off near 20th Avenue West, including trips to the Ship Canal Trail or to Fremont. After 20th Avenue the trail curves. A sign directs you to Smith Cove Park at approximately mile 3.35 (1.75 miles from Galer Street). Mount Rainier stands white and tall across the water, dwarfing the freighters attached to the pier.

From here you may want to continue 0.5 mile to the restaurants at Smith Cove Marina or enjoy a spectacular view of the Olympic Mountains across the sound. The marina allows public access until dusk.

The Smith Cove Park area has interesting rail and shipping history. The Northern Pacific coal bunker pier was completed here in 1891. Steamers and sailing vessels berthed on either side of this 2,500-foot trestle, loading coal from railroad cars until 1899, when the Great Northern Railway built Piers 88 and 89. This linked the transcontinental railroad to the Orient. In 1912 the Port of Seattle bought the tidal flats that were to become Piers 90 and 91. The US Navy owned them from 1942 to 1976.

When you're ready, turn around and return the way you came. Once back at Olympic Sculpture Park, take a stroll along the modernized downtown Seattle waterfront promenade. You'll pass through a lively tourist area with restaurants, gift shops, piers, the Seattle Aquarium, the Seattle Great Wheel, and ferry docks.

Travel along the shore between downtown Seattle and Smith Cove Park on the Elliott Bay Trail.

3 COAL CREEK TRAIL

This trek through the Coal Creek Natural Area takes you southeasterly through a bit of coal-mining history on your way to spectacular Cougar Mountain Regional Wildland Park. It offers woodsy tranquility and a pleasant outing close to town.

Activities:

Location: Cougar Mountain, Bellevue, in King County

Length: 2.5 miles

Surface: Chip bark and dirt

Wheelchair access: The trail is not wheelchair-accessible.

Difficulty: This nature trail is moderate to easy. There are additional trails within the Coal Creek Natural Area and the Cougar Mountain Regional Wildland Park.

Food: No food is available along the trail.

Restrooms: There is a portable toilet at the Red Cedar Trailhead and restrooms at the Lewis Creek Visitor Center near the Red Town Trailhead.

Seasons: The trail can be used year-round; conditions vary and are affected by weather.

Rentals: There are no rentals along the route.

Contacts: Bellevue Parks and Community Services, (425) 452-6881, https://bellevuewa.gov/city-government/departments/parks. Visit the Lewis Creek Visitor Center on Lakemont Boulevard, 0.6 mile from the Red Town Trailhead, (425) 452-4195. Find further trail information at Washington Trails Association, www.wta.org and at Cougar Mountain Regional Wildland Park, https://kingcounty.gov.

Bus routes: None currently. For more information, call Metro Transit at (206) 553-3000, or visit www.kingcounty.gov.

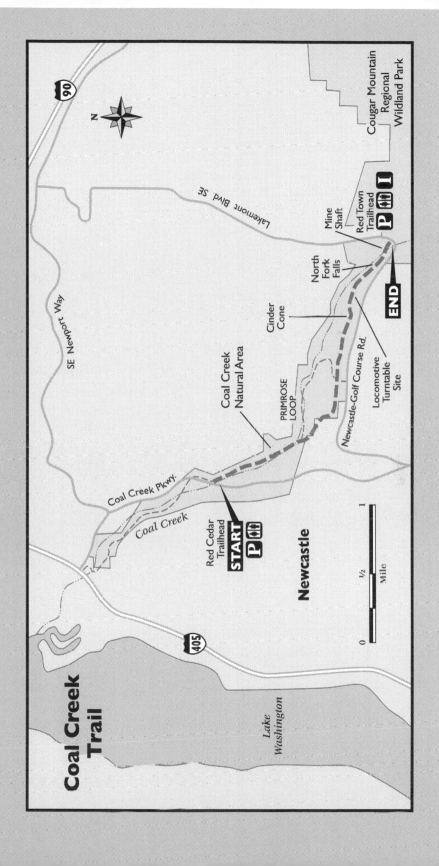

Access and parking: You can park your car and access the trail at either the Red Cedar Trailhead (this trail description's northwestern terminus) or the Red Town Trailhead (its southeastern end). Access the Red Cedar Trailhead by taking exit 10 (Coal Creek Parkway) off I-405. Drive east 1.3 miles to the trailhead on the left. This turn is 0.2 mile past the light at Forest Drive. GPS: N47 33.25' / W122 09.99'

Newcastle coal was once the best in the Northwest, and the mining industry reached its zenith here from the late nineteenth century through the early twentieth. Unfortunately, Washington State let owner- ship of the mines fall into the hands of San Francisco moguls. While they reaped the mining profits, Seattle businessmen made what money they could by moving the coal—via the Seattle Walla Walla Railroad—from the mines to steamers destined for transport to San Francisco and beyond. This railroad, Seattle's own, ran to Renton and to the bunkers at the King Street Pier. Due to the powerful politics of railroading and the interests of the Tacoma-based Northern Pacific, however, it never actually reached Walla Walla.

The Coal Creek Trail described here offers a 2.5-mile segment through this rich history. Much of the land in this area and in surrounding neigh- borhoods was mined for coal, and it's now riddled with underground, arti- ficial caves. In the mines' heyday, disposal of coal tailings built the ravine walls you'll see above the trail. Due to unstable ground and slides, little of the pathway remains on the railroad grade, but it will take you up and down small hills, beside a creek, and to a waterfall on your way to Cougar Mountain Park. You'll cross a variety of bridges along the way.

This description begins at the northwestern side at Red Cedar Trail- head and travels southeast to Cougar Mountain. Leaving the trailhead, the trail descends into a man-made ravine as it follows the creek, rising above and crossing it several times. The trail can be muddy. Leave the creek to climb to an open plateau at about 1.0 mile. The Primrose Loop intersects the trail several times, offering an alternate route.

Before climbing up to Newcastle–Golf Course Road and the Red Town Trailhead, you'll arrive at a peaceful rest stop. Watch a waterfall slide down

Check out the colorful waterfall along Coal Creek Trail near the Red Town Trailhead.

a rust-colored rock face into the creek. Arrive at the trail's end, cross Lake-mont Boulevard Southeast (which becomes Newcastle–Golf Course Road) to reach the Red Town Trailhead. In 1883, Red Town Trailhead was a mining town, due to coal mining on Cougar Mountain.

You're now in Cougar Mountain Regional Wildland Park, which covers more than 3,000 acres and is one of the largest of King County's parks. The Issaquah Alps range here predates the Cascade Mountains. Hiking and equestrian trails await exploration. Wetlands and creeks originate within the park, which is forested by western red cedar, western hem-lock, Douglas fir, Sitka spruce, and bigleaf maple. Keep your eyes open for black-tailed deer, black bears, bobcats, coyotes, bald eagles, ravens, pile-ated woodpeckers, and great horned owls.

Other Cougar Mountain attractions include spectacular waterfalls, mountaintop views, and large glacial boulders. The park offers interpre-tive programs covering the park's history and natural resources. When you're ready, turn around and return the way you came.

4 KING COUNTY INTERURBAN TRAIL (SOUTH)

This trail offers a study in contrasts: from the bustling Outlet Collection Seattle with its endless shops to small-town Algona, which looks straight out of the nineteenth century; from the imposing architecture of the Emerald Downs racetrack to the majesty of Mount Rainier—from industry to agriculture, it's all here.

Activities:

Location: King County, from Tukwila to Pacific; including the towns of Kent, Auburn, and Algona

Length: 15.5 miles

Surface: Asphalt with soft shoulders

Wheelchair access: Most of the trail is wheelchair-accessible.

Difficulty: Easy

Food: In the towns of Algona, Auburn, and Kent.

Restrooms: You'll find restrooms at Fort Dent Park / Starfire Soccer Complex, Bicentennial Park, seasonally at Kent Uplands Playfield, and at the General Services Administration (GSA) Ballfield Park in Auburn.

Seasons: The trail can be used year-round.

Rentals: See appendix A for a list of bike rentals in the Puget Sound area.

Contacts: King County Parks and Recreation Division, www.kingcounty.gov; Washington Trails Association, www.wta.org. View the King County Trail Map at https://gismaps.kingcounty.gov/TrailFinder

Bus routes: For more information, call Metro Transit at (206) 553-3000, or visit www.kingcounty.gov.

Access and parking: Access the trail from several points along the way. At the King County Interurban Trail (South) northern terminus in Tukwila, you can start near Fort Dent Park / Starfire Soccer Complex, near the King County Interurban Trail's intersection with the Green River Trail near

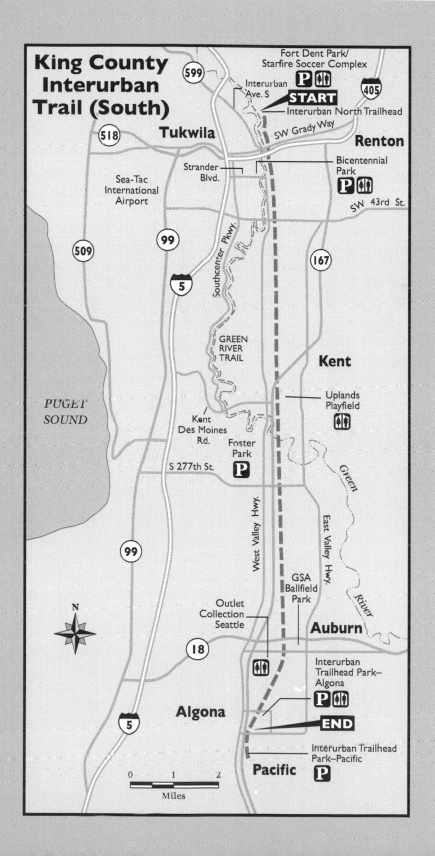

Interurban Avenue and Fort Dent Way at the Interurban North Trailhead. GPS: N47 27.96' / W122 14.88'

Alternately, you can park slightly further south at Bicentennial Park, located on the west side of the Green River and Green River Trail on Strander Boulevard, 1 block west of West Valley Highway. Access the Interurban Trail by crossing West Valley Highway on Strander and following Stander until it dead-ends at the trail.

The Green River Trail—which is depicted on the map but not described here—passes through Bicentennial Park and Fort Dent Park / Starfire Soccer Complex. You can create a loop outing by heading south on the Green River Trail then returning to the north via the King County Interurban Trail, or the reverse. The trails intersect again at Foster Park.

You can also start at either Algona or Pacific, at the southern end of the trail. To park at Interurban Trailhead Park in Algona, exit WA 167 at Algona-Pacific and head east on Ellingson Road. Turn north onto Milwaukee Boulevard South to park along 1st Avenue North in Algona. To reach Interurban Trailhead Park in Pacific, head south on Milwaukee Boulevard and then west on 3rd Avenue Southwest to trail parking on the north side of the road.

||||||||||||||||||||||||||||||||||||||||||||||||||||||||||||||||||||||||||||||||||||||||||||||||||||||||||||||||||||||||||

The electric Interurban Railway transported people between Seattle and Tacoma from September 1902 until December 1928. It ran first as the Interurban Railway, then the Seattle Electric Company, and finally the Puget Sound Electric Railway. The transportation of goods from the productive soil of the Green River Valley to local markets accounted for a portion of the load.

Farming and manufacturing still dominate this route. Large warehouses, office parks, highways, malls, and hotels are near the King County Interurban Trail (South), south from Tukwila to Pacific. Pastureland, rivers, and parks parallel the trail as well. The location of the trail near industry, highways, and bus stations allows commuters to travel via a combination of trails and vehicles. It also provides miles of parkland for residents of industrial neighborhoods.

Although the trail can be accessed from many points along the way, this description carries you from its northern end, in Tukwila, and heads south to Pacific. Begin the journey where the trail intersects the Green River Trail at a bridge crossing the river near Fort Dent Park / Starfire Soccer Complex (near Interurban Avenue at Fort Dent Way). Start on the trail as it crosses over the bridge to the south, goes under I-405, and passes several hotels. You'll travel between an active railroad and office parks, under power lines, and through open fields.

At mile 5.5 pass under WA 167 and continue to the Uplands Playfield near Smith Street in downtown Kent. Safely cross Willis Street at mile 6.5 by jogging right to cross at the light; then jog back left, crossing 74th Avenue South, to regain the trail.

Arrive at Foster Park at 7.0 miles. The park lies at the base of a trestle and could serve as an entry point for the Green River and Interurban Trails. Pause for a view of the Green River below. Note the active railroad trestle beside you. The trail bridge was built in the image of its big brother. Portions of the trail pass under power lines. Utility trucks may occasionally be on the trail for repair work.

Near mile 8.0 the trail goes under the South 277th Street overpass. Next cross a bridge over the wetlands. On clear days, Mount Rainier fills the sky here, as it does along most of your route. At mile 10.0 you are dwarfed by the Emerald Downs racetrack, looming high above the other structures along the pathway. After you cross under several highways, you're suddenly hit by neon signs. This is the popular Outlet Collection Seattle. Shop, eat, rest—it's all here. Otherwise, cross the four lanes of 15th Street Southwest at the light as you continue on the trail.

Once you're past the mall, every sense of urban life disappears. All at once, at mile 14.5, you encounter a casual, small-town atmosphere— a grassy park, people meandering along side streets, and kids on their bikes. Meet Algona, a little town just a few blocks from the city of Auburn. The nearby town of Pacific is 1 mile down the trail and the end of this trail description. Between the two towns you'll cross several roads. When you're ready, turn around and return the way you came. Or consider probing a bit further south, or form a loop through the Green River Valley via the Interurban and Green River Trails.

5 CEDAR RIVER TRAIL AND GREEN-TO-CEDAR RIVERS TRAIL

Beginning as a paved trail near Boeing in Renton, the Cedar River Trail heads east toward Maple Valley and Landsburg Park. The final miles of rural, wooded pathway visit the Cedar River at its most dramatic. A side trip on the Green-to-Cedar Rivers Trail to Lake Wilderness offers the chance for waterfront activities.

Activities:

Location: The cities of Renton and Maple Valley, along with Lake Wilderness, all in King County

Length: The Cedar River Trail runs 17 miles. A Green-to-Cedar Rivers Trail side tour from Lake Wilderness Park to Landsburg Park is an additional 4-mile round-trip, utilizing a portion of the Green-to-Cedar Rivers Trail and the southern end of the Cedar River Trail.

Surface: Asphalt, gravel. The Cedar River Trail is paved from Lake Washington in Renton to Maple Valley, and gravel from the junction with the Green-to-Cedar Rivers Trail to the end of the Cedar River Trail at Landsburg. The Green-to-Cedar Rivers Trail is mostly gravel from its junction with Cedar River Trail in Maple Valley to Black Diamond Open Area near Lake Sawyer. Plans are under way to pave these gravel sections.

Wheelchair access: Find access at Cedar River Trail Park, Liberty Park, and Cedar River Park.

Difficulty: Mostly easy

Food: Grocery stores and restaurants can be found in Renton, Lake Wilderness, and Maple Valley.

Restrooms: Find restrooms at the Cedar River Trail Park, Liberty Park, Cedar River Park, Maplewood Park, Landsburg Park, and Lake Wilderness Park.

Seasons: The trail can be used year-round.

Rentals: See appendix A for bike rentals in the Puget Sound area. Boat rentals are available at Lake Wilderness.

Contacts: King County Parks, www.kingcounty.gov; Washington Trails Association, www.wta.org; City of Renton Parks and Recreation Department, (425) 430-6600, www.rentonwa.gov; City of Maple Valley, https://www.maplevalleywa.gov/departments-services/parks-recreation.   View the King County Trail Map at https://gismaps.kingcounty.gov/TrailFinder/.

Bus routes: Visit the Metro Transit website at www.kingcountry.gov or call (206) 553-3000.

Access and parking: North 6th Street at the Cedar River Trail Park: If you're coming from I-405 South, take exit 5 (Park Avenue / Sunset Boulevard Northeast). Turn right from the exit onto Park Avenue and then right onto North 6th Street. Continue straight for several blocks until you dead-end at the trail. The road turns right to parallel the trail. You can park near the shore of Lake Washington at the Cedar River Trail Park. This is the western terminus of the Cedar River Trail. GPS: N47 29.99' / W122 12.90'

From I-405 North, take exit 5 (Issaquah / Sunset Boulevard Northeast). Turn left onto Sunset Boulevard, which will eventually become Park Avenue. Turn right onto North 6th Street and continue as directed above.

- Landsburg Park: This is the eastern terminus of the Cedar River Trail. Park in the lot at Landsburg Road SE and SE 252nd Place.

- Lake Wilderness Park in Maple Valley: Find the park at 22500 SE 248th Street.

|||||||||||||||||||||||||||||||||||||||||||||||||||||||||||||||||||||||||||||||||||||||||||||||

From 1884 to the 1940s, the converted rail lines you'll be traveling on served the coal industry, which was largely responsible for the area's economic growth. The Columbia & Puget Sound Railway, once called the Seattle Coal & Transportation Company, moved coal from the mines of Maple Valley and Renton to Seattle starting in 1884. The Chicago, Milwaukee & Puget Sound Railway, part of the same parent company, ran the lines from Maple Valley to Cedar Falls and Rattlesnake Lake. The mines

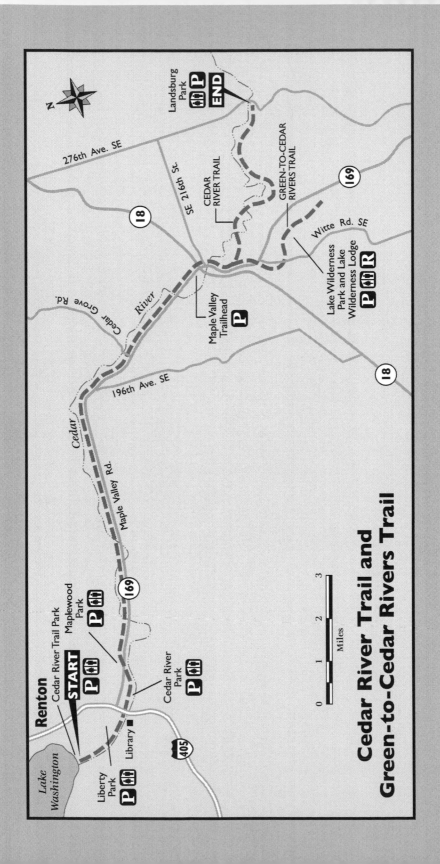

**Cedar River Trail and
Green-to-Cedar Rivers Trail**

The western side of the Cedar River Trail travels between the Boeing property and the Cedar River.

around Puget Sound produced most of Washington's coal in 1890, and the best coal was from this area—in particular, the Newcastle mine on this line just north of Renton. (See Trail 3, Coal Creek Trail.) The coal was taken to the coal docks in Seattle for transport to San Francisco.

You can access the set of trails discussed here from many points; this description begins at the northwestern end at Cedar River Trail Park, in Renton, and proceeds southeastwardly. In the city of Renton, the Cedar River Trail originates as a paved path on the banks of the canal-like Cedar River. Farther down the trail, view the impressive city library. The paved trail then ascends to street level at Liberty Park to head east beside WA 169. This section with its shaded parks is especially popular with skaters; horseback riding is allowed once you're outside the Renton city limits. It's hard to believe you're only a few hundred yards from WA 169. The trail follows the Cedar River along WA 169, dropping below the highway at times to provide a respite from traffic. It continues close to the highway for the next 5 miles, with the trail meeting the river now and again and then wandering off, only to return under an old trestle and along the river. Continue past 196th Avenue Southeast and beyond.

Pass through a tunnel under Southeast 216th Street, then cross a trestle over the Cedar River. Retreat from the highway here and travel through a quiet, rural corridor near the river and its rural riverfront homes all the way to Landsburg Park. You'll reach the Lake Wilderness cutoff 0.8 mile from the WA 18 overpass. If you like, you can take a soft right uphill on the 1.8-mile trail here to reach Lake Wilderness on the Green-to-Cedar Rivers Trail.

This description continues straight 4.8 miles toward Landsburg Park. Along the final 2 miles of this pathway, the Cedar River leaves the trail then sneaks back, crossing back and forth. Stop on the trestle to watch the river rush, especially when the waters are high. The surrounding terrain is hillier here. Arrive at the Landsburg trailhead and the nearby Landsburg Park. When you're ready, turn around and return the way you came. Or you could extend your outing and try a 4-mile round-trip between Lake Wilderness and Landsburg Parks. Lake Wilderness Park is the prior site of historical resorts. Visit the Lake Wilderness Lodge, a modern replacement. This large park offers waterfront opportunities, programs, and an arboretum.

6 PRESTON–SNOQUALMIE TRAIL

This peaceful, wooded trail in the Cascade foothills ends with a view of spectacular Snoqualmie Falls. For a dog walk, an evening ride, your daily jog, or a pleasant skate, this trail is the ticket.

Activities:

Location: Preston, in King County

Length: 7.0 miles

Surface: Asphalt with brief, steep gravel switchbacks

Wheelchair access: The trail is wheelchair-accessible except for the descent and switchbacks noted below.

Difficulty: Easy, except for a steep paved descent to a road crossing and gravel switchbacks back up to the trail.

Food: In Preston, at the I-90 interchange, and in Fall City

Restrooms: There is a toilet at the Preston and Lake Alice Trailheads.

Seasons: The trail can be used year-round.

Rentals: There are no rentals along the route. See appendix A for rentals in the Puget Sound area.

Contacts: King County Parks Division, www.kingcounty.gov; Washington Trails Association, www.wta.org.

Bus routes: Contact Metro Transit at (206) 553-3000 or www.kingcounty.gov.

Access and parking: You can access the trail from either the Preston or Lake Alice Trailhead. To reach the Preston Trailhead, near the trail's western terminus, leave I-90 at exit 22 (Fall City). Turn north and drive to the T intersection with Preston–Fall City Road. Turn right (east), drive 2 blocks, and then turn left onto Southeast 87th Street. The small parking lot is on your right. GPS: N47 31.35' / W121 56.00'

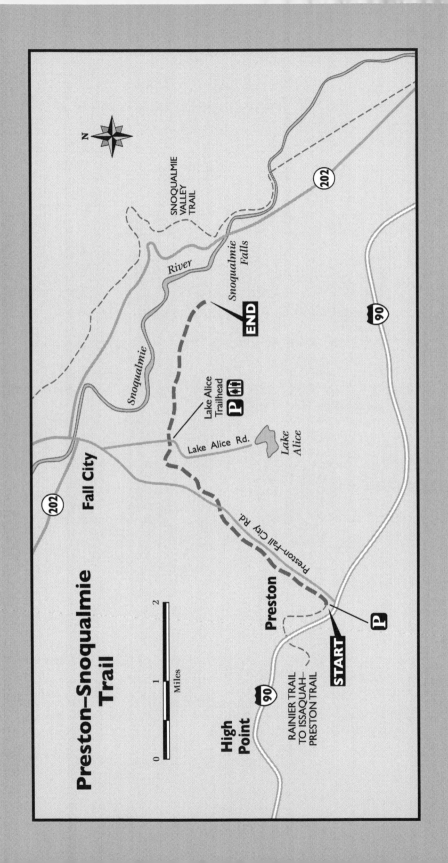

Only a 20-minute drive from the suburbs on the east side of Lake Washington, the Preston–Snoqualmie Trail makes for a pleasant, woodsy outing. Parents stroll the pathway with their children and locals walk their dogs, enjoying the valley views. The trail ends with a view of Snoqualmie Falls, which drop 268 feet into the Snoqualmie River—100 feet more than the drop at Niagara Falls. The pavement is smooth and relatively flat except for a road crossing with a steep hill on both sides, one paved and the other featuring gravel switchbacks. The Seattle, Lake Shore & Eastern Railway was built in 1890; the trail opened in 1978.

This description follows the trail from west to east. The trail actually extends about 1 mile farther west from its western trailhead in Preston to its intersection with the Issaquah–Preston Trail (Trail E) near Northeast 79th Street and High Point Way. To head east toward scenic Snoqualmie Falls, start at the edge of the parking lot where the trail traverses a sidehill. The hillside down to the streets of Preston Mill and the valley below affords fine views and brightens your jaunt. You may see deer, Steller's jays, cougars, and bears. Though the animals usually retreat when humans are around, please read—and follow—the wildlife guidelines at the trailhead.

A large trestle once crossed the Raging River Valley 2.5 miles out, replaced with a steep descent to the road. Watch for traffic veering around the curve as you cross Preston–Fall City Road. The trail climbs back up several steep gravel switchbacks. Follow the trail along the north side of Snoqualmie Ridge. Arrive at the Lake Alice Trailhead, 3.5 miles from Preston.

The final 1.8 miles of trail south from Lake Alice Road offer Snoqualmie River Valley vistas and a distant view of Snoqualmie Falls, framed by tall fir and cedar trees. Far from the throngs of tourists at the Salish Lodge, you'll observe the falls from a quiet viewpoint at the end of the Preston–Snoqualmie Trail.

When you're ready, turn around and return the way you came. From the western portion of the Preston-Snoqualmie Trail, you can connect with the Issaquah–Preston Trail (Trail E) for a longer outing. Or head up to the Salish Lodge for a bird's-eye view of the falls from the attic lounge or the tourist overlook. Sightseeing trains run from the old Snoqualmie depot of the Great Northern Railway—also a railroad museum—and enables an enjoyable, historical look above the falls. In Snoqualmie, access the Snoqualmie Valley Trail (Trail 7) and the Snoqualmie Centennial Trail–Corridor Trail (Trail L).

Enjoy your own private scenic viewing point of Snoqualmie Falls from the trail.

7 SNOQUALMIE VALLEY TRAIL

Wander the foothills of rural Snoqualmie Valley from Duvall through Carnation, to Snoqualmie Falls near Snoqualmie, on to North Bend, and finally to Rattlesnake Lake Recreation Area. You'll travel near the highway, through wetlands, along ridges, above the valley, through a golf course, minutes from Snoqualmie Falls, and into charming and historic downtown areas. Enjoy an elegant lodge, a 268-foot waterfall, bakeries, bridges, rivers, and lakes.

Activities:

Location: Duvall to North Bend, in King County

Length: 31 miles, with a 2.4-mile roadside trail detour

Surface: Crushed rock and original ballast

Wheelchair access: The trail is not wheelchair-accessible.

Difficulty: Easy to moderate. The 2.6 percent average grade above the valley floor requires a few climbs. The 2.5-mile roadside trail detour from along Tokul, Stearns / Mill Pond, and Reinig Roads includes steps.

Food: Restaurants, cafes, and grocery stores are all available within 1 mile of the trail in Snoqualmie, Duvall, Carnation, Snoqualmie Falls, and North Bend.

Restrooms: Public restrooms are available at Depot & McCormick Parks, Duvall Park, Snoqualmie Depot, and Rattlesnake Lake Recreation Area.

Seasons: The trail can be used year-round.

Rentals: There are no rentals along the route. See appendix A for bike rentals in the Puget Sound area.

Contacts: Washington Trails Association, www.wta.org; King County Parks and Recreation, www.kingcounty.gov. View the King County trail finder at https://gismaps.kingcounty.gov/TrailFinder/.

Bus routes: Check the Metro Transit website at www.kingcounty.gov or call (206) 553-3000.

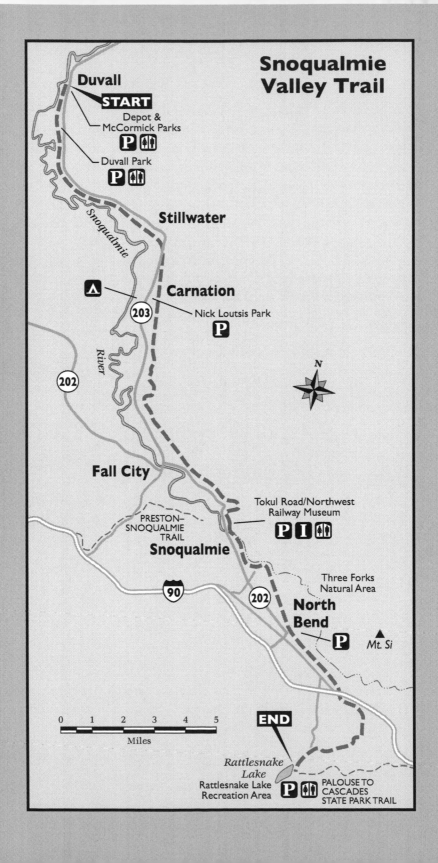

Access and parking: There are several spots along the Snoqualmie Valley Trail, with a sampling indicated below. This description follows the trail from Duvall (at its northern end) to Rattlesnake Lake in the south.

To start at the northern end of the trail in Duvall, take Woodinville–Duvall Road east to WA 203, then turn into the parking area just north of the bridge north of Northeast Virginia Street and Northeast Woodinville Road. GPS: N47 44.61' / W121 59.20'

An alternative is at the Depot & McCormick Parks just south of the bridge in Duvall. Access the trail via a paved path. Head south (left) toward Carnation on the trail.

To start in Carnation at Nick Loutsis Park, take WA 203 to Entwistle Street and turn east.

To start in North Bend, turn north off North Bend Way onto Ballarat Avenue to reach the lot along Northeast 4th Street.

To begin at Rattlesnake Lake, take exit 32 (436th Avenue Northeast) off I-90. Turn south and follow 436th Avenue Northeast / Cedar Falls Road southeast for approximately 3.0 miles to the Rattlesnake Lake Recreation Area parking area.

B eginning in Duvall, it's a 9-mile jaunt on a generally flat trail to Carnation. While in Duvall enjoy the shops and visit the Depot & McCormick Parks. Take in local history at the old Chicago, Milwaukee, St. Paul & Pacific Railroad depot.

The trail travels southeast on the west side of WA 203, close to the road yet separated by wetlands and open fields. You'll pass road crossings and lots of blackberry bushes. Watch for waterfowl and listen for songbirds. Cross WA 203 just north of Carnation. Reach the Nick Loutsis Trailhead at mile 9.0 at Entwistle Street. You can turn west (right) for a neighborhood tour of Carnation and a snack, or take a side trip to the riverfront at Tolt-MacDonald Park.

From Carnation, the trail rises above the Snoqualmie Valley and heads 10 miles to Tokul Road. Trestle crossings offer views of the river and valley through a canopy of evergreens. Cross the Tolt River at 0.5 mile from the town of Carnation. At 7.0 miles, pass the 356th Drive Southeast Trailhead.

The Duvall 1912 depot at the Depot & McCormick Parks.
Dave Lindsay

A high bridge crosses Tokul Creek at 9.0 miles, affording valley views and a peek at the creek below. The trail climbs near Snoqualmie Falls and encounters a 2.5-mile on-street detour. This detour provides an ideal opportunity for a side trip to Snoqualmie Falls, the Snoqualmie Centennial Trail–Corridor Trail (Trail L), and the Northwest Railroad Museum in Snoqualmie.

It's a 5.0-mile stretch between Tokul Road to Meadowbrook. To continue on the Snoqualmie Valley Trail, complete the 2.5-mile on-road detour on mostly country roads. Use the stairs and then follow the Tokul Road southward. Turn east onto Stearns Road and continue as it becomes Mill Pond Road, then Reinig Road. The former Weyerhaeuser mill site is nearby to the north. Continue on Reinig Road to the old Reinig railroad bridge across the river, located on your right. Ascend steps to continue southeast on the trail. The trail passes the Three Forks Natural Area. Mount Si Golf Course appears, surrounding the trail. Pass through the golf course. Look up at Mount Si, towering above the upper Snoqualmie River valley.

Visit the historic Snoqualmie Depot and ride the tourist train.

Continue southeast from the golf course, beside fields and along the river. Cross several small roads before you reach the parking lot at 4th and Ballarat in North Bend. Consider a visit to the library for some railroad history, or visit downtown North Bend.

The Snoqualmie Valley Trail continues north of the parking lot for over 7.0 miles to Rattlesnake Lake Recreation Area. Mount Si remains in sight as you cross several streets. At 2.0 miles, cross North Bend Way and then go under I-90. In 4.8 miles, arrive at Rattlesnake Lake and the Cedar Falls Trailhead. You can reach the extensive Palouse to Cascades State Trail (Trail 22) from here, or enjoy the Rattlesnake Lake Recreation Area.

8 IRON GOAT TRAIL

This interpretive hiking trail in the Stevens Pass historic district climbs a constant 2.2 percent grade. Kiosks guide you through a trail decorated with wildflowers and forests of ferns, alders, and evergreens. The route offers you views of the Alpine Lakes Wilderness and mountain peaks, rivers and streams, remnants of the railroad, and the 7.8-mile Cascade Tunnel. Mileage markers reflect the original railroad signs, indicating mileage to St. Paul, Minnesota. The trail is named for the logo on the Great Northern trains.

Activities:

Location: King County, near Stevens Pass

Length: 10.2 miles, plus 3 connecting trails between the upper and lower grades

Surface: 3.8 miles are gravel / crushed limestone; the remainder consists of native soils or original fill used by the Great Northern Railway. Trail users may encounter snow where the trail passes avalanche paths, even in summer.

Wheelchair access: The 2.8-mile lower grade is barrier-free and wheelchair-accessible from Martin Creek Trailhead to Scenic Iron Goat Trail Interpretive Site, conditions permitting. Also, 2.7 miles of barrier-free trail (moderate difficulty) is available from the Wellington Trailhead to the Windy Point Tunnel.

Difficulty: Easy to moderate

Food: No food is available along this trail.

Restrooms: There are restrooms at the Martin Creek and Wellington Trailheads and the Scenic Iron Goat Trail Interpretive Site; there is a pit toilet at Windy Point.

Seasons: Winter travel is discouraged due to avalanche risks and snow-covered access.

Rentals: No rentals are available along this trail.

Contacts: USDA Forest Service, Skykomish Ranger Station, (360) 677-2414, or visit https://www.fs.usda.gov/recmain/mbs/recreation. Obtain current Forest Service Road conditions and a trail flyer from the Ranger Station (or online). To volunteer through the Washington Trails Association, visit www.wta.org. For avalanche conditions during winter travel, visit www. csac.org.

Bus routes: None

Access and parking: To reach the Martin Creek Trailhead, take US 2 to milepost 55, 6 miles east of the town of Skykomish, or to milepost 58.3 at Scenic, 5.6 miles west of the summit. Turn north onto Old Cascade Highway, FR 67. Proceed to FR 6710 (2.3 miles from milepost 55 or 1.4 miles from milepost 58.3). Take FR 6710 1.4 miles to the trailhead. GPS: N47 43.76' / W121 12.40'

To access the trail at the Scenic Iron Goat Trail Interpretive Site Trailhead, drive US 2 to milepost 58.3 at Scenic. Turn north onto Old Cascade Highway, then immediately turn right into the Iron Goat Interpretive Site, maintained by the Washington State Department of Transportation. Look for the red caboose.

To reach the Wellington Trailhead from the east, take US 2 to milepost 64.4 and take the first right (0.3 mile) onto Old Stevens Pass Highway. After 2.8 miles turn right onto a short gravel spur road marked "Iron Goat Trail #1074." Continue to the trailhead parking by the restrooms.

If heading west, for safety reasons continue past milepost 64.4 to the summit and turn around. Then head west on US 2, return to milepost 64.4, and follow directions above. If parking at the Wellington Trailhead, a Northwest Forest Pass (day-use or annual) is required, and is valid in

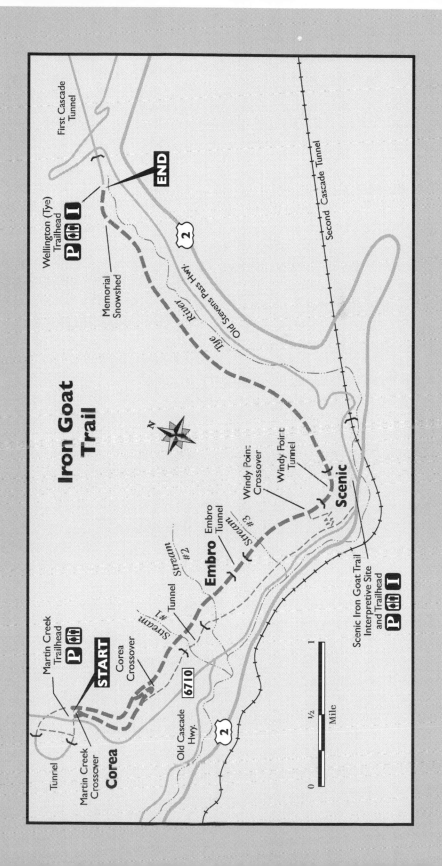

Washington and Oregon national forests. Purchase information is available at the above USDA Forest Service website. Payment locations may include a ranger station, select local vendors, and on the website.

|||||||||||||||||||||||||||||||||||||||||||||||||||||||||||||||||||||||||||||||||||||||||||||||||||||||||||||||||||||

The route of the Iron Goat Trail is best known for two things: for the impressive engineering of the mountainside switchbacks and the Cascade Tunnel, and for the tragedy of 1910, when an avalanche knocked fifteen cars off the rails and killed ninety-six people. The tragedy was but the final blow for the train's passengers, who had been stalled for seven days watching hillsides of rocks, snow, and trees sliding over the tracks.

The drama of the railroad started back in 1891 when engineers like Charles Haskell and John Stevens forced their way to Stevens Pass through challenging terrain and difficult weather. Then came the construction of intricate switchbacks cut into the mountainside. In 1900 the completion of the original 2.6-mile Cascade Tunnel eliminated the need for the tedious switchbacks. Though snowsheds were added to protect trains from avalanches, trains were still halted for days at a time in winter storms. These historic events are documented in the *Iron Goat Trail Guidebook*.

Today many of the tunnels are collapsed or covered with slide debris. They can be viewed from the trail, but do not attempt to enter any tunnels or to walk on rotten timbers. Please stay on the trail to protect the wildflowers.

Nearly fifty interpretive signs dot the trail system and add depth to a visit to the area. Although you can access the trail from three trailheads, this description begins at the Martin Creek Trailhead. Trains once climbed through a 170-degree horseshoe-shaped tunnel (now collapsed) at Martin Creek, creating an upper and a lower track. The trailhead lies at the elevation of the lower track section, called the lower trail. In 2013, 1 mile of the Horseshoe Tunnel / Kelly Creek Trail #1076 opened, accessible from the north end of Martin Creek Trailhead. It contains three viewpoints—two at historic trestle abutments, and one at the lower portal. This trail eventually will connect with the old Kelly Creek Trail in the Wild Sky Wilderness.

For a short, flat hike from the Martin Creek Trailhead, follow the lower trail for 1.5 miles. Listen for the rustling leaves of hardwood trees as you travel across Stream #1 to the Twin Tunnels and the 96-foot-high concrete arch of a snowshed. The trail continues another 1.5 miles to the town of Scenic, the Scenic Iron Goat Trail Interpretive Site and Trailhead, and the red caboose.

For a longer outing from the Martin Creek Trailhead (elevation 2,380 feet), you can take either of two crossover trails (which avoid the collapsed tunnel) up to the upper grade. It is 6.2 miles from Martin Creek Trailhead to Wellington Trailhead via the upper grade.

This tunnel serves as an example of the many tunnels visitors see on the Iron Goat Trail.

From the trailhead the trail crosses wetlands on a boardwalk. The Martin Creek Crossover appears after the boardwalk and takes you up a short, steep trail to the upper grade. You can take this crossover and turn right when you reach the upper grade, or, for a longer trail with less slope, continue on the lower grade to the Corea Crossover at 0.5 mile. This crossover is about 0.3 mile long; turn right at the top.

At just under 2 miles from Martin Creek, you'll find one of the remaining back walls of eleven massive concrete snowsheds just before Embro, once the site of a telegraph station and workers' shacks. A spur trail leads you to the spillway and reservoir built to manage fires caused by sparks from passing trains.

Just beyond, follow the spur trail around the Embro Tunnel. After the tunnel's east portal, head to the Windy Point Crossover, where a trail option is to take the switchbacks down to the Iron Goat Trail Interpretive Site at Scenic. You could end your journey at the interpretive site, having enjoyed Windy Point and the loop trails from Martin Creek. Otherwise, continue on the Iron Goat Trail past the Windy Point Crossover, around Windy Point Tunnel, and east to Wellington.

At the Windy Point Tunnel, the trail follows the original grade around the tunnel on the edge of the mountainside. Check out the active tunnel below from the viewpoint, and follow the trail on the 2-foot-wide ledge of the snowshed archway to view the east portal. Continue east past several snowsheds.

At mile 6.0 you'll start through the all-concrete snowshed that now serves as a memorial to those who died here in the avalanche of 1910. The Wellington depot was built just beyond this point in 1883. It was moved east when this snowshed was built. A year after the avalanche disaster, both the depot and the town of Wellington were renamed "Tye"; the railroad knew that passengers simply would not want to pass through "Wellington."

Pass a runaway track and cross Haskell Creek to reach the Wellington Trailhead, 3,100 feet in elevation. Continue 0.25 mile to the interpretive signs and viewpoint to see the west portal of the Cascade Tunnel. When you're ready, turn around and return the way you came.

9 CASCADE TRAIL

The Cascade Trail reaches into the Cascade foothills in rural northwestern Washington. It parallels WA 20 on the flats until it climbs to a wooded hillside near Concrete. The trail crosses over twenty trestles, which range from 10 to 2,200 feet long.

Activities:

Location: Sedro Woolley to Concrete, in Skagit County

Length: 23 miles

Surface: Crushed rock and ballast

Wheelchair access: This trail is not wheelchair-accessible except at the Fruitdale Road Trailhead, where the trail is paved for about 1 mile in total to the east and west.

Difficulty: Easy, although the ballast is difficult to bike on at times

Food: You'll find things to eat in the towns of Sedro Woolley and Concrete.

Restrooms: Public restrooms are available at the trailheads in Sedro Woolley and Concrete.

Seasons: The trail can be used year-round.

Rentals: Near Sedro Woolley, you can rent bicycles from the Willowbrook Manor English Tea House and Chamomile Farm, (360) 218-4585, www.teaandtour.com.

Contacts: Skagit County Parks and Recreation, (360) 416-1350, www.skagitcounty.net; Sedro Woolley Chamber of Commerce, (360) 855-1841, www.sedro-woolley.com; Concrete Chamber of Commerce, (360) 853-8784, www.concrete-wa.com

Bus routes: Skagit Transit #70X, (360) 757-4433, www.skagittransit.org

Access and parking: To reach the western trailhead at Sedro Woolley, take I-5 to exit 232 (Cook Road) and navigate the roundabouts to eastbound WA 20. Drive about 6 miles to the trailhead parking at Fruitdale Road. GPS:

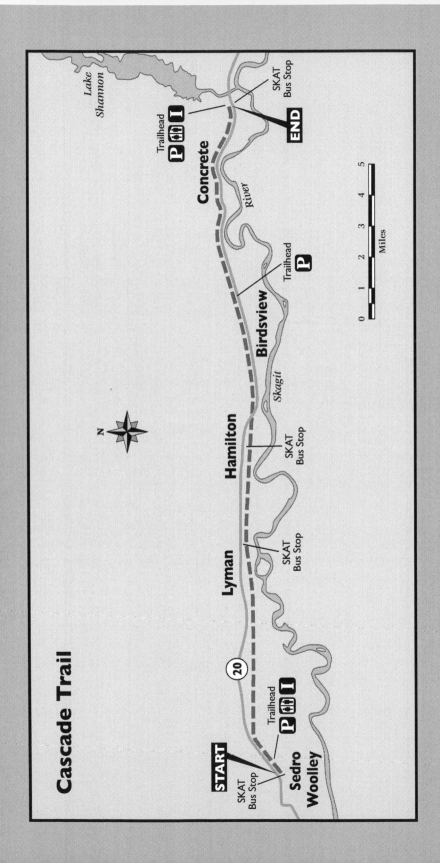

Cascade Trail

Lake
Shannon

Concrete

River

Birdsview

Skagit

Hamilton

Lyman

Sedro
Woolley

Trailhead

START

END

SKAT
Bus Stop

SKAT
Bus Stop

SKAT
Bus Stop

SKAT
Bus Stop

Trailhead

Trailhead

N

20

0 1 2 3 4 5
Miles

N48 30.92' / W122 12.66' (**Note:** Horse trailer parking is available at this and all trailheads.)

Find the eastern terminus at the Concrete Center in the town of Concrete.

||||||||||||||||||||||||||||||||||||||||||||||||||||||||||||||||||||||||||||||||||||||||||||||

The Great Northern Railway (GN) once connected downriver towns with the wooded areas along the upper Skagit where the Cascade Trail now runs. Independent businessmen sought their riches among the forests of cedar trees that filled the valley. In Sedro Woolley, P. A. Woolley made a fortune supplying ties for the GN; merchants also prospered from the passengers traveling through town. The line transported cement, lumber, and shakes. The GN arrived in the town of Concrete in 1900. Concrete's cement plants, opened in 1904 and 1907, supplied building material for the Grand Coulee Dam, Baker River Dam, and Ballard Locks, and shipped cement as far as the Pacific during World War II. Eleven miles of the line—from Sedro Woolley to Hamilton—ran freight until 1990. The trail was completed in 1999.

You can access the trail from several points along the way; this description takes you from west to east. The trail starts on a short paved section on the outskirts of Sedro Woolley among the trees, turning to gravel a short distance east from the Fruitdale Road trailhead. Mileage is well marked. At mile 7.0 the Skagit River comes up to the trail for a brief, scenic passage. Three miles out of Lyman you'll cross Lyman-Hamilton Road; there's a SKAT bus stop here if you're ready to turn back. At the second trestle after you cross the Lyman-Hamilton Road, a brief detour from the trail along a road and back on the trail avoids the washed-out trestle. You'll next cross numerous creeks before reaching WA 20. The trail runs beside the highway here. Just past mile 14, pass Lusk Road. (Head south on Lusk Road to reach the Rasar State Park on the Skagit River.)

At mile 18.0, on a lush hillside, you begin to see the mountains to the east. If you look south you'll spot the unusual building that bridges the road (it's the Concrete High School). Pass the concrete silos, where concrete dust was stored, and cross Douglas Vose III Way to the trail's end at the Concrete Center in Concrete.

Cascade Trail passes through rural farmlands near the Skagit River.
Dave Lindsay

Turn up Douglas Vose III Way to tour Concrete and get a snack or din-ner. You'll find public restrooms adjacent to the old 1936 schoolhouse. Continue touring Concrete by crossing the historic Thompson Bridge to rest at the riverside at the Baker River Fish Facility Visitor Center. This bridge connected the towns of Baker and Cement City in 1918; at the time it was the longest single-span cement bridge in the world.

Enjoy this little town, and then ride the bus back to your starting point.

10 SNOHOMISH COUNTY CENTENNIAL TRAIL

This trail leaves the city of Snohomish and travels north through farmland, wetlands, and fields. At Lake Stevens it continues through rural and wooded country, on to Arlington, then out to the terminus at the Nakashima Heritage Barn near the Snohomish–Skagit county border. Skaters savor the wide, smooth pavement, while equestrians enjoy the soft, 6-foot-wide parallel path. Multiple access points, fun towns, and several parks and lakes contribute to a relaxing destination.

Activities:

Location: Snohomish, Lake Stevens, Marysville, Arlington, Bryant, and to the Snohomish–Skagit county line, all in Snohomish County

Length: 29.5 miles

Surface: Asphalt for 29.5 miles, with parallel dirt path for equestrians. Check with trail managers or website for current equestrian exclusions on a few sections.

Wheelchair access: All trailheads indicated are wheelchair-accessible.

Difficulty: Easy

Food: Snohomish and Lake Stevens offer restaurants, espresso shops, and markets within 1 mile of the trail.

Restrooms: There are restrooms or chemical toilets at all trailheads.

Seasons: The trail can be used year-round.

Rentals: Bicycle Centres, 707 Pine Avenue, Unit B101, Snohomish, (360) 862-8300, www.bicyclecentres.com

Contacts: Snohomish County Parks, Recreation, and Tourism Department, (425) 388-6600, https://snohomishcountywa.gov/5168/Parks-Recreation; Snohomish County Tourism Bureau at (888) 338-0976, or www.snohomish.org

Bus routes: Take bus #201 or #202 from Smokey Point to Marysville. For more information, call Community Transit at (425) 353-RIDE (7433), or visit www.communitytransit.org.

Access and parking: Moving from the southern end of the trail to the northern terminus, there are several trailheads with vehicle access points. The directions provided here are for the trail as described.

The intersection of Maple and Pine Avenues in Snohomish is near the trail's southern terminus. Exit I-5 at US 2 eastbound to Snohomish and Wenatchee. Take the 88th Street SE exit off US 2 toward Snohomish. Turn right onto Pine Avenue at the stoplight and drive to Maple Avenue. The trail northward begins at this intersection. GPS: N47 55.24' / W122 05.12' (The city of Snohomish extended the trail from this point to about 0.5 mile south to 1st Street, and named this short section the City of Snohomish Centennial Trail.)

The northern terminus at Nakashima Farm is the Nakashima Heritage Barn North Trailhead and is accessed off WA 9 near the Snohomish–Skagit county border, about 6 miles north of Arlington.

||||||||||||||||||||||||||||||||||||||||||||||||||||||||||||||||||||||||||||||||||||||||||||||||

If the sunny summer crowds of Seattle are not your style, head north to the Snohomish Valley, 40 miles northeast of Seattle. The valley's hundred-year history of dairying and farming is evident along the Snohomish County Centennial Trail that begins in Snohomish and ends at Nakashima Heritage Barn North Trailhead along WA 9 near the county border. Trail mile marker and trail map mileage numbers go from 29 in the south to 0 at the northern terminus. Along the trail, enjoy the antiques shops and eateries of Snohomish and the Lake Stevens town center and lake.

This trail is peaceful and thoughtfully planned. Smooth, wide pavement attracts skaters, and a 6-foot-wide natural trail lures equestrians. The calm, rural setting takes you back to the heyday of the dairy and farming industries, when this area was served by the Seattle, Lake Shore & Eastern Railway and the Northern Pacific Railroad. Past years of heavy logging have left no scars. Well-placed benches and picnic tables and occasional interpretive and historical signs invite you to stop, rest, look, and imagine.

Machias Trailhead lends a railroad theme to the trail experience.

You can access the trail from many points along the way; this description begins in Snohomish, its southern end, and proceeds northward. From the trailhead at Pine Avenue and Maple Street, begin your journey along the Pilchuck River. Benches and picnic tables are thoughtfully placed for views and serenity.

Railroad history and trail mileage are all listed at the Pilchuck parking lot, 2 miles up the trail. The Snohomish–Arlington run of the Seattle, Lake Shore & Eastern Railway's Sumas line came to town in 1889 and continued through the 1950s. In 1989 the rail trail was planned and named for this hundred-year history. It opened in 1991, with additional pavement northward to the Nakashima Heritage Barn North Trailhead dedicated in 2012 at the Nakashima Farm.

The train came from Woodinville to Snohomish, Arlington, and Bryant—the site of a big mill and a 100-foot-high trestle—through the town of Pilchuck and on to the Canadian border. The Seattle–North Bend run completed the route to Seattle for shipping lumber and carrying mail and livestock. Shingle mills were big business in the railroad's peak years; they required little investment, and the Snohomish Valley had plenty of cedar. Snohomish had four shingle mills; Marysville had seven.

Machias Trailhead near Division Street, 5 miles up the trail from the Snohomish Trailhead, provides a sense of heritage. Restrooms are housed in the blue replica of a depot built in the late 1890s. The photos of the town of Machias take you back to the early 1900s. The trail continues past the 20th Street Trailhead in Lake Stevens. Or turn left here, or at the previous crossing at 16th Street, and continue 0.25 mile to the old section of town and grab a meal.

If you'd like to continue your trek northward, return to the trail and travel past trailheads at Highway 92 Overpass and Rhododendron. At 84th Street Northeast, use caution with the vehicle traffic when crossing the road. You'll cross under WA 9 near trail mile marker 20.7 and then under Lauck Road. At the Lake Cassidy Wetlands near trail mile marker 18, take the access path to enjoy the lake. Getchell Trailhead (trail mile marker 17) and the large Armar Road Trailhead (152nd Street East at trail mile marker 12) are ahead, located south of the city of Arlington.

Get some views of valley farms as the trail traverses a ridge. Follow the trail through Arlington near trail mile marker 8. Continue north to the trailhead at Bryant, at trail mile marker 4.

The trail ends 4 miles farther north at the Nakashima Heritage Barn North Trailhead near the Snohomish–Skagit county line. Check out the interpretive signs describing the varied history of the site. The red barn, built circa 1908, is on the Washington State Heritage Barn Register.

11 WHATCOM COUNTY AND BELLINGHAM INTERURBAN TRAIL

The Interurban Electric Trolley motored passengers between Mount Vernon and Bellingham Bay from 1889 to 1903. This retired trolley route takes you high above Chuckanut Drive and Bellingham Bay on a path amid evergreens, deciduous trees, and the occasional home. Though Chuckanut Drive is a hilly, curvy street, the trail is quite flat except for one section.

Activities:

Location: Larrabee State Park to the historic Fairhaven district in Bellingham, in Whatcom County

Length: 7.0 miles

Surface: Crushed stone; short road sections

Wheelchair access: Fairhaven Park and the trail north of Old Samish Way are wheelchair-accessible.

Difficulty: Easy in the southern portion and north of Arroyo Park; difficult near California Street through Arroyo Park

Food: You'll find things to eat in Fairhaven.

Restrooms: All trailheads except Arroyo Park offer restrooms.

Seasons: The trail can be used year-round.

Rentals: Jack's Bicycle Center, 1907 Iowa Street, Bellingham, (360) 733-1955, www.jacksbicyclecenter.com

Contacts: City of Bellingham Parks and Recreation, (360) 778-7000, https://cob.org/services/recreation/parks-trails; Whatcom County Parks and Recreation, (360) 733-2900, https://www.whatcomcounty.us/1787/Parks-Recreation; Bellingham/Whatcom County Tourism, (360) 671-3990, www.bellingham.org; Larrabee State Park, (360) 676-2093, www.parks.wa.gov

Bus routes: Contact the Whatcom Transit Authority (WTA), (360) 676-RIDE (7433), www.ridewta.com.

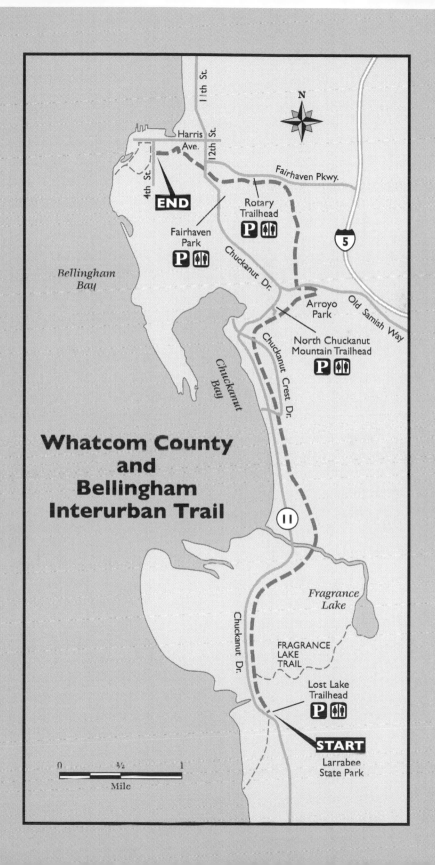

Whatcom County and Bellingham Interurban Trail

Access and parking: Follow the signs for Larrabee State Park from exit 250 (Fairhaven Parkway) off I-5. Drive west on Fairhaven Parkway for 1.5 miles to 12th Street. Turn left onto 12th Street and after 2 blocks bear left onto Chuckanut Drive. Continue about 5.0 miles. Turn left into the Lost Lake parking lot / trailhead located 0.5 mile past the main entrance to the park. GPS: N48 38.89' / W122 29.23'

A state park Discover Pass is required to park here, and is valid at Washington's state recreation lands. Find information on the Washington Parks website at www.parks.wa.gov. Purchase options include one-day passes and annual passes, available online, at select automated pay-stations at trailheads, or at specified local vendors.

|||||||||||||||||||||||||||||||||||||||||||||||||||||||||||||||||||||||||||||||||||||||||||||||

In 1915 the Larrabee family donated the 20 acres that became Larrabee State Park, the first state park in Washington. The park's Chuckanut Mountain includes a network of signed hiking and mountain biking pathways that take off from the Interurban Trail.

You can park your car and access the trail from many points along its way; this description begins at its southern end, the Lost Lake Trailhead. Jump on the Interurban Trail and watch for the 0.5-mile markers along the trail. Heading north on the main trail, you'll run into hikers coming from the Fragrance Lake Trailhead at 0.5 mile. Bicycles are not allowed on this side trail.

A forest of second-growth and deciduous trees begins to open up to a view of the bay and the islands in 2 miles. Cross several streets and meet Chuckanut Drive where it rises up to the level of the trail at Chuckanut Crest Drive. If you want to avoid steep hills, exit the trail to a second shuttle car parked on the road here, or turn back and retrace your steps.

After this brief encounter with civilization, you'll reach a couple of hills and then a drop to a sudden stop sign at California Street, at 4.5 miles. Due to a missing railroad trestle, trail users choose between a road detour and a forested switchback trail through the Arroyo Park's mountainous singletrack trails. For the road option, turn left onto California Street, then right onto Chuckanut Drive to Old Samish Way for a roadside detour of about 1 mile. Turn right and regain the trail across the street from the Arroyo Park lot.

View Chuckanut Bay from along the Whatcom County and Bellingham Interurban Trail.

For the singletrack route, you'll continue across California Street to the trail. Take the right fork and head into a mossy forest with creeks, bridges, a small waterfall, and the Chuckanut Creek. Cross the long wooden bridge. Turn left at the trail across the bridge for an uphill haul to Old Samish Way.

Cross Old Samish Way and continue on an easier section of the Interurban Trail.

Head into a pleasant, more open area on the fringes of town. Cross several small streets and parallel Fairhaven Parkway. You'll cross 20th Street 1 mile from the Arroyo Park Trailhead. Get onto Clementine Street briefly. Shortly rejoin the trail where it heads right as the street curves left. Pass the Rotary Trailhead and leave the neighborhood to enter the wooded Padden Creek area. You'll reach Donovan Avenue and 10th Street at Padden Creek, less than 1 mile from the Rotary Trailhead.

To travel near the bay for 1 mile, continue on the trail now named "Lower Padden Creek and Larrabee Trail." Another option is to turn onto 10th Street to head into Fairhaven for a refreshing meal and to reach the South Bay Trail (Trail 12). Otherwise, turn around and return on the Interurban Trail to your starting trailhead.

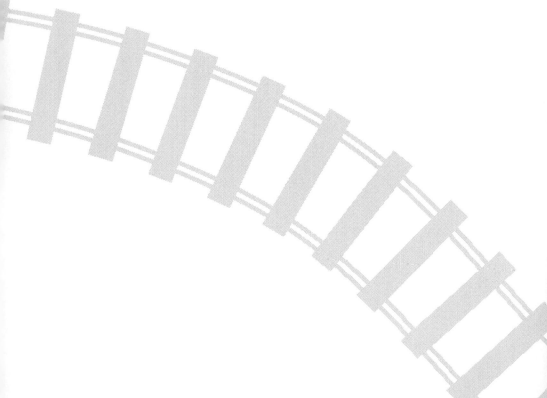

12 SOUTH BAY TRAIL

Read about local history, see a sunset, walk the waterfront, pass through a park, and enjoy the shops and eateries of downtown Bellingham. Starting at the historic Fairhaven district, most of the South Bay Trail hugs the shore of Bellingham Bay.

Activities:

Location: Bellingham, in Whatcom County

Length: 2.5 miles

Surface: Asphalt, crushed stone, concrete

Wheelchair access: Boulevard Park and the Taylor Avenue Dock are wheelchair-accessible.

Difficulty: Easy, except for steep section on the historic Taylor Avenue Dock

Food: You can stock up in downtown Bellingham and the historic Fairhaven district.

Restrooms: There are restrooms and drinking water at Boulevard Park and the Fairhaven Village area. Find restrooms at Taylor Dock.

Seasons: The trail can be used year-round.

Rentals: Jack's Bicycle Center, 1907 Iowa Street, Bellingham, (360) 733-1955, www.jacksbicyclecenter.com

Contacts: City of Bellingham Parks and Recreation, (360) 778-7000, https://cob.org/services/recreation/parks-trails; Bellingham/Whatcom County Tourism, (360) 671-3990, www.bellingham.org

Bus routes: Contact the Whatcom Transit Authority, (360) 676-RIDE (7433), www.ridewta.com.

Access and parking: Take exit 250 (Fairhaven Parkway) off I-5 and drive west on Fairhaven for 1.5 miles to 12th Street. Turn right, then left in 4

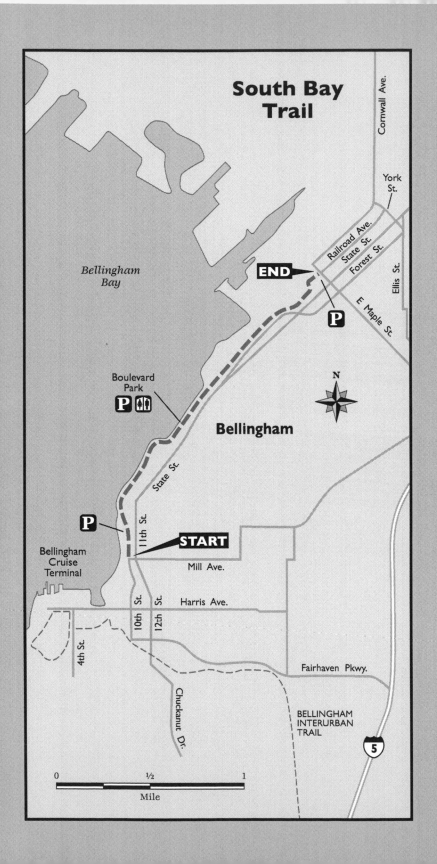

South Bay Trail

Cornwall Ave.

York St.

Railroad Ave.

State St.

Forest St.

Ellis St.

E. Maple St.

END

P

Bellingham Bay

Boulevard Park

P 🚻

N

Bellingham

State St.

P

11th St.

START

Bellingham Cruise Terminal

Mill Ave.

10th St.

12th St.

Harris Ave.

4th St.

Chuckanut Dr.

Fairhaven Pkwy.

BELLINGHAM INTERURBAN TRAIL

5

0   ½   1

Mile

blocks onto Mill Avenue. It dead-ends at the trailhead on 10th Street; you can park on the street. GPS: N48 43.26' / W122 30.26'

|||||||||||||||||||||||||||||||||||||||||||||||||||||||||||||||||||||||||||||||||||||||||||||||||||||||||||||||||||||

This line of the Bellingham Bay & Eastern Railway once pulled coal, sawlogs, and lumber from the Lake Whatcom watershed to ship to developing West Coast cities. The first mill in the area—Henry Roeder's Mill—was built in 1850, and there were no fewer than sixty-eight shingle mills in Whatcom County by 1900. The largest mill in the world, the Puget Sound Sawmill and Timber Company, operated in Fairhaven.

You can park your car and access the right-of-way—now the South Bay Trail—from many spots along its way. This description takes you from its southern terminus, 10th Street and Mill Avenue, northward. Watch for mile markers every 0.5 mile along the route. As you head north, the trail takes you onto 10th briefly until you reach Taylor Avenue Dock, a refurbished wooden trestle and reconstructed boardwalk. Cross over the tracks

Trail users cross the Taylor Avenue Dock on the South Bay Trail in Bellingham.

and enjoy the 0.25-mile over-water walkway. Bicycle riders should move slowly or consider dismounting.

Continue into Boulevard Park and enjoy the sparkling water, or perhaps a scenic sunset. Note that at the north end of the park the trail used to cross a bridge over the tracks. This overpass was removed. Trail users carefully cross the active tracks or seek northward progress by exiting the southern portion of the park and continuing via street sidewalks and street bicycle lanes, reentering the trail further north. Once back on the paved trail, you'll pass waterfront property, businesses, and industries until you reach East Maple Street, where the trail ends.

A mile and a half further on city streets takes you to the Railroad Trail (Trail 13). If you're traveling southbound on the South Bay Trail, you can connect with the Whatcom County and Bellingham Interurban Trail (Trail 11). Whale-watching tours and ferries to the San Juan Islands, Victoria, and Alaska leave from the Bellingham Cruise Terminal at 4th and Harris. A nearby boat launch is convenient for kayaking, sailing, and pleasure boating. Summer rentals are available.

13 RAILROAD TRAIL

This trail makes a gradual climb through quiet neighborhoods to Whatcom Falls Park and Bloedel Donovan Park. Railroad Trail is lightly wooded for most of its length. Each park has a network of trails and water-based attractions. You might enjoy a planned detour to the creek or Lake Whatcom. Picnic facilities are available at both parks.

Activities:

Location: Bellingham, in Whatcom County

Length: 3.5 miles

Surface: Asphalt, crushed stone

Wheelchair access: The trail is wheelchair-accessible at Whatcom Falls and Bloedel Donovan Parks.

Difficulty: Easy to moderate. Traveling from west to east, the trail offers a gradual uphill grade with one moderate slope.

Food: Barkley Village Shopping Center on Woburn Street offers things to eat.

Restrooms: There are restrooms and drinking water at Bloedel Donovan and Whatcom Falls Parks.

Seasons: The trail can be used year-round.

Rentals: Jack's Bicycle Center, 1907 Iowa Street, Bellingham, (360) 733-1955, www.jacksbicyclecenter.com

Contacts: City of Bellingham Parks and Recreation, (360) 778-7000, https://cob.org/services/recreation/parks-trails; Bellingham/Whatcom County Tourism, (360)671-3990, www.bellingham.org

Bus routes: Contact the Whatcom Transit Authority, (360) 676-RIDE (7433), www.ridewta.com.

Access and parking: To reach the western trailhead near Memorial Park, get off I-5 at Sunset Drive (exit 255). From I-5 southbound, go straight,

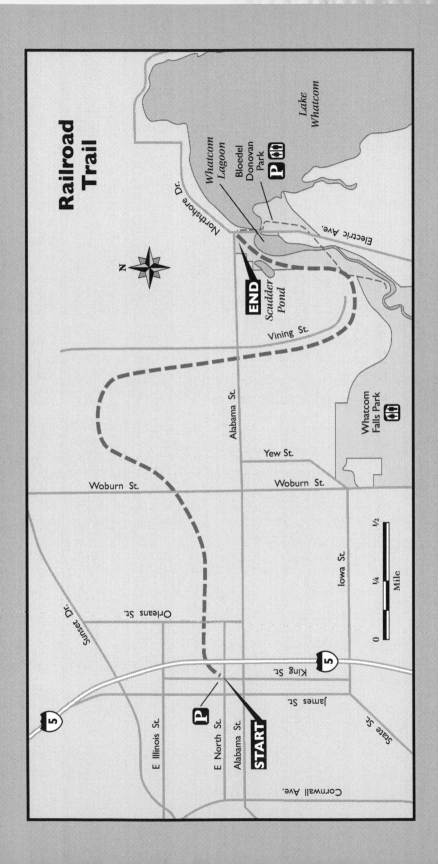

down James Street. From I-5 northbound, turn left onto Sunset to cross the highway and then left onto James. After several blocks, turn left onto East North Street, then left again onto King Street. The trailhead is on your right. GPS: N48 45.89' / W122 27.80'

Find the eastern trailhead by turning east onto Sunset Drive / Mount Baker Highway, south (right) onto Orleans Street, and east (left) onto Alabama Street. Turn right onto Electric Avenue at Lake Whatcom. The trailhead is immediately on your right.

|||||||||||||||||||||||||||||||||||||||||||||||||||||||||||||||||||||||||||||||||||||||||||||||||||||

Y̶ou can travel the Railroad Trail in either direction; this description takes you from west to east. Starting from King Street, the trail crosses I-5 and enters a quiet neighborhood with several streets to cross. There is a nice buffer between the small homes and the trail. Cross Woburn Street at 0.9 mile. A well-used side trail lures you to Barkley Village with a variety of restaurants.

Urban and waterfront views greet trail users along the trail crossing the Alabama Hills Bridge.

Back on the trail, continue past pilings from an old trestle. In years past, the Bellingham Bay & Eastern Railway occupied the Railroad Trail for 4 miles from New Whatcom to Lake Whatcom. In 1882 the Blue Canyon Mines used the railway to send coal to bunkers on Bellingham Bay. Later the tracks brought lumber from Lake Whatcom to the docks of New Whatcom and Fairhaven for transport to developing western cities, such as San Francisco. Remnants of trestles are found along the trail to Lake Whatcom, around Lake Whatcom, and even across Lake Whatcom. The BB&E merged with the Northern Pacific Railway in 1903.

Just past these pilings, head up a hill to an opening beside a pond at 1.4 miles. As the trail curves north beyond the peaceful pond, you can take in views of town and the bay below. An overpass takes you safely over Alabama Street. The trail parallels Vining Street before it heads up a short, steeper hill into Whatcom Falls Park. Turn left at the fork (2.9 miles) to go north to Scudder Pond, or follow the signs leading off the Railroad Trail to cross the bridge and Electric Avenue to Bloedel Donovan Park.

If you continue on Railroad Trail, you'll end at the eastern terminus by Lake Whatcom and another access point for Bloedel Donovan Park. After visiting the park, return the way you came. Enjoy the downhill grade on the trip back.

14 WALLACE FALLS STATE PARK: OLD RAILROAD GRADE TRAIL

On this trek you'll start uphill on a railroad grade or along a river side trail and then continue on a narrow walking trail up steep switchbacks, through deep woods, and over wooden bridges to spectacular views of Wallace River waterfalls. Get ready for a workout as you enjoy a rural road trip and a scenic trail system with the convenience of camping and the proximity of good food.

Activities:

Location: Wallace Falls State Park, town of Gold Bar, in Snohomish County

Length: Old Railroad Grade Trail is 2.5 miles long and good for mountain biking. Several trails depart from the Old Railroad Grade Trail. At 1.5 mile the 0.9-mile Bicycle Trail leaves the park and connects to the gravel DNR–Wallace Mainline Road. Then at 2.0 miles the 800-foot long cutoff trail connects to the 1.0-mile mark on the Woody Trail. At 2.4 miles the second cutoff trail connects to the 1.4-mile mark on the Woody Trail. At the end of the Old Railroad Grade find the 1.9-mile Greg Ball Trail. It heads north and is the best route to Wallace Lake. To the Upper Falls, it's 2.5 miles on Old Railroad Grade Trail to Greg Ball Trail, plus 1.5 miles on Woody Trail. Alternately, from the parking lot the 2.75-mile pedestrian-only Woody Trail takes you to the Upper Falls. A 4.1-mile hiking trail and the 6.5-mile biking route take you to Wallace Lake and the Upper Grade Trail. The trails are well signed.

Surface: Dirt, somewhat rocky

Wheelchair access: This trail is not wheelchair-accessible.

Difficulty: The rail trail is moderate; the hiking trail to the falls is steep.

Food: You'll find restaurants, grocery stores, bakeries, and espresso shops in Gold Bar and other towns along US 2.

Restrooms: There are restrooms and water at the trailhead.

Seasons: The trail can be used year-round, from dawn to dusk.

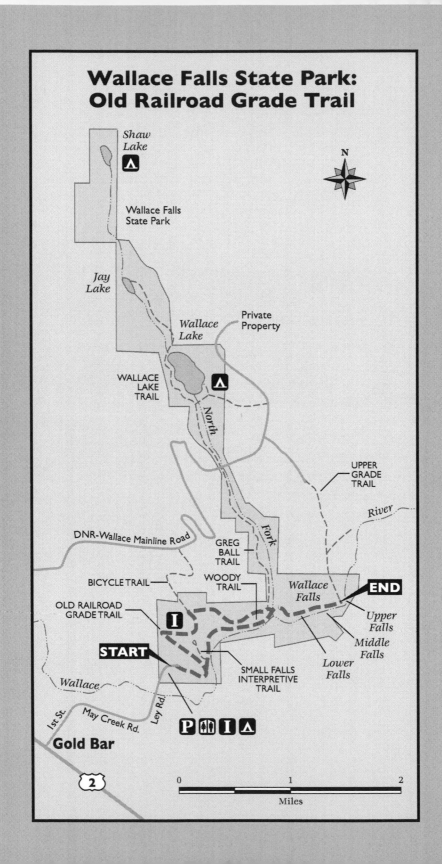

Rentals: No rentals are available along this trail.

Contacts: Wallace Falls State Park, (360) 793-0420, www.parks.wa.gov

Bus routes: Bus #270/271 from Everett. For information check the Community Transit website at www.communitytransit.org or call (425) 353-RIDE (7433). In Washington call toll-free (800) 562-1375.

Access and parking: Access the trail from Wallace Falls State Park. Take US 2 to Gold Bar, 30 miles east of Everett. Follow signs to the Wallace Falls State Park entrance. Turn left into the park and travel 0.3 mile to the trailhead, adjacent to the restrooms in the parking lot. GPS: N47 52.01' / W121 40.68'

A state park Discover Pass is required to park here, and is valid at Washington's state recreation lands. Find information on the Washington Parks website at www.parks.wa.gov. Purchase options include one-day passes and annual passes, available online, at select automated pay-stations at trailheads, or at specified local vendors.

The Wallace River rushes, plummets, and jams up against large river boulders along its course. Nine waterfalls, ranging in height from 50 to 265 feet, plunge into the river from tributaries, while the waterway itself drops 800 feet in 0.5 mile. Wallace Falls State Park, the site of this riverside trek, is located off US 2 in Gold Bar and near several small towns in the Cascade foothills.

This lush trail system runs along a few of several logging railroad routes built in these hills. The railroad grade is steeper than most rail trails because it was built for wood-fired engines with winches mounted on log sleds, known as steam donkeys. When anchored to a stump, this machine pulled logs out of the woods to a loading area, reaching high into the hills after timber. The invention of the steam donkey and the arrival of the Great Northern Railway in 1882 put Gold Bar on the map as a "great northern town." Success of the logging industry here became a sure thing when Frederick Weyerhaeuser bought 900,000 acres of land from J. J. Hill, Great Northern's owner. The logs were taken to a nearby mill and shipped out from the depot at Gold Bar.

View Wallace River waterfalls from the Woody Trail.

Washington State eventually purchased the park site from the Weyerhaeuser timber company. The park opened in 1977. It was built through the efforts of the Youth Development and Conservation Corps programs, thanks to the legislative initiative of Senator Frank Woody, for whom the Woody Trail is named.

This description includes the Old Railroad Grade Trail, Woody Trail, and scenic waterfalls along the trail system. Stop to examine the mosaic of the bright green, fuzzy moss that carpets each branch of the forest and each stump top in pleasing designs. You'll hear the distant sound of the river as you climb through the woods on broad switchbacks. Birds and deer roam here. The area is home to coyotes, bobcats, bears, and cougars. You'll access the falls by walking or via a combination of mountain biking and walking.

Find the trailhead near the parking lot. The Old Railroad Grade Trail splits from the Woody Trail at 0.4 miles. It's a nice alternative to the much busier and challenging Woody Trail; just be prepared to add another mile to a hike to the waterfalls. Woody Trail is to the right of the intersection. Two cutoff trails beyond this intersection go from the Old Railroad Grade down to the Woody Trail. If you're riding, secure your bike and continue via foot on this pedestrian-only trail.

Continuing left on the Old Railroad Grade Trail you'll find an interpretive panel at 1.5 miles, detailing local logging history. This is the site of an old railroad trestle where supports are still visible. At the end of the Old Railroad Grade Trail at 2.5 miles, the Greg Ball Trail and Wallace Lake Trail depart, to the left of the intersection. Continue another 1.5 miles on the pedestrian-only Woody Trail to the Upper Falls.

If you take the Woody Trail at the intersection, departing from Old Railroad Grade Trail at 0.4 miles from the parking lot, the trail hugs the river for 1.5 miles and ultimately traverses away from the river, leading you to a series of waterfalls. Via this footpath, Upper Falls is 2.75 miles from the parking lot. Mountain bikers and hikers can continue to the left on the Old Railroad Grade Trail.

Turn left when you reach the river. A bridge crosses the North Fork and the trail climbs to the falls. Steps are built into some of the steeper portions. The riverside picnic shelter at Lower Falls is your first viewpoint, 0.3 mile from the bridge. Less than 0.25 mile ahead is a dramatic view of Middle Falls. The trail steepens progressively into shorter switchbacks over the next 0.5 mile until you reach the Upper Falls viewpoint at 1,570 vertical feet. Consider exploring the upper trails, consisting of Greg Ball Trail, Wallace Lake Trail, and the Upper Grade Trail. Enjoy the mountains peeking through the trees on your descent.

15 OLYMPIC DISCOVERY TRAIL: DEER PARK SCENIC GATEWAY CENTER TO SEQUIM

Leave US 101 to tour a pathway with wildflowers, a covered bridge, and a beautifully restored trestle. This segment of the Olympic Discovery Trail offers a combination of flat and rolling terrain with some steep hills.

Activities: 🚶 🚴 🚴 ⛸ 🚣 🐟 🦆 🦌

Location: Clallam County, east of Port Angeles

Length: 15 miles plus an 8.0-mile option to continue east to Blyn

Surface: Asphalt

Wheelchair access: Deer Park Scenic Gateway Center, Robin Hill County Park, Railroad Bridge Park, and Carrie Blake Park are wheelchair-accessible.

Difficulty: Moderate

Food: Sequim

Restrooms: Restrooms are found along the trail at Robin County Hill Park, Railroad Bridge Park, and Carrie Blake Park Trailhead and Deer Park Scenic Gateway Center.

Seasons: The trail can be used year-round.

Rentals: Paddle-sport and bicycle rentals are found at Adventures through Kayaking, 2358 West Highway 101, Port Angeles, (360) 417-3015, https://atkayaking.com/. For bicycle rentals in Sequim, there's Ben's Bikes, 1251 West Washington Street, Sequim, (360) 683-2666, www.bensbikessequim.com

Contacts: Clallam County Public Works, (360) 417-2290; Port Angeles Regional Chamber of Commerce and Visitor Center, (360) 452-2363, www.portangeles.org; Olympic Discovery Trail, www.olympicdiscoverytrail.org

Bus routes: Contact Clallam Transit, (800) 858-3747, www.clallamtransit.com.

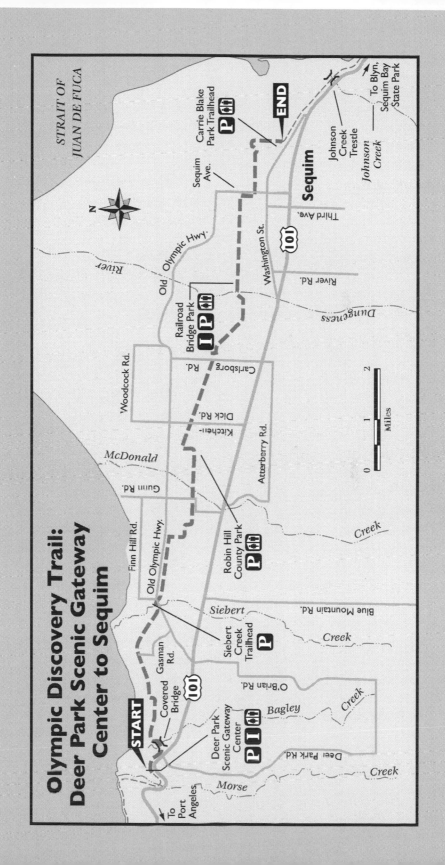

Olympic Discovery Trail: Deer Park Scenic Gateway Center to Sequim

STRAT OF JUAN DE FUCA

N

STRAIT

END

Carrie Blake Park Trailhead

P

Sequim Ave.

To Blyn, Sequim Bay State Park

Johnson Creek Trestle

Johnson Creek

Sequim

Third Ave.

101

Washington St.

River Rd.

Dungeness

Old Olympic Hwy.

River

Railroad Bridge Park

i P

Woodcock Rd.

Carlsborg Rd.

Kitchen-Dick Rd.

Atterberry Rd.

0   1   2
Miles

McDonald

Gunn Rd.

Finn Hill Rd.

Old Olympic Hwy.

Robin Hill County Park

P i

Creek

Blue Mountain Rd.

Siebert

Siebert Creek Trailhead

P

Creek

Gasman Rd.

Covered Bridge

101

O'Brian Rd.

Bagley

Creek

START

Deer Park Scenic Gateway Center

P i

Deer Park Rd.

Morse

To Port Angeles

Creek

Access and parking: To reach the Deer Park Scenic Gateway Center, when westbound on US 101, exit directly onto the road beside the parking area. If eastbound on US 101, turn north off US 101 onto Buchanan Road, just west of Deer Park Cinemas. Turn left onto Cedar Park Drive and take the second left at the Scenic View sign. Turn right into the parking lot. GPS: N48 06.41' / W123 20.83'

The eastern trail terminus at Sequim is accessed by taking US 101 westbound to the first Sequim exit (Washington Street). Turn north onto Blake Avenue, go 0.5 mile north, and turn into Carrie Blake Park.

IIIIIIIIIIIIIIIIIIIIIIIIIIIIIIIIIIIIIIIIIIIIIIIIIIIIIIIIIIIIIIIIIIIIIIIIIIIIIIIIIIIIIIIIIIII

The Olympic Discovery Trail is planned to connect Forks and La Push on the Pacific Ocean with Port Angeles, Sequim, and Port Townsend. Sections of the trail run on old railroad rights-of-way. Completed trail segments in this area extend from west of Port Angeles, to beyond Blyn. See Trail 16 and Trail 17 for other segments of this ambitious rail trail.

The Seattle, Port Angeles & Western Railway Company purchased the Seattle, Port Angeles & Lake Crescent Railway Company (1911–15) in 1916 and then sold it to the Chicago, Milwaukee & St. Paul in 1918. Two round-trips a day reached Discovery Junction from Majestic, with connections to Port Townsend. The line to Twin Rivers, west of Port Angeles, was built for logging; in the industry's glory days, three large logging concerns competed to bring 1 million board feet of logs to the trains each day for shipment to the Orient. When trucking logs became competitive, the rail line was abandoned. The current rail trail moves on and off the right-of-way to avoid private property.

Although you can access this segment of the Olympic Discovery Trail from Deer Park or Sequim, this description begins on the western side at Deer Park Scenic Gateway Center parking lot, between trail mileposts 5 and 6.

Head east on the trail, accessed by turning left from the parking lot onto the road and heading to the second stop sign at the Cedar Park Drive and Buchanan Road intersection. The trail is across the road, indicated by cement bollards. You'll briefly travel along the trail beside US 101 until the trail turns left.

Enjoy the paved trail down a steep hill to the renovated covered bridge before milepost 6, formerly a Bainbridge ferry ramp. You can smell the moisture of the forested ravine. After crossing the covered bridge, you climb up a short, steep hill out of the Bagley Creek ravine. The next 4.0 miles are up and down past private land. Once you've moved away from the highway, you'll hear birds chirping and see yellow, violet, and white wildflowers. A few cedar trees provide a green background in this open country.

See bright red berries beside the trail. You'll come to the intersection of the trail and Old Olympic Highway between mileposts 9 and 10. The Siebert Creek Trailhead is just ahead on the shallow Siebert Creek Ravine, near the end of Wild Current Way.

At milepost 9.5 the Siebert Creek Trail Bridge connects the forested western trail with pastures and farms. Proceed east on the paved trail and on Spring Road. Your next major attractions are the McDonald Creek Bridge between mileposts 12 and 13 and the Robin Hill County Park, used as an access point by equestrians, located between mileposts 13 and 14.

The trail heads north from Robin Hill Farm beside Vautier Road for 0.5 mile before turning sharply east past the Sequim Valley Airport. Railroad Bridge Park and the Audubon Center are at milepost 17 beside the Dungeness River. Major renovations in this area may change the routing and mile-markers.

When you get near the end of this trail section in Sequim, you will encounter a detour that takes you off the trail and east onto Hendrickson Road, then south onto North Sequim Avenue for about 0.25 mile. Follow the street marking "sharrow" lanes, where bikes have equal status with vehicles. Then join Fir Street and go about 0.75 mile east into Carrie Blake Park, an eastern-end trailhead located between mileposts 22 and 23.

For a 7.0-mile extension to your journey, head east from the park toward Blyn. Between mileposts 22 and 23 you will journey across Johnson Creek Trestle near Whitefeather Way. By milepost 25 you'll pass through Sequim Bay State Park. The trail travels on Dawley Road for about a mile to milepost 28, a mile from the Jamestown S'Klallam Tribe trailhead parking and toilets. Alternately, return to the Deer Park Scenic Gateway and take a brief detour to the long Morse Creek Trestle, built in 1915. This fully decked and railed trestle curves under a maple canopy and over Morse Creek. The trail heads west from Morse Creek for 5.0 miles to downtown Port Angeles, and then travels another 4.0 miles west through Port Angeles to Ediz Hook (see Trail 16).

16 OLYMPIC DISCOVERY TRAIL: PORT ANGELES WATERFRONT

What better place to tour Washington State's coast than on the turbulent Strait of Juan de Fuca? Especially when you can also see Victoria in front of you and the Olympic Mountain Range behind you. This stretch of the Olympic Discovery Trail lets you stroll along the downtown waterfront, through lumber holding areas, and past an active mill. By continuing east you'll travel right beside an undeveloped shoreline of the strait.

Activities:

Location: City of Port Angeles on the Olympic Peninsula, in Clallam County

Length: 9.0 miles from Harbor View Park on Ediz Hook to Deer Park Scenic Gateway Center

Surface: Asphalt

Wheelchair access: The entire trail is wheelchair-accessible, although the trail runs on the roadside at Ediz Hook.

Difficulty: Easy

Food: Find plenty to eat and drink at local eateries near the route.

Restrooms: You'll find restrooms at the marina on Marine Drive, at the tip of Ediz Hook, at the City Pier, and at Deer Park Scenic Gateway Center.

Seasons: The trail can be used year-round.

Rentals: Paddle-sport and bicycle rentals are found at Adventures through Kayaking, 2358 West Highway 101, Port Angeles, (360) 417-3015, https://atkayaking.com/.

Contacts: Port Angeles Regional Chamber of Commerce and Visitor Center, (360) 452-2363, www.portangeles.org; Olympic Discovery Trail, www.olympicdiscoverytrail.org

Bus routes: Contact Clallam Transit, (800) 858-3747, www.clallamtransit.com.

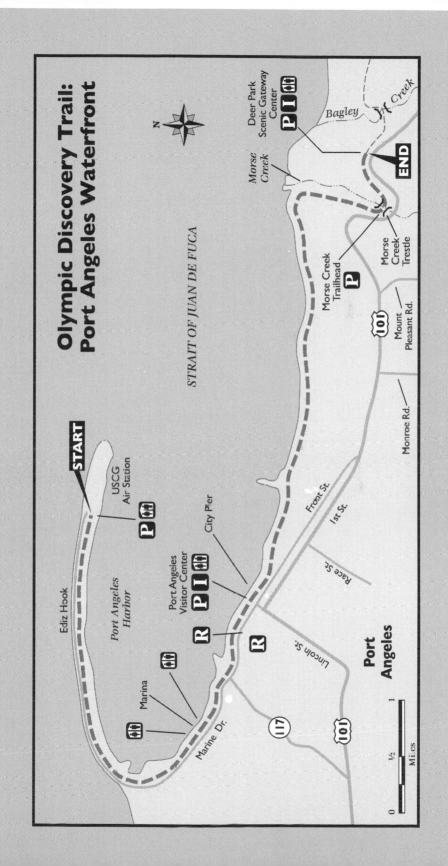

Olympic Discovery Trail: Port Angeles Waterfront

N

START

Ediz Hook

USCG
Air Station

P 🚻

Port Angeles
Harbor

Marina

🚻

🚻

R

Port Angeles
Visitor Center

P I 🚻

City Pier

R

Marine Dr.

STRAIT OF JUAN DE FUCA

Front St.

1st St.

Race St.

Lincoln St.

**Port
Angeles**

117

101

0   ½   1
Miles

101

Monroe Rd.

Mount
Pleasant Rd.

P

Morse Creek
Trailhead

Morse Creek
Trestle

*Morse
Creek*

Deer Park
Scenic Gateway
Center

P I 🚻

P 🚻

Bagley

H Creek

END

Access and parking: To start by the trail's terminus by Harbor View Park, located near the restricted area of the Port Angeles Coast Guard Station at the tip of Ediz Hook (the spit), drive northwest on Marine Drive, which continues as Ediz Hook Road. GPS: N48 08.50' / W123 25.77'

To start at the City Pier, follow US 101 into Port Angeles, where it becomes Front Street. At the intersection with Lincoln Street, turn north onto Lincoln and drive 1 block to the waterfront and pier. You can park in downtown Port Angeles.

||||||||||||||||||||||||||||||||||||||||||||||||||||||||||||||||||||||||||||||||||||||||||||||||||||||||||||

Port Angeles is the largest city on the northern Olympic Peninsula, headquarters for Olympic National Park, and site of the ferry dock for Vancouver Island. The waterfront trail here is one of several sections of the Olympic Discovery Trail, which will reach from Port Townsend to Forks and on to the Pacific Coast.

An ideal spot to start your trip is at the City Pier on Railroad Avenue near Lincoln Street. It is the starting point for the trail mileposts, which increase in number as you head east toward Sequim. (See Trail 15 for more information on the Deer Park Scenic Gateway Center to Sequim section.)

As you head east from the City Pier toward Morse Creek Trailhead, you leave the city life behind you. Along the way you will find benches, interpretive signs, and serenity. At 1.0 mile east of the City Pier, the trail passes the former mill site and continues eastward along the Strait of Juan de Fuca for 2.0 additional miles past the mill site before it turns south near Morse Creek. When you turn south away from the strait, you are less than a mile from the Morse Creek Trestle and the Morse Creek Trailhead.

If you opt to start your trip by heading west from the City Pier on Railroad Avenue, you'll travel on a 10-foot-wide concrete sidewalk. It follows Railroad Avenue, then turns west onto the sidewalk beside Marine Drive. Pass the marina, ducks, and a host of fishing boats. The trail sneaks into the little Valley Creek estuary and on toward the mill, an impressive operation. Continue on the shoulder off the road from here to the tip of the spit, about 3 miles. Use caution. Check out the ships docked in the harbor and traveling through the strait, with Canada in the distance and

View the Port Angeles City Pier from the trail.

the snowcapped Olympic Mountains above. The trail ends at the US Coast Guard station.

For other nearby sections of the Olympic Discovery Trail, continue west on US 101 to Spruce Railroad (Trail 17) or east to the Deer Park Scenic Gateway Center to Sequim (Trail 15).

17 OLYMPIC DISCOVERY TRAIL: SPRUCE RAILROAD TRAIL

This fun and scenic trail runs along the north shore of Lake Crescent in Olympic National Park. It's bounded by steep slate walls above and the water below. Travel through tunnels and, after your workout, relax beside mountains mirrored in the turquoise lake.

Activities:

Location: Olympic National Park, 16 miles west of Port Angeles on the Olympic Peninsula, in Clallam County

Length: The Spruce Railroad Trail is 4.0 miles in length and completes the 10.0-mile length of the Olympic Discovery Trail section on the north shore of Lake Crescent. Trail users may continue westward on the Olympic Discovery Trail heading west from the Fairholme Hill Trailhead.

Surface: The previously gravel section is now paved to universal accessibility standards with a gravel shoulder for equestrians.

Wheelchair access: The trail is specifically designed for wheelchair accessibility. Wheelchair access is provided at the eastern trailhead off East Beach Road, at the US 101 access point at Fairholme Trailhead on US 101 opposite Sol Duc Hot Springs Road, and at the North Shore Picnic Area off Camp David Jr. Road.

Difficulty: Easy to moderate

Food: You'll find many restaurants in Port Angeles (see Trail 16). In summer only, try the Fairholme General Store on US 101 at Camp David Jr. Road, the Log Cabin Resort near the eastern trailhead, and Lake Crescent Lodge on US 101.

Restrooms: There are vault toilets at the eastern end of the trail off East Beach Road, at the North Shore Picnic Area, and the Fairholme Hill Trailhead. Fairholme Campground, open spring through autumn, has flush toilets and water.

Seasons: The trail can be used year-round. At only 800 feet in elevation, snow usually isn't a problem. Most services in the area are open May through Sept.

Rentals: Paddle-sport and bicycle rentals are found at Adventures through Kayaking, 2358 West Highway 101, Port Angeles, (360) 417-3015, https://atkayaking.com/. Find boat rentals available at Log Cabin Resort and Lake Crescent Lodge.

Contacts: Olympic National Park Visitor Center, Port Angeles (hours vary by season), (360) 565-3130, www.nps.gov/olym; Olympic National Park Wilderness Information Center, (360) 565-3100, www.nps.gov/olym. For fishing regulations view https://www.nps.gov/olym/planyourvisit/fishing.htm. For information on the Olympic Discovery Trail visit www.olympic-discoverytrail.org.

Bus routes: Contact Clallam Transit, (800) 858-3747, www.clallamtransit.com.

Access and parking: Take US 101 west from Port Angeles for 16 miles, then turn right (northwest) onto East Beach Road. Follow the signs for 2.2 miles to just past the Log Cabin Resort (accommodations available), turning left shortly after the trail sign. You'll reach the trailhead 0.8 mile beyond. GPS: N48 05.59' / W123 48.13'

To reach the Fairholme Hill Trailhead, continue on US 101 West past Lake Crescent to Sol Duc Hot Springs Road, then turn right into the parking area off of US 101.

The Spruce Railway was a war effort during World War I, when the US Army needed the light, strong wood of the Sitka spruce to build airplane frames. This tree grows only along the Pacific coastal region from northern California to Alaska, with vast stands located in the roadless Olympic Peninsula. The army's Spruce Production Division built the Olympic Spruce Railroad #1 around Lake Crescent in 1918. Armistice Day arrived on November 11, 1918; nineteen days later, the line was completed. The army sold the railway before a single log was hauled. It was used for

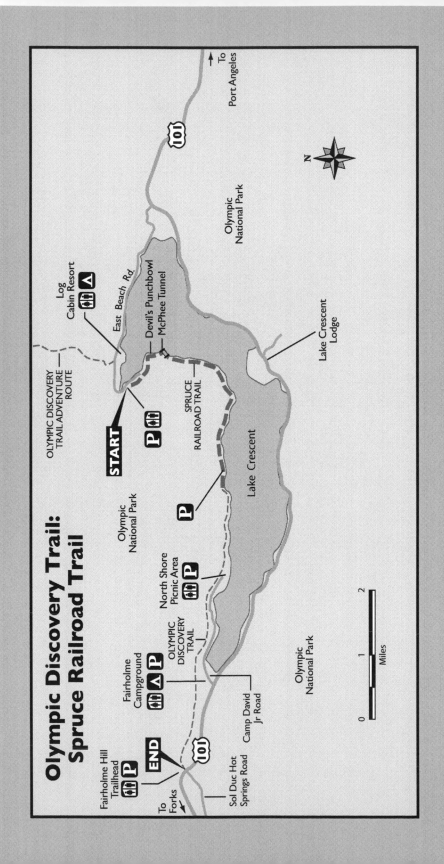

commercial logging until 1954, when it was abandoned. A 4.0-mile single-track dirt trail was completed in 1981. By 2020, a multiyear collaborative project resulted in the opening of two refurbished railroad tunnels and the creation of a paved wheelchair-accessible trail, with a gravel shoulder for equestrian use. The updates now link the paved Spruce Railroad Trail segment through the park with other parts of the 135-mile Olympic Discovery Trail, ultimately linking Port Townsend to La Push, Washington.

For more information about the trails or the national park, stop at the Olympic National Park Visitor Center on Mount Angeles Road, a short distance east from US 101, in Port Angeles. The park is designated as both a World Heritage Site and an International Biosphere Reserve.

Although you can access the trail from either end, this description begins at its eastern trailhead. From here the trail heads into the woods and remains beside the lake, either at water level or on a bank 100 to 200 feet high. You will travel through the refurbished 450-foot McFee Tunnel, with the option to visit the Devil's Punch Bowl Bridge via a side-trail-on-foot detour. Trail users may want to use a light while in this tunnel, as it's not

A bridge passes over a small inlet on Crescent Lake along the Spruce Railroad Trail.
Dave Lindsay

possible to see from one end to the other. At 3.0 miles encounter the Daley-Rankin Tunnel.

Though Pacific madrone trees, with their peeling red bark, shade these lower slopes of Pyramid Peak, the southern exposure creates a dry microclimate. In addition to cougars, bears, deer, and raccoons, you might see a golden eagle or a peregrine falcon dropping in from its nesting spot on Pyramid Peak. Look and listen for the pileated woodpecker.

Near 4.0 miles you have a choice: Exit at a western trailhead parking area and ride Camp David Jr. Road to the Fairholme Campground, or continue your ride another 6.4 miles to US 101. At about 5.6 miles from the eastern trailhead, you'll pass the North Shore Picnic Area to the south. The start of the rugged Pyramid Peak Trail, which climbs 2,400 feet to the peak, is to the north of the trail. The paved trail exits at a gated state disabled-parking permit area. Access it from the Fairholme Hill Trailhead across from Sol Duc Hot Springs Road, 1.7 miles from the turnoff into the campground.

While in the area, consider exploring the 9.5 miles of paved trail on the Olympic Discovery Trail that goes from Mount Muller Trailhead and along the Sol Duc River west to Cooper Ranch Road. Mountain bikers may want to ride the Olympic Discovery Trail Adventure Route starting on the east side of Lake Crescent to the Elwha River. Access the route near the eastern trailhead for Spruce Railroad Trail.

In this region you might also visit the Deer Park Scenic Gateway Center to Sequim (Trail 15) and Port Angeles Waterfront (Trail 16) sections of the Olympic Discovery Trail.

18 FOOTHILLS TRAIL

The foothills of Mount Rainier and the southern Cascades, green valleys, rivers, creeks, eagles and salmon, small towns, and families at play—this is the Foothills Trail. Mount Rainier towers above at such close range that you can almost feel its 14,000 feet of rock, glaciers, and snowfields. Though segments total 30 miles, the Foothills Trail is a group of unconnected trails between rural communities along the prior Burlington Northern Railway.

Activities:

Location: Puyallup to Buckley, in Pierce County

Length: This description covers 15 continuous miles of paved trails between the East Puyallup (Meeker) and South Prairie Trailheads, a portion of the developing 30-mile network of trails.

Surface: Asphalt with a narrow equestrian path

Wheelchair access: The trail is accessible where paved.

Difficulty: Easy, except one hill climb

Food: You'll find restaurants, espresso shops, and grocery stores in the towns of Puyallup, South Prairie, and Orting.

Restrooms: Restrooms are available at the trailheads.

Seasons: The trail can be used year-round.

Rentals: None

Contacts: Foothills Rail-to-Trails Coalition, https://foothillscoalition.org/; Pierce County Parks and Recreation, (253) 798-4177, https://www.pierce-countywa.gov/1292/Parks-Facilities-Trails

Bus routes: None

Access and parking: There are several spots from which to access this trail. To begin at the northwest terminus and enjoy 15 miles of 21-mile paved trail, use the East Puyallup (Meeker) Trailhead on 80th Street East, 0.2 mile east of 134th Avenue East and Pioneer Way East (shown as Pioneer Avenue on some maps), located 1 mile west of WA 162 in Puyallup. GPS: N47 11.04' / W122 14.69'

This intersection can be reached from WA 512 by taking the Pioneer Way East exit and continuing east for 1.8 miles.

To get to the South Prairie Trailhead, follow WA 162 toward South Prairie and Buckley. In South Prairie, find the trailhead along WA 162 / Pioneer Way East between Emery Street South and Rainer Avenue South.

|||||||||||||||||||||||||||||||||||||||||||||||||||||||||||||||||||||||||||||||||||||||||||||||||||||||||||||||||

While much of the Foothills Trail's eventual 30-mile length is paved, this description covers a popular 15-mile asphalt segment. It starts at Puyallup's eastern city limit at the East Puyallup (Meeker) Trailhead, then continues by McMillin, through the town of Orting, then to a trailhead at South Prairie. Travelers cross rivers and wetlands along the way. Additional trail sections continue to Buckley's eastern terminus, with future plans connecting the trail northeast through Enumclaw, and south from South Prairie to Wilkeson and Carbonado.

From Puyallup you'll travel to McMillin through rural farmland and experience breathtaking views of Mount Rainier. South of the McMillin Trailhead, the trail parallels WA 162 through a corridor of housing developments and schools for a distance of 2.5 miles into the Orting park complex and business district. Enjoy the landscaped greenway with flowering fruit trees planted by the Foothills Rails-to-Trails Coalition.

The grade on the trail is minimal, but you may notice it if you're a beginner skater or bicyclist. At 2.3 miles from the McMillin Trailhead, the trail turns right and crosses Whitesell Street Northwest. Shortly you'll reach Orting's North, Central, and South Main Parks, with the trailhead located at Central Park at Calistoga Street West. Enjoy the history of the area depicted on the building murals in town.

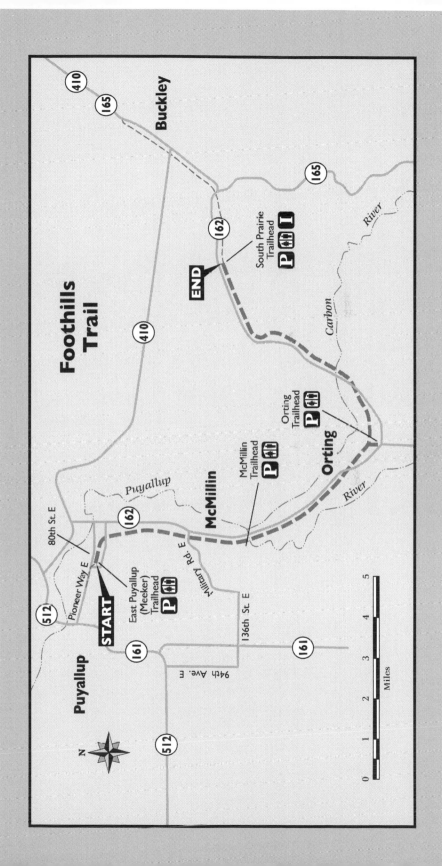

Check out the Carbon River from a trestle along the Foothills Trail between South Prairie and Orting.

The Orting parkland was purchased by the Northern Pacific Railway in 1887 for $1 from the city of Orting. Trains carried passengers to Spokane on one line and across the country on another. Coal and coke were transported from Carbonado, Fairfax, and Wilkeson; timber was shipped from the forestlands by the St. Paul & Tacoma Lumber Company. Burlington Northern took up the tracks starting in 1985, and the city and Pierce County Parks department bought the right-of-way in 1994. Trail construction began in 1996 and is an ongoing project.

Continue through the park area and over to the WA 162 crossing, where the highway turns north toward Buckley. The trail leaves WA 162 and crosses the rushing Carbon River. Additional trestle crossing are ahead. The trail passes along South Prairie Creek. Stay on the paved trail to the South Prairie Trailhead. When you are ready, turn around and return to the trailhead you started from.

The 6.0-mile paved trail segment from South Prairie Trailhead to Buckley's eastern terminus awaits your exploration. Ultimately the Foothills Trail network will connect to other regional trails.

19 CHEHALIS WESTERN TRAIL

This peaceful trail segment takes you from the Woodard Bay Natural Resources Conservation Area near Puget Sound, through a commercial district near I-5 just a few miles from the state capitol building in Olympia, then on to Chambers Lake Trailhead. Travel beside homes, farms, and ponds in the north and near stores and eateries in the south, culminating near the water at Chambers Lake. Enjoy the sounds of birds, ducks, and cows on this delightful trail smartly designed for all users.

Activities:

Location: Olympia, in Thurston County

Length: 7.0-mile section of 21.0-mile trail

Surface: Asphalt with a dirt horse trail (separated for much of the distance)

Wheelchair access: The entire trail is wheelchair-accessible.

Difficulty: Easy

Food: You'll find restaurants in Olympia along Pacific Avenue.

Restrooms: There are restrooms at the Woodard Bay and Chamber Lake Trailheads and at 41st Avenue.

Seasons: The trail can be used year-round.

Rentals: There are no rentals directly along the trail.

Contacts: For trail information contact Thurston County Recreation Services, (360) 786-5595, http://www.co.thurston.wa.us/publicworks/parksandtrails.html. For Woodard Bay Natural Resources Conservation Area, contact Washington State Department of Natural Resources, (360) 577-2025, www.dnr.wa.gov.

Bus routes: None

Access and parking: To start at the northern terminus at Woodard Bay Natural Resources Conservation Area, exit I-5 at Sleater Kinney Road (exit 108). Turn north and go about 5 miles. The road turns sharply left and becomes

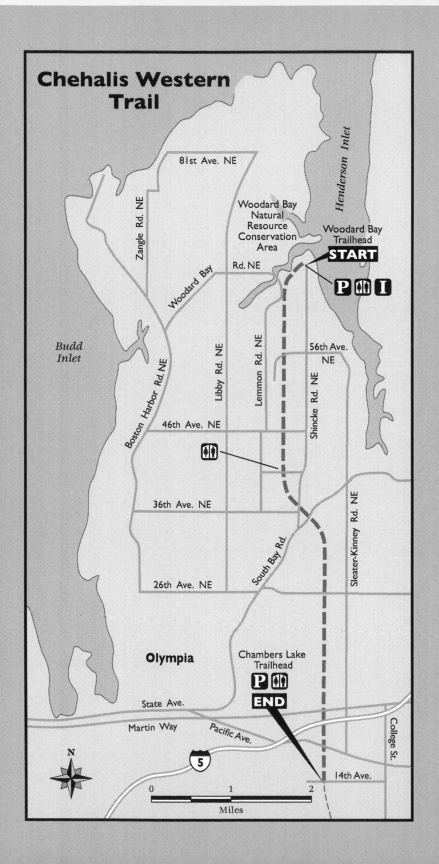

Chehalis Western Trail

81st Ave. NE

Zangle Rd. NE

Woodard Bay Natural Resource Conservation Area

Henderson Inlet

Woodard Bay Rd. NE

Woodard Bay Trailhead

START

P 🚻 I

Budd Inlet

Libby Rd. NE

Lemmon Rd. NE

56th Ave. NE

Shincke Rd. NE

46th Ave. NE

Boston Harbor Rd. NE

🚻

36th Ave. NE

Sleater-Kinney Rd. NE

26th Ave. NE

South Bay Rd.

Olympia

Chambers Lake Trailhead

P 🚻

END

State Ave.

Martin Way

Pacific Ave.

College St.

N

5

14th Ave.

0   1   2

Miles

56th Avenue Northeast. Take 56th Avenue north to Shincke Road, and turn right. Follow Shincke Road to the trailhead parking area on the west side of the road. GPS: N47 07.46' / W122 51.03'

Reach the Chambers Lake Trailhead at the southern end of the trail by taking exit 108 (Sleater-Kinney Road) off I-5 and heading south. Cross over Pacific Avenue. Turn right onto 14th Avenue at a four-way stop. Continue about 0.5 mile to the entrance, on the left after the trestle. Equestrians are allowed from the Woodard Bay Trailhead to South Bay Road and south of Fir Tree Road.

This description takes you from the trail's northern terminus at Woodard Bay Natural Resources Conservation Area to Chambers Lake Trailhead. While at the Woodard Bay Trailhead, consider taking the 0.5-mile walk on the Overlook Trail to Henderson Inlet. Rest at this wooded waterfront spot, which was once a bustling logging transfer area.

For the Chehalis Western Trail, start from the edge of the parking lot at the Woodard Bay Trailhead. Mileage markers occur every mile, starting at the northern terminus and increasing as you head south. Interpretive and map signs are placed at each road intersection. See pictures of locomotives and read the history of timber transport along this route. Logs were hauled to Henderson Inlet by rail and then to the Everett mills by water.

After leaving the trailhead, you pass through a forest and then travel past horse pastures and wetlands, through evergreens and blackberry vines. You'll encounter street crossings within the first 2.5 miles, including 56th and 46th Avenues.

Near mile 3.5, the trail crosses South Bay Road. The horse trail for the northern section, starting at Woodard Bay Trailhead, ends here.

Continue south toward the overpass across Martin Way and the overpass over I-5, both located between miles 5.5 and 6.0. Along the way you'll pass by homes. This stretch is mostly flat, with a bit of grade here and there. The overpass smoothly transitions trail users over the two busy roads and exits at the South Sound Center mall. Follow the trail along the edge of the mall to Pacific Avenue, and then cross the bridge over Pacific Avenue.

It is worth the effort to continue on the trail as it leaves the busy avenue at about 6.5 miles and heads south. At the four-way trail intersection, continue straight (south) for about another 0.5 mile to the Chambers Lake

Blackberries are prolific along the trail in late summer.

Trailhead near mile 7.0. Enjoy a rest by the lake before you return the way you came. When you return to Woodard Bay, consider a drive out to Boston Harbor for a waterfront view and some birding.

Another option is to continue another 14 miles south from the Chambers Lake Trailhead on the Chehalis Western Trail along another section of the trail, administered by Thurston County Parks. The southernmost portion of the trail connects with the Yelm–Rainier–Tenino Trail. While in the area, consider visiting the Foothills Trail (Trail 18) in Orting, or head to Olympia to tour the capital city.

20 WILLAPA HILLS TRAIL: RAYMOND TO SOUTH BEND RIVERFRONT TRAIL

Experience these unique rural communities loaded with regional pride, history, and art. Enjoy viewing blue herons and outdoor sculptures. Raymond and South Bend, Washington, are on the coastal route to the Pacific Ocean destinations of Long Beach, Washington, and Astoria, Oregon. Break up your drive with a stroll or bicycle ride on the Raymond to South Bend Riverfront Trail, a paved portion of the 56-mile Willapa Hills Trail.

Activities:

Location: Between Raymond and South Bend, in Pacific County

Length: 4.8 miles

Surface: Asphalt

Wheelchair access: The trail is wheelchair-accessible.

Difficulty: Easy

Food: You'll find things to eat in Raymond and South Bend.

Restrooms: Restrooms are located at the Raymond Trailhead. Public restrooms are also located at the South Bend Trailhead on Summit Street and at the Joe Krupa Wayside along US 101 in Raymond, about midway along the trail.

Seasons: The trail can be used year-round, but it's often windy and wet in winter.

Rentals: There are no rentals available along this trail.

Contacts: Willapa Harbor Chamber of Commerce and Visitor Center, (360) 942-5419; Raymond City Hall, (360) 942-4100

Bus routes: Pacific Transit System, (360) 875-9418, www.pacifictransit.org

Access and parking: Travel north on US 101 to South Bend and turn left (north) onto Summit Avenue. Take an immediate right into the trailhead parking lot, adjacent to the public restroom. GPS: N46 40.18' / W123 47.08'

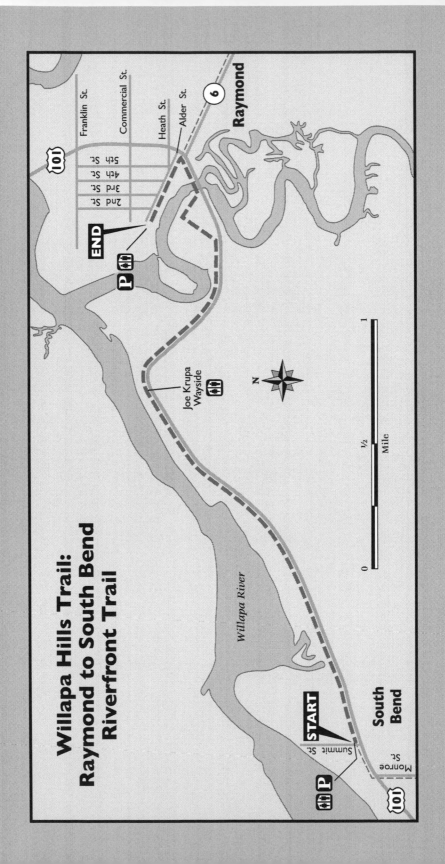

The Raymond Trailhead is located in South Fork Landing Park at the Willapa Seaport and Northwest Carriage Museums. If traveling north on US 101 (WA 105), turn west onto Heath Street (which turns into Alder Street) kitty-corner from the gas station and convenience store in Raymond. The museums and trailhead are on your left and visible from US 101. Take a short walk westerly along the trail from the museums to see the old metal-framed Burlington Northern railroad bridge.

||||||||||||||||||||||||||||||||||||||||||||||||||||||||||||||||||||||||||||||||||||||

Explore a pair of rewarding small towns on the Willapa Hills Trail (Raymond to South Bend Riverfront Trail). Your starting point, off the beaten track in South Bend, is more than its claim as the prior oyster capital of the world. The Pacific County Courthouse is also listed on the National Register of Historic Places. Plus there's the Robert Bush Memorial Park at the South Bend public dock, adjacent to the Pacific Seafood Company, one of the largest processors of fresh oysters on the West Coast.

Raymond, on the other hand, boasts a Wildlife-Heritage Sculpture Corridor, funded by the US Coastal Corridor Program to visually enhance US 101. The community worked together to determine the essence of Raymond. Artists then developed images to portray that essence: Willapa Bay with its nearby hills and native flora and fauna; the community's history; logging, fishing and farming.

You can access the trail from either end, but this description takes you from the South Bend side into Raymond. The trail follows the abandoned Burlington Northern railroad right-of-way and parallels US 101. At the start you'll travel closely between US 101 and the Willapa River for a while. As the trail passes the Joe Krupa Wayside in Raymond, the trail leaves the railroad right-of-way briefly and heads toward the Stan Hatfield Industrial Park via a short detour along streets. To continue, leave the trail, turn left onto the street, and follow the street around the corner to the right. At a stop sign, a short distance ahead, move onto the sidewalk to the right side and follow the sidewalk until it returns to the trail. You get a break from the highway before crossing the South Fork of the Willapa River on US 101 as the trail passes through a commercial district. The trail then turns left toward the Northwest Carriage Museum on Heath Street, taking you to

Life-size sculptures grace Raymond's Wildlife-Heritage Sculpture Corridor, near the Raymond Riverfront Public Pier.

the Raymond Trailhead and the interpretive area near the museums at the Raymond Riverfront Public Pier.

The Willapa Seaport Museum and Northwest Carriage Museum at the trailhead offer more glimpses into local history. Head to Raymond's 3rd Street to see the Historic Raymond Theater and more sculptures.

When you're ready, turn around and return to South Bend. You could continue another 0.6 mile on the trail by heading west from the South Bend Trailhead toward the huge pile of oyster shells, so large it is visible on aerial photos. Cross US 101, follow Monroe Street south, and then turn right onto 1st Street. You'll arrive at the South Bend elementary/high school.

While in South Bend, take in the artistic highlight of this town—the 1911 Pacific County Courthouse, 2 blocks off US 101 on the hill overlooking the pristine Willapa Bay. Walk among the faux marble pillars; look down at the mosaic tile floor and gaze up at the lit art glass dome, 29 feet in diameter. Outside you can picnic by the duck pond and watch the trout swim about. The Pacific County Historical Society Museum, located 2 blocks west of the courthouse, also offers glimpses of local history.

The Raymond to South Bend Riverfront Trail travels farther east from the Raymond Trailhead. It crosses US 101 and is paved for another 0.7 mile to the Raymond City limits. The trail then continues as a gravel trail for about 45 more miles to the approximately 5-mile paved portion approaching Chehalis, Washington, following WA 6. If you're up for a mountain bike ride, Lake Sylvia State Park (Trail 21) is about 35 minutes from Raymond. Or continue the coastal theme and head down the coast on US 101 and take in the Astoria Riverwalk (Trail 27) in Oregon.

21 LAKE SYLVIA STATE PARK

Lake Sylvia State Park has something for everyone: logging history and operations, a dam, a 30-acre lake, camping, picnicking, and any number of great trails to explore. Two of these trails—the Sylvia Creek Forestry Trail and the Lake Trail—are featured here. Both are secluded in a forest of western hemlock and Douglas fir, some of which are part of a working tree farm. Though the trails are managed by two different agencies and for different purposes, they are contiguous and offer a similar forest experience and a great workout.

Activities:

Location: Grays Harbor County

Length: 3.8 miles total; 2.3 miles for the Sylvia Creek Forestry Trail, 1.5 miles for the Lake Trail

Surface: Dirt and gravel; the trails can be very muddy. Contact park for current conditions.

Wheelchair access: The first 0.5 mile of the Sylvia Creek Forestry Trail is wheelchair-accessible.

Difficulty: The Sylvia Creek Forestry Trail is easy along the railbed and moderate along the singletrack trail. Lake Trail is easy along its 0.75-mile flat stretch and moderately difficult along the 0.75-mile hiking trail.

Food: You'll find restaurants and groceries in Montesano.

Restrooms: The park has restrooms and drinking water.

Seasons: Trails are open year-round, though they can be wet in fall and winter.

Rentals: Rent nonmotorized watercraft at the state park.

Contacts: City of Montesano, (360) 249-3021; Lake Sylvia State Park, (360) 249-3621; Washington State Parks Reservations Service, (888) 226-7688, https://www.parks.wa.gov/

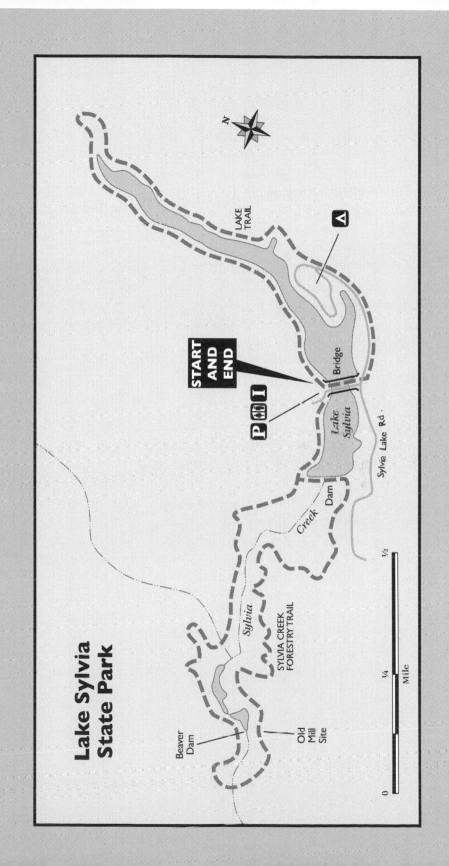

Bus routes: None

Access and parking: To reach Lake Sylvia State Park, travel on US 12 and take the Montesano exit. Take WA 107 north, watching for "Montesano, Lake Sylvia State Park" signs. Turn right into town and follow signs to the park. Go straight at the stoplight, turn left at the stop sign (West Spruce Avenue), and then turn right onto North 3rd Street. You'll arrive at the Lake Sylvia parking area within 3 miles from US 12. GPS: N46 59.82' / W123 35.71'

A state park Discover Pass is required to park here, and is valid at Washington's state recreation lands. Find information on the Washington Parks website at www.parks.wa.gov. Purchase options include one-day passes and annual passes, available online, at select automated pay-stations at trailheads, or at specified local vendors.

Lake Sylvia State Park is a haven for playing. The park's 30-acre lake contains native bass and stocked trout. Coho salmon and trout live in Sylvia Creek; beavers build dams along its banks, while otters play in the water. Bears and birds love the sweet grasses, berries, and bushes in the open replanted areas of the forestry trail. A play area, legacy pavilion, boat launch, and picnic sites combine with interpretive trails to offer a full day of recreation; a campground lets you extend your visit.

History is highlighted throughout the park as well. The original dam was built in 1868 to power the first sawmill in Grays Harbor County and the backwater pond was used for log flotation. You can see the superstructure when the lake is lowered. The present dam was built in the 1920s to provide Montesano with power, and the land became a state park in 1936.

Look for the underwater log dam, sawmill remnants, and old trestles. These 3 miles of railroad were built to haul timber from the pond to the Chehalis County Logging and Timber Company in 1905. Oxen then hauled it to town. The hearty oxen were the sole method of timber transport before the railroad.

A vast network of trails traverses the park and adjoining city-owned forest. The trails on the north side are gravel and follow the old railroad grade, while south-side trails are forested singletrack trails. This description focuses on two of them: The Sylvia Creek Forestry Trail, built in 1991 and improved over the years, is a rugged interpretive trail beside Sylvia Creek with short, steep hills and small bridges; the Lake Trail heads out 0.75 mile on the railroad right-of-way and then loops 0.75 mile around Lake Sylvia on a steep hiking trail. The undeveloped right-of-way continues straight into the forest as part of the network of mountain bike trails. Obtain a park map of the entire trail network, with desirable mountain biking. Some trail segments are also logging roads, so you may encounter logging trucks.

The Sylvia Creek Forestry Trail (SCFT) is a rugged, challenging 2.3-mile-long trail. For the mountain biker it's strewn with obstacles and hazards; for the hiker it provides an interesting and hilly pathway through the forest. Land adjacent to the park boundaries, including this trail, is owned by the city of Montesano and managed as a working tree farm. Logging created this railroad bed over one hundred years ago, and logging is still going strong today. The city developed an interpretive trail along the graveled railbed to exhibit this working forest. Clear-cuts, a second-growth forest, the old Chehalis mill site, and wildlife and plant habitat are all part of this display.

Access the lake outlet via a planked bridge near the parking area.

Enjoy camping and paddle sports at Lake Sylvia State Park.

From the western edge of the large paved parking lot, follow the planked lakeside bridge on the north side of the lake toward the dam outlet. The SCFT starts by an information board near the outlet. Bikers may start on the north side of Sylvia Creek and ride the gravel trail to the bridge and back, avoiding the more difficult south side. If you do bike the south-side singletrack trail, stop or slow at blind curves to avoid collisions with hikers, and be cautious of steep banks below the curving trail, wooden steps placed in steep sections, narrow bridges, and mud holes. Ride in control.

Lake Trail begins adjacent to a small parking area near the road bridge crossing the lake. It runs flat along the lake, then uphill, through a cute covered bridge, and to a bank high above the lake. Be sure to take a bike map if you'd like to venture off to the many trails outside the park boundaries. Ultimately the trail exits into the campground. Use the road to return to the starting point.

Other nearby rail trails include the Willapa Hills Trail (Trail 20), 35 minutes from Montesano, and the Chehalis Western Trail (Trail 19), north of Olympia off I-5.

22 PALOUSE TO CASCADES STATE PARK TRAIL

Standing as one of the longest rail trails in the nation, the Palouse to Cascades State Park Trail crosses most of Washington State and ends at the Idaho border. Along the way it passes through various climatic zones. It was previously known as the John Wayne Pioneer Trail. With the completed renovation of the bridge trestle over the Columbia River at the town of Beverly, Washington's portions of the Chicago, Milwaukee, St. Paul & Pacific Railroad corridor are linked. An ultimate long-distance adventure awaits travelers, while several shorter sections fascinate trail users with scenery and history.

Activities:

Location: Cedar Falls to Columbia River in King and Kittitas Counties in the western segment, and Beverly to Tekoa in Grant, Adams, Whitman, and Spokane Counties in the eastern segment.

Length: 250 miles of the original railbed are managed by the Washington State Parks and Recreation Commission (a 113-mile western segment and a 137-mile eastern segment).

Surface: Western segment contains compacted ballast, gravel, and sand. The section from Cedar Falls to Thorp has the firmer surface. Eastern segment includes crushed stone, original rail ballast, and dirt; the surface is deep and sandy for long sections of the trail.

Wheelchair access: This trail is not wheelchair-accessible.

Difficulty: Easy to moderate in the western segment, with some sandy and rocky surfaces. There's a constant 1.75 percent grade uphill from Cedar

Falls to Hyak. As the trail continues eastward, it flattens. Moderate to difficult on the eastern segment beyond Beverly, where rough surfaces offer tough travel plus mandatory detours on rural roads.

Food: Try Easton, Ellensburg, Kittitas, Beverly, Othello, Warden, Lind, Rosalia, and Tekoa.

Restrooms: You'll find restrooms along the western segment at all trailheads except Ellensburg West, Kittitas, and Army East / Huntzinger. Water is available at some trailheads. Expect limited restrooms and drinking water beyond Army West / Renslow Trailhead and beyond Beverly.

Camping: There are campgrounds at Lake Kachess, Lake Easton State Park, and Kittitas County Fairgrounds. If you prefer primitive trailside campsites, try Alice Creek and Carter Creek, located between Cedar Falls and Hyak, or Cold Creek and Roaring Creek, located between Hyak to Easton. Ponderosa campsite is west of Thorp. Near Beverly there's camping at Wanapum Recreation Area and Crab Creek Wildlife Area.

Seasons: The trail can be used year-round, although the Snoqualmie Tunnel is closed Nov 1 through Apr 30. There's cross-country skiing and snowshoeing between Dec and Mar on some trail sections.

Rentals: Mountain bike rentals are available at the Pavilion at the Suncadia Resort between Roslyn and Cle Elum, (509) 649-6160 (Recreation), 877-220-1438 (Main Lodge). For the eastern trail section, see appendix A for a list of bike rentals in Eastern Washington.

Contacts: For information about the trail and online registration for east segment travel beyond Beverly, visit Washington State Parks, https://www.parks.wa.gov/521/Palouse-to-Cascades, and www.parks.wa.gov. Additional information is at Palouse to Cascades Coalition, www.palousetocascadestrail.org; Palouse to Cascades and Columbia Plateau Trail State Parks, (509) 646-9218; Washington Trails Association, www.wta.org; and Mountains to Sound Greenway, www.mtsgreenway.org. For information on camping, call Washington State Parks Reservations Service, (888) 226-7688; Lake Easton State Park, (509) 656-2586; or Wanapum Recreation Area, (509) 856-2700. For information on camping at the Kittitas County Fairgrounds and for reservations, call the Kittitas County Events Center, (509) 962-7639. To learn about the history of the Milwaukee Road Railroad, visit www.mrha.com.

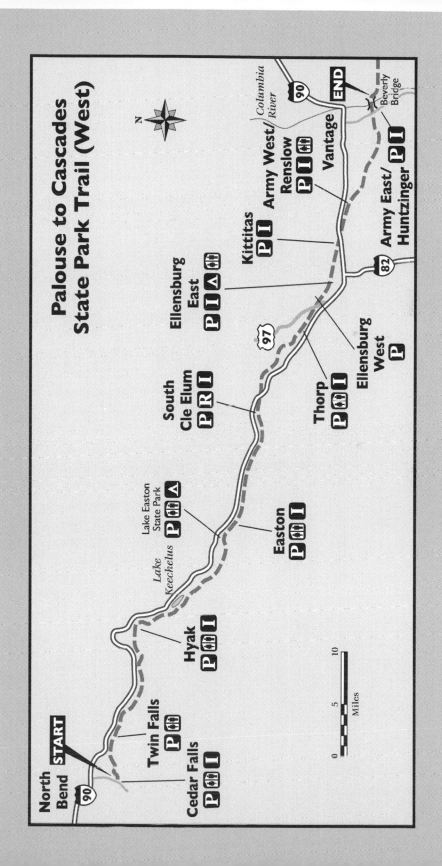

Palouse to Cascades
State Park Trail (West)

North Bend

START

Cedar Falls
P 🚻 I

Twin Falls
P 🚻

Hyak
P 🚻 I

Lake Easton
State Park
P 🚻 ⛺

Lake
Keechelus

Easton
P 🚻 I

South
Cle Elum
P 🚻 I

Ellensburg
East
P I ⛺ 🚻

Kittitas
P I

Army West/
Renslow
P I 🚻

Vantage

Ellensburg
West
P

Thorp
P 🚻 I

Columbia
River

END

Beverly
Bridge

Army East/
Huntzinger
P I

N

0   5   10
Miles

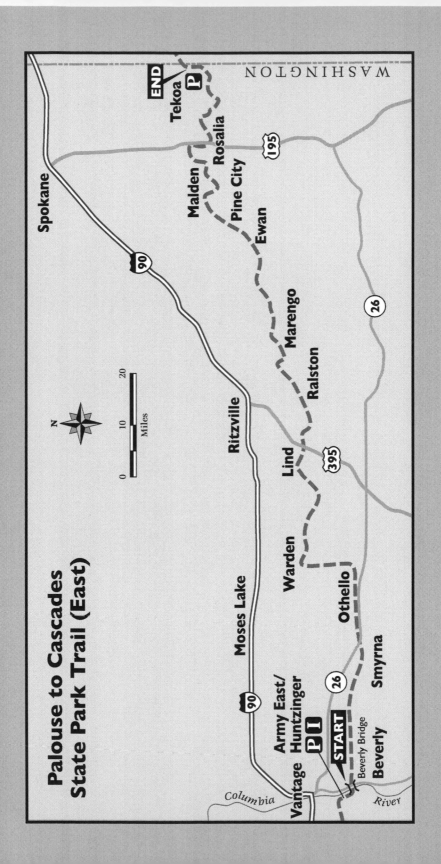

Palouse to Cascades State Park Trail (East)

WASHINGTON

Spokane

END

Tekoa

P

Rosalia

Malden

Pine City

Ewan

195

Marengo

Ralston

26

90

Ritzville

Lind

395

Moses Lake

Warden

Othello

N

10   20

0

Miles

Vantage

Army East/
Huntzinger

P

START

90

26

Beverly Bridge

Beverly

Smyrna

Columbia

River

Bus routes: None

Access and parking: When traveling between Army West / Renslow Trailhead and Army East / Huntzinger Trailhead, you'll self-register at kiosks near these trailheads. If traveling east from Beverly to the Idaho border, you'll need to register online at the Washington State Parks' website, at www.parks.wa.gov. Visitors need a Discover Pass year-round and a Sno-Park permit in winter to park at Hyak, Crystal Springs, Easton Reload, or Lake Easton State Park. Find information on the Washington Parks website at www.parks.wa.gov. Purchase options include one-day passes and annual passes, available online, at select automated pay-stations at trailheads, or at specified local vendors.

Directions are provided to the trailheads for the described sections.

- Cedar Falls: To begin at Rattlesnake Lake, take exit 32 (436th Avenue Northeast) off I-90. Turn south and follow 436th Avenue Northeast / Cedar Falls Road Southeast for approximately 3.0 miles and go beyond the Rattlesnake Lake Recreation Area parking area. Go left into the Palouse to Cascades State Park Trail and the Cedar Falls trailhead. GPS: N47 25.93' / W121 45.99'

- Hyak: Take exit 54 off I-90 and at the end of the ramp, make a soft left onto WA 906. Follow the signs for the Snoqualmie Tunnel. Sno-Park permits required in winter.

- Easton (exit 71): To head east on the trail, follow the signs from the exit to Easton. Cross the railroad tracks and turn left at the trail sign. Depending on snow conditions, this trailhead may not be accessible Dec through Mar.

- South Cle Elum (exit 84): Coming from the west, follow the signs to South Cle Elum and then follow the trail signs.

- Thorp (exit 101): Head 0.25 mile north on Thorp Prairie Highway. Turn left onto Thorp Depot Road and drive another 0.25 mile to the trail crossing and the trailhead beyond.

- Ellensburg West (exit 106): To head west on the trail, follow signs to Central Washington University north of I-90. The trailhead is on Water Street near 15th Avenue.

- Ellensburg East (exit 109): Turn north onto Main Street. Head north for 2.0 miles, then turn right on University Way. Drive 0.8 mile more, watch for the Kittitas County Fairgrounds sign on your right, and continue on University Way, which turns into East 10th Street. Continue past Chestnut Street. Turn right onto North Alder Street and go 2 blocks. The trailhead is on the left. You can park at the fairgrounds or next to the trailhead on the corner of North Alder Street and East 8th Avenue.

- Army East / Huntzinger Road (exit 136): From the freeway, travel south on Huntzinger Road past Wanapum Recreation Area. Continue 2.0 miles farther, passing The Cove. The trailhead parking is on the left, about 3 miles from The Cove. The Beverly Railroad Bridge connects the Palouse to Cascades State Park Trail's west segment with the east segment. Leave Army East / Huntzinger Trailhead and cross the Columbia River, or leave from the town of Beverly.

- Tekoa near the eastern terminus at the Washington–Idaho border: For access to westward travel, take WA 27 southward from Spokane toward Tekoa. On the north side of Tekoa, turn west on Lone Pine Road. Travel about 1 mile and turn south onto Summer Road (as marked on maps, although road sign reads "Soup Road"). Arrive at the small trailhead and kiosk. A newer Tekoa trailhead is in the planning stages.

The Palouse to Cascades State Park Trail includes 250 miles of usable trail and 5,794 acres of adjacent land. This long-distance trail is isolated much of the way.

In 1917 the Milwaukee Road (of the Chicago, Milwaukee, St. Paul & Pacific Railroad) became the first electrified transcontinental railroad and the nation's longest electrified train. The line opened for freight in 1909, and the *Olympian-Hiawatha* passenger train made its debut in 1911. The last Milwaukee train passed over the Cascades in 1980. Washington State opened the first segment of the rail trail in 1984, with improvements ongoing. Now the Washington State Parks and Recreation Commission manages 250 miles of the original railbed from the Washington–Idaho border to Rattlesnake Lake, near North Bend. The following description progresses from the west to the east.

Starting in the west, this section of the historic Milwaukee Road Railroad right-of-way trail parallels I-90 from Cedar Falls, near North Bend, to Kittitas, then drops south through US Army land to the magnificent Columbia River. The 113-mile western segment is the more developed and popular section. In 2022, the completed Beverly Bridge renovations opened the river trestle to trail users. Now adventurers travel 70 feet above the Columbia River for 3,000 feet to the eastern segment. Another 137 miles of remote trail, trestles, and road detours leads to the Washington–Idaho border.

West of the Cascades are the wet and green Cascade foothills. East of the mountains you'll find glacial valleys with coniferous trees and ranchland. Snow cover for cross-country skiing and snowshoeing usually lasts from December through March in the western segment and is most reliable from Hyak to Crystal Springs or Easton. Ski tracks are groomed in winter in the Hyak area. As you continue east, the landscape changes to sagebrush desert, arid scrublands, and the irrigated farmlands of the Columbia Basin. East of Thorp the trail is shadeless and dry, hot in summer and cold in winter. Bears, bobcats, cougars, rattlesnakes, eagles, ospreys, rodents, and rabbits inhabit different parts of the trail.

The adventurous eastern segment of the Palouse to Cascades State Park Trail starts at the Beverly Bridge. You'll pass through several geological zones, some with dramatic scenery and varied wildlife. There's snow for skiing and snowshoeing several weeks of the year—mostly from the Idaho border westward about 20 miles. Trail travel between Beverly to the Idaho border requires registration, completed online on the Washington State Parks website. This segment is less developed than the western segment, with some difficult surfaces. One of the longest detours on the entire trail occurs on country roads around the 38-mile gap from Royal City Junction to Warden.

Cedar Falls to Hyak, 22.5 miles

From near the lowland town of North Bend to the Snoqualmie Pass, this portion of the Palouse to Cascades State Park Trail guides you above the Snoqualmie River Valley. You'll travel on high trestles, below mountain

Stop by the railroad-themed restrooms at the Cedar Falls Trailhead.

peaks, and through a 2.0-mile tunnel. Pass beside creeks and waterfalls, under huge fir trees, and beside a large blue lake. It's a treat to be perched above the valley and dwarfed below the mountain peaks, watching the moving picture of the Cascade Mountains and valleys below you.

Starting at the western terminus at Cedar Falls near Rattlesnake Lake you'll discover the fun 22.5-mile trail section to Hyak. Cedar Falls also serves as the trailhead for a multiday trip across the state via bicycle, horse, ski, or foot. The Snoqualmie Valley Trail reaches Rattlesnake Lake for those connecting from other trails. Bicyclists might prefer to go westward from Hyak because the slight, though constant, uphill grade heading east makes this section an easier downhill ride going west. Many people visit the trail just to see the tunnel near Hyak. This Cedar Falls to Hyak section and the Hyak to Lake Easton section are the most heavily used.

Once on the trail heading toward Hyak, pass a road cutting down to Olallie State Park and more waterfalls. Moving eastward on the Palouse to Cascades State Park Trail you'll pass a rock wall covered with climbers scaling Deception Crags. Just beyond, travelers go across the Hall Creek trestle.

Continuing along the trail, cross creeks, observe valley views, and admire waterfalls against the steep hillsides. Reach a curving trestle at Hansen Creek followed by a wooden snowshed. You soon approach a highlight of this section. You'll enter the west portal of the 2.0-mile Snoqualmie Tunnel, which is closed November 1 through May 1. Bring a flashlight and a jacket. The ceiling drips water in several spots, and it's cold and dark. It's also spooky and a lot of fun. Focus on the beams of light from oncoming walkers, horses, and bicyclists. Eventually the exit archway visibly grows until you depart the tunnel.

Continue on to the Hyak Trailhead. In the Hyak area, skiing and snowshoeing are accessible and popular during the winter. A part of The Summit at Snoqualmie ski area lies directly uphill. Cross-country ski trails are near the rail trail, and the Hyak Sno-Park area is nearby.

Hyak to Easton, 18 miles

Heading east from Hyak, enjoy 18.0 miles of gentle downhill and flat grade as you drop from 2,500 to 2,176 feet. The trail follows the edge of Lake Keechelus until you reach the Keechelus Dam. You will find yourself on a corridor bounded by bright green foliage, rock faces, and the deep blue Lake Keechelus, interrupted by the occasional tiny island. The relaxing sound of water teasing the lake's shoreline makes this a great place to stop. Little white wildflowers color the trail in summer, while frosted peaks and the icy lake change the landscape in winter. Cross Meadows Creek and pass near the road to Lost Lake near mile 6.0. At mile 10.0, pass through the short, dark, restored Whittier Tunnel. Between miles 14.0 and 15.0, you will pass over creeks and high above the Yakima River on the secluded, wooded trail. You will pass the detour off the trail into Lake Easton State Park. Continuing on the Palouse to Cascades State Park Trail, approach the Easton trailhead, where you'll find a trail information kiosk.

Easton to Cle Elum, 11.5 miles

As you depart from the downtown Easton Trailhead, you'll enjoy a slight downhill grade and a good surface. The trail runs close to I-90 in places, though it's buffered by pine and fir trees. The mountains shrink into rounded hills; an occasional ranch appears on the landscape. You'll cross Golf Course Road and an I-90 interchange at 6.0 miles, with the twin trestles beyond. At mile 9.5 the Yakima River rushes under the trail and quickly leaves. Summertime violet and yellow wildflowers grace the trail edges.

Marshes and creek crossings give the trail some interest as you approach the old Cle Elum railroad station. In the depot you'll find the historic museum. This is one of two remaining depots; the second still stands in Kittitas. As you pass the depot, the substation, and a trail kiosk, you can exit at Main Street and head into South Cle Elum for food and lodging. Cle Elum was a lively town in the railroading days.

Cle Elum to Thorp, 18.6 miles

After exploring the historic rail station, pass under I-90 at mile 3.16, leaving it south of the trail. The Yakima River (and WA 10) appears to your left at mile 5.0; in spring and summer look for rafters and anglers in the fast waters below the trail. Green foliage and pine trees create a pleasant pathway while the slight downhill grade eases your journey.

As you enter the Upper Yakima River Canyon, the river widens, trees become sparse, and hills are round and brown. Tall walls of basalt appear. The only shade you'll find is inside Tunnels 46 and 47. If on a bike in the western tunnel, you'll be in darkness for a few seconds—a bit longer on foot. The eastern tunnel is short. While on the trail, perhaps a muskrat or rabbit will scurry away.

Eventually the last cliffs disappear and you emerge into an expanse of ranchland bordered by foothills in the distance. Cows stare from behind barbed wire. Be sure to secure any gates you pass through. Arrive at the Thorp Trailhead at mile 18.6. You are entering another transition zone. Look eastward to miles of prairie grasslands. These merge into sage-covered hills and mingle with fertile farmland in the Columbia River basin.

Thorp to Ellensburg East, 8.4 miles

Hop back on the trail to Ellensburg. You will cross two decked trestles and leave the noise of I-90 behind. It's time to enjoy the flat, open farmland and the occasional shade of a crab apple tree. Take caution on the narrow and slanted terrain passing around several gates. You'll reach the first of two decked trestles at mile 2.2. They cross WA 10 and the active railroad tracks.

Find the Ellensburg West Trailhead at Water Street at 6.8 miles. A kiosk displays the route you might want to use to take a 1.6-mile detour through town. The trail restarts at the fairgrounds trailhead next to North Alder Street, near East 8th Avenue. There are restrooms, showers, and overnight camping for tents and RVs, available by reservation through the Kittitas County Events Center. While in town, cruise to the historic district and enjoy a solid meal.

Ellensburg East to Army East / Huntzinger,
33.7 miles

From the fairgrounds, head through farm country on flat, open trail. At mile 6.0, pull into Kittitas at the second of the two remaining depots. Built in 1909, it's listed on the National Register of Historic Places. The town is smaller than when it was built in a failed attempt to lure the Northern Pacific Railway. Ultimately, the Milwaukee Road built a right-of-way through town to transport the area's grains, fruits, vegetables, and livestock. Once the arid lowlands were irrigated, the fertile soil could produce enough food to support residents.

There are amenities within 2 blocks of the trail. This is your last stop in civilization until near the Army East / Huntzinger Trailhead in 27.7 miles.

Back on the trail it is about 5.7 miles to the next trailhead. Nearing the Army West / Renslow Trailhead, you'll cross the Renslow Trestle over I-90 and Boylston Road. Completed in 2020, the trestle avoids the prior 4-mile road detour. After the trestle you pass an access path from the trailhead parking at Army West / Renslow Trailhead, located off Stevens Road just off of Boylston Road. This upcoming section is popular with equestrians. The next 22 miles are on sandy, rocky, shadeless desert property owned and managed by the Department of Army—Yakima Training Center. Trail use is strictly confined to the railroad bed to ensure user safety and to prevent interference with military training activities. Find the self-registration kiosk once you get on the trail heading east from the Army West / Renslow Trailhead area. The other self-registration kiosk is near the Army East /

Equestrians ride the Palouse to Cascades State Park Trail westward toward the Army West / Renslow Trailhead.

Huntzinger Trailhead and serves trail users heading westward from the Beverly area.

The trail surface is sandy the first 4.0 miles after the Army West / Renslow Trailhead, which may challenge bicyclists. You'll encounter the closed Boylston Tunnel and can follow a trail uphill and around the tunnel. It's downhill for much of the next 18.0 miles. Passages through the rock cuts may be littered with rocks. The trail ahead is a bit rough and the grade is slight, but it's an improvement over the sand.

It's best to drink your water and slather on the sunscreen. There's no exit from this area if you become dehydrated, overheated, or tired. At about mile 30.0, pass near the area formerly known as Doris. In about 3 miles you'll come to the Army East / Huntzinger Trailhead parking area adjacent to Huntzinger Road. The self-registration kiosk for westbound travel is across the road from the parking area.

Continue toward the sparkling Columbia River and the refurbished Beverly Bridge rail trestle over the river, opened in April of 2022. When you reach or cross the bridge, congratulate yourself on completing the western segment.

To get to a campground, turn left at the intersection of the trail and Huntzinger Road and head 5 miles west to the Wanapum Recreation Area. The small town of Vantage, I-90, and the vehicle bridge across the river are 2 miles ahead. Gingko Petrified Forest is 1 mile north of Vantage. From here, grab a motel room or head home. Adventurers may continue on the Palouse to Cascades State Park Trail railbed via the Beverly Bridge, which connects the west and east sides of the Columbia River.

Beverly to the Idaho Border, 137 Miles

After leaving the Beverly Bridge and the town of Beverly, you'll pass through wildlife refuges and farmlands as you head out on the rugged, adventurous eastern segment. Make sure you've completed your online registration with the Washington State Parks for the Beverly to Idaho border segment and have checked their website for updates on conditions. This old Milwaukee Road railway right-of-way trail development is progressing. Anticipate some road detours around private property, missing bridges, and a closed section—all part of the unique experience of this remote trail. When you register, you'll receive maps showing any detours. Plans are under way to improve a 9.0-mile portion from Malden to Rosalia in the east. There is a long road detour around the undeveloped section between Royal City Junction and Warden, which contains still-intact old rail lines and active rail lines. The trail surface is rougher than the western segment described above, yet the challenges increase the sense of adventure. Expect hard-packed sand, railway ballast, rockfall, weeds, and swamp areas. Prepare carefully for your outing. You will need to be self-dependent, as there are limited services along this segment between Beverly and Tekoa and the rough 6.0-mile section to the Idaho border. The Palouse to Cascades State Park Trail is a host trail within the Great American Rail-Trail, with additional linkage plans with other trails in Idaho.

23 COWICHE CANYON TRAIL

Cowiche Canyon Trail takes you through both geological and railroading history. Slicing through a canyon and crossing the creek repeatedly, this rail trail makes for a tour that's both dramatic and peaceful. You'll have many opportunities to observe plant and animal life.

Activities:

Location: Yakima, in Yakima County

Length: 3.0 miles

Surface: Gravel and dirt

Wheelchair access: The trail is not wheelchair-accessible.

Difficulty: Easy

Food: No food is available along this trail.

Restrooms: You'll find a vault toilet at the Cowiche Canyon West and East Trailheads.

Seasons: The trail can be used year-round from dawn to dusk.

Rentals: There are no rentals near this trail.

Contacts: The Cowiche Canyon Conservancy is a nonprofit organization dedicated to protecting the canyon as a natural resource area and ensuring its recreational use and enjoyment. Write PO Box 877, Yakima, WA 98907, call (509) 248-5065, or visit www.cowichecanyon.org.

Bus routes: None

Access and parking: To reach the western terminus, at the West Trailhead, from Yakima exit US 12 onto North 40th Avenue. Head south to Summitview Road, turn right, and drive 7 miles west to Weikel Road. Turn right, drive 0.25 mile, and turn right into the parking area. Continue along the road within the parking area to the historical kiosk at the trailhead. GPS: N46 37.89' / W120 39.94'

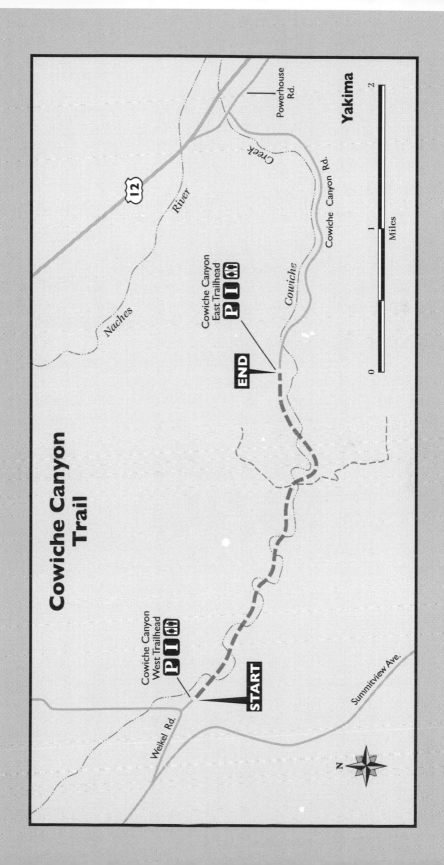

To reach the East Trailhead, take US 12 and exit onto North 40th Avenue. Head south on North 40th Avenue to West Powerhouse Road and turn right. Go 1.1 miles on West Powerhouse Road and take the second left onto Cowiche Canyon Road. Continue another 2.2 miles to the trailhead parking lot to the right.

|||||||||||||||||||||||||||||||||||||||||||||||||||||||||||||||||||||||||||||||||||||||||||||||||||||||

Cowiche Canyon Conservancy owns 2,300 acres and helps manage another 3,000 acres for Washington State Department of Fish and Wildlife, containing over 30 miles of trails, including this rail trail. Cowiche Canyon is the result of geological activity that took place millions of years ago. From Pullman, lava flowed to form the Cowiche Canyon floor and the south wall 17.5 million years ago. This 6,000-foot-thick layer, called the Columbia River Basalt Group, covered eastern Washington. One million years ago, Tieton andesite flowed from the west to create the north wall.

In 1913 the North Yakima & Valley Railroad line of the Northern Pacific was built through the canyon to haul apples to Yakima from the productive orchards in Cowiche and Tieton. Workers blasted through vertical basalt cliffs to create the line, which crossed the Cowiche River eleven times. The constant curve of the canyon frames each rock formation ahead and paints a picture of the trains rumbling down the rails.

From the kiosk at West Trailhead at the western terminus, travel a slight grade downhill to the first of eleven bridges, with bridge numbers ascending west to east. You will cross all but two of the bridges. Portions of the trail contain heavy gravel and a few rocks, making it challenging in places for mountain bikes. Beware of a large step onto and off some of the bridges. Bikers should dismount if in question. Though sightings are rare, rattlesnakes may be present.

Witness the contrast between the lush riparian vegetation along Cowiche Creek and the browns and yellows of the shrub-steppe on the hillsides in late spring. During the hot, dry summer months the plants dehydrate. In autumn the vegetation rebounds with stunning colors. Cold winters put plant life to sleep until the cycle begins again in spring.

Creek crossings give life to the still canyon. Look and listen for wildlife as you travel from bridge to bridge. The western meadowlark sings from

You can take a break near the cliffs along the Cowiche Canyon Trail.

March through June. Marmots, coyotes, canyon wrens, chickadees, and magpies may be seen or heard. Look for big beaver dams near the east end of the trail. Fish occupy Cowiche Creek, thanks to restoration efforts by the Cowiche Canyon Conservancy and their partners.

Near Bridge 8 the Winery Trail departs from the north side of the trail and traverses 0.8 mile up to the Tasting Room at Wilridge Vineyard. The Uplands Trail, another side trail by Bridge 8, rises up the southern slope. Shortly after these trail junctions, the trail detours around Bridges 9 and 10 on a nice riparian trail.

When you emerge at the East Trailhead at Cowiche Canyon Road, turn around and return the way you came. While in the area, consider exploring the Cowiche Canyon Conservancy's trail system at Snow Mountain Ranch, or head over to the Lower Yakima Valley Pathway (Trail 24).

24 LOWER YAKIMA VALLEY PATHWAY

Wineries, sunshine, fresh fruit, and more wineries! This traverse of the world-renowned Yakima Valley wine country will take you past any number of gourmet delights—fine dining, farm stands, candy shops, and of course, the area's many award-winning wine makers—all in a shadeless desert environment.

Activities:

Location: The Yakima Valley towns of Sunnyside, Grandview, and Prosser, in Benton and Yakima Counties

Length: 14.5 miles

Surface: Asphalt

Wheelchair access: The trail is wheelchair-accessible in areas, but note rough spots mentioned below.

Difficulty: Easy; though it's moderate for skaters. The trail is narrow and occasionally has a bit of grade, along with some rough pavement (noticeable for skaters). In Grandview the trail detours on the roadside for 1.5 miles. For smooth skating, start at the East Grandview Trailhead parking area and head to Prosser.

Food: Grocery stores, fruit vendors, fast food, restaurants, and wineries are sprinkled along the way.

Restrooms: There are facilities 3.5 miles east of the western trailhead.

Seasons: The trail can be used year-round, though it may be snowy or cold in winter.

Rentals: None

Contacts: Yakima Valley Visitor and Information Center, (509) 573-3388, www.yakimavalleytourism.com; Grandview Chamber of Commerce, (509) 882-2100; Prosser Chamber of Commerce, (509) 786-3177; Wine Yakima Valley, http://wineyakimavalley.org; Washington Wine Commission, www. washingtonwine.org

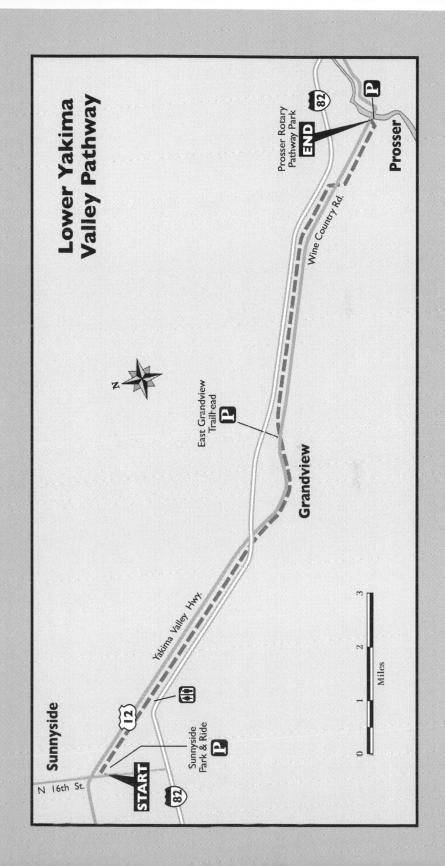

Bus routes: None

Access and parking: Take I-82 from Yakima or from the Tri-Cities of Pasco, Richland, and Kennewick to the exit for Sunnyside (exit 69), Grandview (exit 73), or Prosser (exit 82). The trail parallels US 12. Western terminus parking is located in Sunnyside at an informal paved parking strip east of North 16th Street and Yakima Valley Highway (US 12) on the south side of US 12. GPS: N46 19.58' / W119 59.82'

For the eastern terminus in Prosser, park at the Prosser Rotary Pathway Park near the Les Schwab tire store on Wine Country Road (US 12), 1 block west of the west bridge over the Yakima River.

The Lower Yakima Valley Pathway spans three desert towns between Yakima and the Tri-Cities. The desert clime is dry: hot in summer, cold in winter. It's also just right for producing the fine wines of Washington State. Vintners note its location on the forty-sixth parallel—the same as Burgundy and Bordeaux, the great wine-producing regions of France. The soil is twice as productive as most due to nutrients from rich volcanic ash.

Before the valley's fertile soil and climate were recognized in the 1950s, rail lines were built here to transport the fruit and grains of the Lower Yakima Valley. The North Coast Railroad was incorporated in 1906 and merged with the Oregon-Washington Railroad & Navigation Company, beginning operations in 1910. The Attalia to North Yakima line was then leased to the Union Pacific on January 1, 1936. This line liberated the valley from the domination of the Northern Pacific Railway and their line from Kiona to Yakima City.

You'll be traveling in unshaded desert—bring lots of sunscreen and water. The trail is narrow (about 8 feet wide); please be courteous to other trail users.

Although you can access the trail from several places, this description takes you west to east. From Sunnyside to Grandview (6.5 miles), the trail is sandwiched between I-82 and US 12 (Yakima Valley and Wine Country Roads), beside fast-food spots, gas stations, and the town's commercial districts. The section between Grandview and Prosser has limited services.

Watch for Prosser Rotary Pathway Park, the eastern terminus of the Lower Yakima Valley Pathway in Prosser.

A 1.5-mile gap in the trail starts on the west side of Grandview near North Euclid Street. Continue east on the shoulder of Wine Country Road (US 12) and reenter the trail near Fir Street and the Palacios Parkway stone archway. Look for this archway on the north side of the road about 7 miles from Sunnyside. Continue on the trail to the trailhead parking on the east side of the rose garden just before the I-82 interchange.

On your way through Grandview, detour to the Dykstra House restaurant—a National Historic Site built in 1909—on Birch, 1 block off the highway. Grandview is a rural community based on agriculture, and a good choice for a Mexican food meal.

The trail is smoother much of the way from east of Grandview to Prosser, 6.5 miles farther. There's a touch of a grade here and there as you approach distant Rattlesnake Mountain, visible to the north. View the Horse Heaven Hills south of Prosser. The trail dips down from the rail right-of-way to avoid an active trestle crossing at about 3 miles from Prosser (or about 11.5 miles from Sunnyside). You'll primarily travel rural desert until Chukar Cherries appears about 0.5 mile from the eastern terminus. Stop here for your gourmet sweet treat. If you're lucky, you'll walk in on a tasting.

A short distance ahead the trail ends at Prosser Rotary Pathway Park, near the bridge over the Yakima River, not far from downtown Prosser. The Prosser Historical Museum is down the road. Check your winery map to attend a tasting.

Other area trails include the Umatilla County Lewis and Clark Commemorative Trail (Trail 32), located across the Columbia in Oregon, less than an hour away, and the Cowiche Canyon Trail (Trail 23), near Yakima.

25 SPOKANE RIVER CENTENNIAL TRAIL

Welcome to 40 miles of paved riverfront trail in a dry region. The sun shines on the Spokane River, rapids rush downriver, and bridges criss-cross the water. The Centennial Trail has three different personalities: the bustling and beautiful downtown Riverfront Park; the calm and gentle terrain to the east; and the hilly section high above the river, to the west. Long stretches of the trail are without services other than trailhead restrooms. Riverside benches and picnic tables offer views of the river.

Activities:

Location: Nine Mile Recreation Area of Riverside State Park to the Idaho border, in Spokane County

Length: 40 miles

Surface: Asphalt, with some shared road sections. Portions of the trail are favorable to horseback riding. There is a trail-side equestrian area with camping and parking located between Military Cemetery Trailhead and Morin Trailhead in Riverside State Park.

Wheelchair access: Most of the trail is wheelchair-accessible. The area west of downtown Spokane is quite hilly. Contact the agencies listed below for a list of accessible parking areas.

Difficulty: The trail ranges from easy to difficult; see the description for each section.

Food: You'll find eateries in downtown Spokane, at the Spokane Valley Mall, and at the Idaho border.

Restrooms: There are many restrooms along the trail. See map for approximate locations.

Seasons: The trail is used year-round dawn to dusk. Some restrooms are closed Oct through Mar.

Rentals: You can rent bikes in Spokane at Spoke N Sport, 212 North Division Street, (509) 838-8842, www.spokensportinc.net.

Contacts: Riverside State Park, (509) 465–5064, www.parks.wa.gov; Riverside State Park's Bowl and Pitcher Office (509) 327-2635; Riverfront Park, (509) 625-6600; Spokane Regional Visitor Center, 888-SPOKANE (776-5263), www.visitspokane.com; Friends of the Centennial Trail, (509) 624-7188, http://spokanecentennialtrail.org

Bus routes: For information, call (509) 328-RIDE (7433), or visit www.spokanetransit.com.

Access and parking: You can access both the westbound and eastbound segments of the trail from Riverfront Park in downtown Spokane. To take the trail westward, begin at Riverfront Park at the Howard Street Bridge near the Spokane Arena. GPS: N47 39.86' / W117 25.24'

For the section to the east, start in Riverfront Park on the south side of the river by the Convention Center and Doubletree Hotel. GPS: N47 39.68' / W117 24.95'

Nine Mile Recreation Area to the west and the Idaho border to the east mark the western and eastern termini. Parking is available at most trailheads. The trail numbering starts at the Idaho state line at mile 1.0 and continues west, ending at mile 40.0.

A state park Discover Pass is required for state park trailhead parking, and is valid at Washington's state recreation lands. Find information on the Washington Parks website at www.parks.wa.gov. Purchase options include one-day passes and annual passes, available online, at select automated pay-stations at trailheads, or at specified local vendors.

‖‖

By 1883 a nationwide rail connection was established in Spokane, and the small town experienced a population explosion. The legacy of the rails is evident throughout the Spokane River Centennial Trail. Numerous railroads sketched a matrix of tracks in this area. The Inland Empire Paper Company, owned by the local newspaper company, completed a land exchange with the state parks from Argonne to the state line. Great

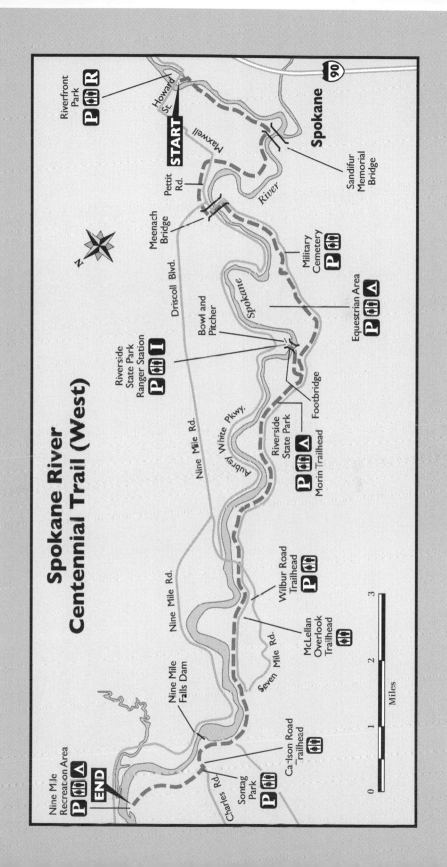

Spokane River
Centennial Trail (West)

Riverfront Park

Spokane

90

Howard St.

Maxwell

START

Sandifur Memorial Bridge

Pettit Rd.

Spokane River

Meenach Bridge

Driscoll Blvd.

Military Cemetery

Bowl and Pitcher

Riverside State Park Ranger Station

Equestrian Area

Footbridge

Nine Mile Rd.

Aubrey White Pkwy.

Riverside State Park

Morin Trailhead

Nine Mile Rd.

Wilbur Road Trailhead

McLellan Overlook Trailhead

Seven Mile Rd.

Nine Mile Falls Dam

Charles Rd.

Carlson Road Trailhead

Sontag Park

Nine Mile Recreation Area

END

Miles

0   1   2   3

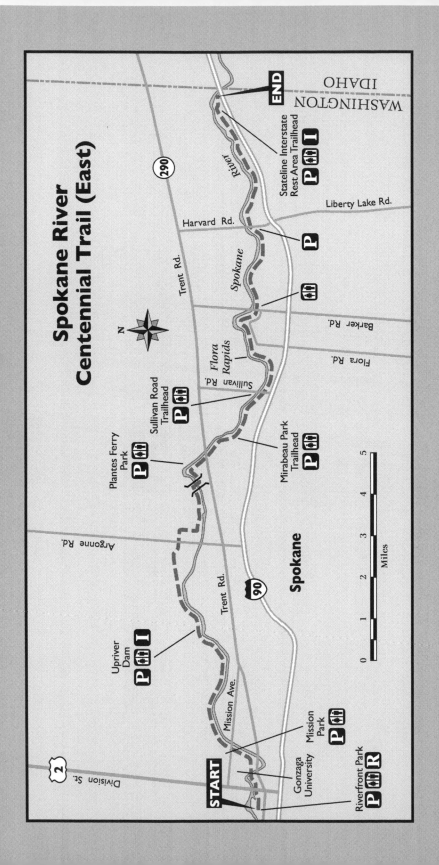

Spokane is a city of bridges viewable from the Spokane River Centennial Trail through Riverfront Park.

Northern contributed the Don Kardong Bridge. Spokane's Great Northern Station sat on Havermale Island on the river.

The Riverfront Park in downtown Spokane is popular with visitors and locals and serves as the starting point for descriptions of trail segments heading west and east. This 100-acre park blends a natural setting with a hearty history reflected in bridges, dams, and turn-of-the-twentieth-century buildings. The rail trail rolls by downtown hotels and runs blocks from pubs, coffeehouses, restaurants, and shopping. Spokane turned the abandoned railroad tracks into this unique park and outdoor amusement center for the 1974 Expo.

You can use Riverfront Park to begin an exploration of the Centennial Trail. The eastern trip is gentle and dry; to the west, look for hilly terrain. If you're new to this area, you'll learn about boulder fields and basalt cliffs, ice floods and aquifers. You'll also see exquisite homes and parks created by the prosperous mining of silver and gold and nurtured by the railroad. Check with the visitor bureau to locate historic homes, restaurants, bed-and-breakfasts, parks, and gardens reminiscent of the mining era.

Riverfront Park to Nine Mile Falls Dam and Nine Mile Recreation Area, 17 miles westbound

The hilly route from the park west to Nine Mile Falls Dam and Nine Mile Recreation Area passes through ponderosa pines, pastures, and Riverside State Park, all beside the Spokane River. It's a rural area with restrooms along the way. There are several trailheads providing access, including a handful with horse trailer parking access available.

After leaving Riverfront Park and residential areas, you'll travel through pines and over hills. Pass a trailhead parking area at the military cemetery. Continue by the equestrian area and on toward the Morin Trailhead. Ahead is an opportunity for a fun detour to a famous scenic site. A mile past this trailhead, watch for a restroom where a side trail (Trail 211) splits off from the main trail and heads down to the swinging bridge over the river. Cross the bridge and follow the trail to the north side of Riverside State Park and the overlook above the fascinating Bowl and Pitcher rock formations. You could also access this famous area by vehicle after you complete your trail outing.

Once you're back on the main trail, pass through an area with a basalt ridge above and river rapids below. Several side trails drop to the river along the way. Near mile 34, explore the history of Seven Mile Camp, a Civilian Conservation Corps operation of the 1930s. Just beyond are the Wilbur Road Trailhead and McLellan Overlook Trailhead. Soon you'll return to the river and cruise the hills toward Nine Mile Falls Dam.

The trail drops down to Deep Creek Bridge and a picnic area just past mile 36.0. There are plenty of benches and overlooks along the way. From here the trail passes next to Carlson Road Trailhead and to Sontag Park. For the best view of the gushing water released at Nine Mile Falls Dam, go to the viewing point across the bridge or go to the end of the road by the cottages. Return to the trail and continue on to the western terminus at the Nine Mile Recreation Area.

Riverfront Park to Idaho Border, 23 miles eastbound

The eastern half of the Centennial Trail is nothing like the west, except that it starts in downtown Spokane and runs by the river. Once you leave downtown at Upriver Drive, a calm river follows close beside a gentle grade most of the way to Idaho. Pines decorate the desert landscape; the sun warms you.

Depart from Riverfront Park on the southeast side of the river by the Convention Center and the DoubleTree Hotel. Mileage numbers descends as you travel eastward. The city section gives way to the suburbs and turns into wide-open spaces. The Upriver Dam is around mile 18.0. Rock jocks and mountain bikers hang out at the Minnehaha Rocks near mile 17.0. This is one of the rock deposits dumped here from the collapse of the Purcell ice lobe, a 2,000-foot-high ice dam in Idaho. This glacial flood occurred at the tail end of the last ice age, 20,000 years ago.

Enjoy a wide, smoothly paved scenic tour from Maringo to Mirabeau Park. Watch for deer, ospreys, and herons as you wander through the open pine forest. Cross the bridge at Plante's Ferry Park. Pass under Trent Road; reach Sullivan Road near milepost 10.0, then wake up to the traffic of the Spokane Valley Mall. Here you can grab some food and a bus to downtown Spokane (I-90).

From Sullivan Road the trail returns to a rural riverside route with birds, boaters, and rapids. It opens up to the prevailing winds 3 miles from the border. Pass along the Gateway Regional Park and arrive at the eastern terminus at Stateline Interstate Rest Area at the Washington–Idaho border. Though the Spokane River Centennial trail ends here, trail users can immediately connect with the North Idaho Centennial Trail (Trail 36). Get on the Idaho trail via a spur trail that crosses under I-90 and continues into Idaho. Follow the North Idaho Centennial Trail from the border to Post Falls and Coeur d'Alene.

26 BILL CHIPMAN PALOUSE TRAIL: PULLMAN, WASHINGTON

Connecting one university town to another, this trail—spanning two states—is popular with commuters and visitors. It weaves along Paradise Creek and features extensive interpretive signs detailing rail history and local points of interest.

Activities:

Location: City of Pullman, Washington, in Whitman County; city of Moscow, Idaho, in Latah County

Length: 6.0 miles in Washington and 1.0 mile in Idaho

Surface: Asphalt

Wheelchair access: Wheelchair access is available at the western terminus trailhead in Pullman, the Sunshine Trailhead, and the eastern terminus trailhead in Moscow, Idaho.

Difficulty: Easy

Food: There are many restaurants and gas stations in Pullman near the western trailhead and in Moscow near the eastern trailhead.

Restrooms: Emergency phones and restrooms are located near miles 1.5, 4.0, and 5.0, as measured from the western terminus in Pullman.

Seasons: The trail can be used year-round.

Rentals: In Pullman you can rent bicycles at B & L Bicycles, 219 East Main Street, (509) 332-1703, www.bandlbicycles.com. See appendix A for additional bicycle rentals in Moscow, Idaho, just across the state border.

Contacts: Whitman County Parks and Recreation, (509) 397-6238, https://whitmancounty.org/362/County-Parks; the Pullman Civic Trust, https://www.pullmancivictrust.org/trails

Bus routes: Contact Starline Luxury Coaches / Wheatland Express for Pullman-to-Moscow routes, (509) 334-2200, www.wheatlandexpress.com.

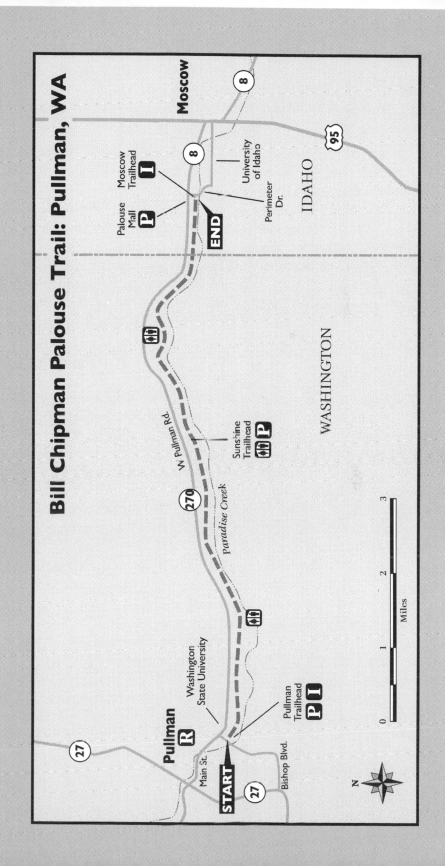

Bill Chipman Palouse Trail: Pullman, WA

For Pullman routes, contact Pullman Transit, (509) 332-6535, www.pull-mantransit.com.

Access and parking: To begin in Pullman, Washington, take WA 270 east or WA 27 south into Pullman and turn left onto Main Street. Continue on Main Street and turn right onto Bishop Boulevard. If coming from Moscow, Idaho, take ID-WA 270 West for about 6 miles. When you reach the location where WA 270 becomes Main Street, continue another 2 miles on Main Street to the first stoplight and turn left onto Bishop Boulevard. Bishop Boulevard winds toward the left, and within 1 block you turn left into the Quality Inn hotel parking lot. The trail starts at the northwest edge of the parking lot by the railroad station shelter replica. GPS: N46 43.29' / W117 09.84'

C leverly themed "All Aboard" and capturing the spirit of rail history, this trail is an adventure in learning. Discover commonly used rail terms and learn about the natural environment as you travel the route.

Opened in 1998, thanks to the work of the Pullman Civic Trust, the trail is jointly managed by Moscow, Pullman, the University of Idaho, Washington State University, and Whitman County. Since this smooth, easy trail is heavily used by bicycle commuters traveling between the two border cities of Pullman and Moscow, trail users need to be alert at all times and use proper trail etiquette.

Start at trail mile 0 on the east side of Pullman at the Pullman Trailhead, on the edge of the Quality Inn parking lot. End in Idaho at trail mile 7.0, just on the edge of the University of Idaho campus in Moscow. Educational rest stops with detailed interpretive signs, frequent benches, restrooms, and emergency phones smooth the way for visitors. The trail runs parallel to WA-ID 270 as it wanders back and forth across Paradise Creek and over thirteen bridges.

The first rail service to the area originally was the Oregon Railway and Navigation Company, which arrived in Pullman in 1885. It later became the Union Pacific Railroad. The trail follows a part of the line that eventually extended to Moscow. "Student Specials" carried students from various parts of Washington to school at Washington State University.

The Bill Chipman Palouse Trail heads east from the Pullman Trailhead at mile 0.

On the present-day trail you can learn loads of railroad lingo, such as the term *jerkwater*, which refers to a small town that has no water source. Train crews had to "jerk" buckets of water from a local source, like a creek, to provide the water to power their steam engines. Be sure to stop and enjoy the numerous educational signs along this well-documented rail trail.

After the first 0.5 mile out of the Pullman Trailhead, grain silos and a grain elevator loom large. They used to hold white wheat—a major crop of the region used for crackers, noodles, and cakes. A sign identifies the elevator spur as Lava Siding. A siding is a brief section of track that connects at both ends to the main tracks. The siding enables a train to wait on the side, where it can be loaded and unloaded—in this case, with wheat. Interesting geological features are visible in the area. Note the basalt rocks, which indicate old lava flows that were 50 to 100 feet thick.

Farther down the trail, read about the Homestead Flag Stop, at 3.0 miles. Near 5.0 miles the active track runs beside Paradise Creek and the trail. The small creek you are following originates in the Palouse Mountain

Range to the south, ultimately traveling to Moscow, then Pullman, on to the Snake and Columbia Rivers, and then into the Pacific Ocean. Paradise Creek provides a habitat for local birds and wildlife. Western meadowlarks, killdeer, and tree swallows are among the creatures supported by the creek ecosystem.

Beyond 6.0 miles you cross the Washington–Idaho border and enter the fringes of Moscow, Idaho. Continue the last mile to the eastern terminus, indicated by a train station replica and interpretive signs. After soaking up all the information offered at the kiosks, return the way you came.

There are loop trails in Pullman accessing the Bill Chipman Palouse Trail. The Paradise Path in Moscow connects with the trail at the eastern terminus.

While you are in the area, consider visiting other Washington trails, including the Spokane River Centennial Trail (Trail 25), and the Colfax Trail (Trail B). You can easily route onto the Latah Trail (Trail 37) in Idaho from the Bill Chipman Palouse Trail.

More Rail Trails

![A] TIGER MOUNTAIN STATE FOREST: EAST TIGER MOUNTAIN TRAIL SYSTEM

Tiger Mountain State Forest offers a variety of trails and serves as one of Seattle's top mountain biking destinations. In the East Tiger Mountain Trail System, multiuse Preston Railroad Trail and Iverson Railroad Trail follow portions of old railroad grades and interconnect via old logging roads. The TMT Connector passes by a historic train wreck site. Northwest Timber, East Tiger Summit, Joy Ride, Silent Swamp, Inside Passage, Easy Tiger, and other trails are traveled individually or combined as a loop. Logging in Tiger Mountain State Forest started in the 1920s and continues today. Timber was transported by switchback or incline railways to the base of the mountain and then by local railroads to mills in Preston, Issaquah, Hobart, and High Point. Both the Preston and Northwest Timber Trails were originally switchback railways. The Iverson Trail was part of the Wooden Pacific incline railway, which climbed 2 straight miles to the summit. The trails are named for the companies that logged them. The Department of Natural Resources, together with mountain bikers, built the trails in the early 1990s and continues improving the trails. You're in a forest of fir, cedar, hemlock, alder, and maple trees with bears, bobcats, grouse, ducks, and dozens of bird species. Logging activities provide trail users with far-reaching views of Mount Rainier and the Green, Cedar, and White River Valleys. You can further enjoy the Tiger Mountain State Forest system with a trip to the West Tiger Railroad Grade. It's deep within the boundaries of the West Tiger Mountain Natural Resources Conservation Area, and you reach the railroad grade only after hiking other trails that begin from street-level in Issaquah.

Activities:

Location: King County

Length: 25 miles of beginner through expert trails. Some are mountain bike–only trails, while other trails require directional travel.

Surface: Natural surface, with some crushed rock in places

Wheelchair access: The trail is not wheelchair-accessible.

Difficulty: Moderate to advanced

Food: No food is available along this trail.

Restrooms: You'll find facilities at the second upper parking lot at Tiger Summit Trailhead. From the eastern lower parking area, the restrooms can be accessed via a path from the gravel lot.

Seasons: The trails can be used year-round.

Rentals: See appendix A for bike rentals in the Puget Sound area.

Contacts: Washington State Department of Natural Resources, South Puget Sound Region Office, (360) 825-1631, www.dnr.wa.gov, and their website for Tiger Mountain at https://www.dnr.wa.gov/Tiger; Evergreen Mountain Bike Alliance, http://trails.evergreenmtb.org/wiki/Trail:Tiger_ Mountain; King County trail finder at https://gismaps.kingcounty.gov/ TrailFinder/

Bus routes: None

Access and parking: To reach the East Tiger Mountain Summit parking lot, get off I-90 at exit 25 (WA 18). Head west 4.3 miles to the Tiger Mountain Summit sign. The large gravel parking lot next to the information kiosk is just beyond on the right. GPS: N47 27.99' / W121 55.85'

Access the second parking area, Tiger Summit Trailhead, from the eastern lower parking lot. Tiger Summit Trailhead is located west and slightly above the first parking area. Follow West Side Road (the left-hand, ungated road off the first parking area), for about 0.25 mile toward the upper parking lot to the west. Turn right into the parking lot.

A state park Discover Pass is required to park here, and is valid at Washington's state recreation lands. Find information on the Washington

Parks website at www.parks.wa.gov. Purchase options include one-day passes and annual passes, available online, at select automated pay-stations at trailheads, or at specified local vendors.

B COLFAX TRAIL

The remote and woodsy Colfax Trail, originally an electric interurban railway hauling passengers, and later, freight, currently follows the Palouse River. Cattle graze across the first portion of the trail. Keep alert for bald eagle, deer, and other wildlife. This trail is one of the few horse trails in Whitman County, so be ready for interactions with horseback riders.

Activities:

Location: City of Colfax, in Whitman County

Length: 2.5 miles

Surface: Dirt

Wheelchair access: This trail is not wheelchair-accessible.

Difficulty: Easy

Food: No food is available along the Colfax Trail.

Restrooms: There are no restrooms along the trail.

Seasons: The trail can be used year-round.

Rentals: No rentals are available near this trail.

Contacts: Whitman County Parks, (509) 397-6238

Bus routes: None

Access and parking: From Colfax take WA 26 westbound for less than 1 mile. Cross the bridge over the Palouse River and take an immediate right onto West River Drive. Keep the faith that the trailhead is ahead and continue to your left through the working gravel pit compound until you reach the gate at the end of the property. GPS: N46 53.54' / W117 23.34'

The trail starts at the gate near the agriculture fields. Please close all gates after passing through.

C DRY CREEK TRAIL

Dry Creek Trail #194 parallels Dry Creek and passes through pockets of old-growth timber. It starts out flat and then climbs; your total elevation gain is nearly 400 feet. The end of the route is after Bourbon Creek, at the junction with Big Hollow Trail #158. The last half-mile passes through the Big Hollow Fire zone that blazed in 2020.

Activities:

Location: Gifford Pinchot National Forest in Skamania County, 15 miles north of the Columbia Gorge

Length: 3.75 miles

Surface: Natural dirt surface

Wheelchair access: The trail is not wheelchair-accessible.

Difficulty: Moderate

Food: No food is available along the trail.

Restrooms: Find restrooms at the nearby Government Springs Campground.

Seasons: You can enjoy the Dry Creek Trail May through Nov.

Rentals: No rentals are available along this trail.

Contacts: Mount Adams Ranger Station, (509) 395-3402, www.fs.usda.gov/giffordpinchot

Bus routes: None

Access and parking: Exit WA 14 at Wind River Road in Carson. Drive past mile marker 14, the location of the Carson National Fish Hatchery. Shortly after the fish hatchery, leave Wind River Road by continuing straight on Mineral Springs Road. About 1 mile from the fish hatchery, turn right at a Trapper Creek Wilderness Trailhead sign onto FR 5401. The road ends at the trailhead in approximately 0.5 mile. Start on Trapper Creek Trail #192 then turn right onto Dry Creek Trail #194. GPS: N45 52.90' / W121 58.80'

A Northwest Forest Pass (day-use or annual) is required to park at the Forest Service trailheads, and is valid in Washington and Oregon national forests. Purchase information is available at the above USDA Forest Service website. Payment locations may include a ranger station, select local vendors, and on the website.

D ALKI TRAIL

Picture-perfect views of the Seattle skyline across Elliott Bay blend with the sounds of barking sea lions. The north end of the Alki Trail starts west of Alki Beach near the Alki Point Lighthouse. Follow the trail as it extends south toward an industrial area along the Duwamish River near the West Seattle Bridge. From there it's possible to connect with the West Seattle Bridge Trail and, via neighborhood roads, the Duwamish and Green River Trails.

Activities:

Location: West Seattle to South Seattle, in King County

Length: 4.4 miles

Surface: Asphalt, with brief sections along the roadside

Wheelchair access: The trail is wheelchair-accessible.

Difficulty: Easy

Food: You'll find things to eat in the town of Alki.

Restrooms: There are restrooms at Alki Beach.

Seasons: The trail can be used year-round.

Rentals: See appendix A for a list of rentals in the Puget Sound area.

Contacts: Seattle Parks and Recreation Department, (206) 684-4075, https://www.seattle.gov/parks; Washington Trails Association, www.wta. org

Bus routes: For information, call Metro Transit at (206) 553-3000, or visit www.kingcounty.gov.

Access and parking: To reach the trail, take the West Seattle Bridge to the Harbor Avenue exit. Turn right. The sidewalk on your right is the trail. GPS: N47 34.33' / W122 22.24'

Drive as far north as you like and park on the street.

E ISSAQUAH–PRESTON TRAIL

This scenic trail starts in Issaquah at a junction with the East Sammamish Trail. The Issaquah–Preston Trail continues as an urban paved trail for a little over 1 mile, paralleling I-90, and then passes under Issaquah Highlands Drive Northeast. It continues east through forestlands as a gravel trail above I-90, and Issaquah Creek for 2 miles, to where it passes through a small parking area at High Point Road near the I-90 High Point interchange. The trail continues east another 1.1 miles between the freeway and Issaquah Creek. The gravel segment ends and the trail continues 0.7 mile as the Issaquah–Preston Trail Track, a delineated and dedicated two-way trail along the south side of rural High Point Way. Next, the trail crosses the road and meets the west side of the Preston–Snoqualmie Trail. Offering pleasant hiking and mountain biking the Issaquah–Preston Trail connects the East Lake Sammamish Trail with the Preston–Snoqualmie Trail.

Activities:

Location: Issaquah and Preston, in King County

Length: 7.0 miles

Surface: Asphalt and ballast

Wheelchair access: The trail is not wheelchair-accessible.

Difficulty: Easy

Food: No food is available near the trail.

Restrooms: There are no restrooms along the trail.

Seasons: The trail can be used year-round.

Rentals: See appendix A for a list of rentals in the Puget Sound area.

Contacts: King County Parks and Recreation Division, www.kingcounty. gov, https://gismaps.kingcounty.gov/TrailFinder

Bus routes: None

Access and parking: Take exit 20 (High Point Way) off I-90. Turn north and then left into the unmarked parking lot on the north edge of the I-90 on-ramp, westbound. This is the High Point Trailhead. GPS: N47 31.92' / W121 58.82'

F INTERURBAN TRAIL NORTH: SNOHOMISH COUNTY SEGMENT

This excursion takes you down a historic trolley corridor in and out of view of busy I-5. A sea of red taillights competes in autumn with the orange gold of maple trees, a forest of deeply colored evergreens, and tangles of blackberry bushes. Now a public utilities corridor, this portion of the Interurban Trail North in Snohomish County reaches from South Lynnwood north to Everett as it passes through urbanized areas and towns. The southern end of the trail extends to north Seattle, replicating the original trolley route. People came to town first by canoe, then riverboat, and finally, train. On April 30, 1910, the Everett–Seattle Interurban introduced an elegant and effective way to move people between neighborhoods. This—the longest-lasting interurban line in Washington—connected Seattle with Everett for twenty-nine years, over a distance of 29 miles. In the end, however, the trolley could not compete with cars and buses.

Activities:

Location: The cities of Everett, Lynnwood, and Mountlake Terrace in Snohomish County and Shoreline and Seattle in King County

Length: 24 miles

Surface: Asphalt

Wheelchair access: Most of the trail is wheelchair-accessible.

Difficulty: Easy. The trail is mostly flat, with several hills and several areas that run on the roadside shoulders, bike lanes, and sidewalks.

Food: There are roadside eateries along the way.

Restrooms: Restrooms are found in commercial establishments along the way and in the parks.

Seasons: Year-round. Some sections may be closed for short periods while the Public Utility District (PUD) works on power lines.

Rentals: See appendix A for a list of rentals in the western Washington area.

Contacts: Snohomish County Parks, Recreation, and Tourism (425) 388-6600, https://snohomishcountywa.gov/5168/Parks-Recreation; Everett Parks and Recreation Department, (425) 257-8300, www.everettwa.gov/parks; Washington Trails Association, www.wta.org. View the King County Trail Map at https://gismaps.kingcounty.gov/TrailFinder.

Bus routes: View the Community Transit website at www.communitytransit.org or call (425) 353-RIDE (7433).

Access and parking: There are numerous access points beside or near the trail. To reach South Lynnwood Neighborhood Park, near the trail's southern portion in Snohomish County, leave I-5 at exit 179 and drive west on Southwest 220th Street. Turn north onto 66th Avenue West, east onto Southwest 212th Street, north onto 63rd Avenue West, east onto 211th Street, and north onto 61st Avenue. Leave your car beside the park. GPS: N47 48.49' / W122 18.91'

Head north on the trail toward Everett for approximately 19 miles, or as an alternative, head about 5 miles south toward Seattle.

G MIDDLE FORK TRAIL

The Middle Fork Trail is a narrow pathway through a dense forest of western hemlock, around pockets of old-growth forest, across bridges over wetlands and streams, and occasionally beside the Middle Fork of the Snoqualmie River. Eventually you can reach the Alpine Lakes Wilderness. The terrain becomes more rugged in the upper reaches of the trail. Check out the privately owned Goldmyer Hot Springs, located in the area. Reservations are required; call in advance.

Activities:

Location: North Bend, in King County

Length: 14.5 miles

Surface: Gravel, dirt, and clay

Wheelchair access: The trail is not wheelchair-accessible.

Difficulty: Moderate; there are some narrow, steep sections.

Food: No food is available along the trail.

Restrooms: You'll find restrooms at the Middle Fork Trailhead.

Seasons: Although the trail can be used year-round, it's not maintained in winter.

Rentals: No rentals are available along the trail.

Contacts: Mount Baker-Snoqualmie National Forest, https://www.fs.usda. gov/recmain/mbs/recreation; North Bend Station in the Snoqualmie Ranger District, (425) 888-1421; Goldmyer Hot Springs, (206) 789-5631, www.goldmyer.org; Washington Trails Association, www.wta.org

Bus routes: None

Access and parking: Take exit 34 off I-90 (468 Avenue Southeast). Turn north, drive 0.4 mile, and turn right onto Southeast Middle Fork Road. Go about 3 miles, continuing past the Mailbox Peak Trailhead. The dirt NF 5600 takes you to the trailheads and a campground. You'll find the Middle Fork Trailhead about 12.3 miles from I-90. GPS: N47 32.91' / W121 32.22'

Dingford Creek is 5.5 miles farther, at the end of the road. Access the Middle Fork Trail from either trailhead by crossing the river on footbridges to the trail. Mountain bikes are allowed on the trail on odd-numbered calendar days June 1 through Oct 31, and horseback riding is allowed daily between July 15 and Oct 31. You can snowshoe or cross-country ski (when there's enough snow) from any point you can reach by car.

A Northwest Forest Pass (day-use or annual) is required to park at the Forest Service trailheads, and is valid in Washington and Oregon national forests. Purchase information is available at the above USDA Forest Service website. Payment locations may include a ranger station, select local vendors, and on the website.

H NECKLACE VALLEY TRAIL

Necklace Valley Trail is named for the loop of lakes it travels, resembling a jeweled necklace. It's a steep trail entering the Alpine Lakes Wilderness. The old railroad right-of-way portion of the trail extends for 1.5 miles and was logged in the 1920s. Continue for 3.5 miles on a flat trail through old-growth forest and then climb steeply for the last 2.5 miles to Jade Lake.

Activities:

Location: Mount Baker–Snoqualmie National Forest, in King County

Length: 7.5 miles, 1.5 miles of which travel on the railroad right-of-way

Surface: Dirt

Wheelchair access: The trail is not wheelchair-accessible.

Difficulty: Easy for 5.0 miles; very difficult for 2.5 miles

Food: No food is available along the trail.

Restrooms: Restrooms are available at the trailhead.

Seasons: The trail can be used year-round.

Rentals: No rentals are available along the trail.

Contacts: Mount Baker–Snoqualmie National Forest, Skykomish Ranger Station, (360) 677-2414; https://www.fs.usda.gov/recmain/mbs/recreation

Bus routes: None

Access and parking: From US 2 east of Skykomish, turn south onto Foss River Road, which name turns into FR 68. Drive 4.1 miles to the Necklace Valley Trailhead, on the left, signed Trail #1062. GPS: N47 39.88' / W121 17.27'

Approximately 2.0 miles of the Foss River Road are plowed during the winter. Snow is in the area six to nine months of the year.

A Northwest Forest Pass (day-use or annual) is required to park at the Forest Service trailheads, and is valid in Washington and Oregon national forests. Purchase information is available at the above USDA Forest Service website. Payment locations may include a ranger station, select local vendors, and on the website. Obtain the free self-issued Wilderness Permit at the trailheads.

PACIFIC CREST NATIONAL SCENIC TRAIL: STEVENS PASS RIGHT-OF-WAY SECTION

The Pacific Crest National Scenic Trail spans 2,650 miles. A 1.5-mile railroad right-of-way begins at Stevens Pass and follows the path of the upper switchback of the rail line. The trail then leaves the right-of-way and enters the Henry M. Jackson Wilderness Area.

Activities:

Location: US 2, Stevens Pass, in Chelan County

Length: 1.5 miles

Surface: Dirt

Wheelchair access: The trail is not wheelchair-accessible.

Difficulty: Easy. There may be avalanche danger on the trail during winter months.

Food: No food is available along the trail.

Restrooms: There are no restrooms along this trail; however, there is a forest service restroom across the highway at the south trailhead for the Pacific Crest National Scenic Trail.

Seasons: The trail can be used year-round.

Rentals: No rentals are available along the trail.

Contacts: USDA Forest Service, Wenatchee River Ranger District, (509) 548-2550, https://www.fs.usda.gov/activity/okawen/recreation/hiking; Washington Trails Association, www.wta.org

Bus routes: None

Access and parking: The trail begins at Stevens Pass at the lot directly across from Stevens Pass Resort off US 2. The trail leaves from the north corner of the lot by the Chelan County Power Company Summit Substation. GPS: N47 44.86' / W121 05.27'

A Northwest Forest Pass (day-use or annual) is required to park at the Forest Service trailheads, and is valid in Washington and Oregon national forests. Purchase information is available at the above USDA Forest Service website. Payment locations may include a ranger station, select local vendors, and on the website.

J RAINIER TRAIL

Enjoy this quaint historic town's stores and history while getting some exercise. The paved trail begins on Rainier Boulevard at Gilman Boulevard, 1 block west of Front Street. It passes the community center, the historic railroad depot, the logging railroad display, and eateries of downtown Issaquah. After crossing 2nd Avenue, it becomes a narrow, undeveloped dirt-and-gravel trail that heads uphill behind the high school. At 1.0 mile you'll reach a three-way intersection. The Rainier Trail drops down to the left onto Sunset Way and crosses the Sunset interchange. It then connects to the Issaquah–Preston Trail. You can also connect with the East Lakes Sammamish Trail across from the visitor information center on Gilman Boulevard / Rainier Boulevard.

Activities:

Location: Issaquah, King County

Length: 2.5 miles

Surface: Paved for 1.5 miles; dirt and ballast for 1.0 mile

Wheelchair access: The paved portion of the trail is wheelchair-accessible.

Difficulty: Easy to difficult

Food: You'll find groceries and restaurants in the town of Issaquah.

Restrooms: There are restrooms at the city park near the visitor information center, the city hall / police station, and the community center.

Seasons: The trail can be used year-round.

Rentals: Ride Bicycles Bike Shop, 160 NW Gilman Boulevard, #102, Issaquah, (425) 961-9061, www.ridebicycles.com

Contacts: City of Issaquah, www.issaquahwa.gov; Washington Trails Association, www.wta.org

Bus routes: For information, call (206) 553-3000, or visit King County Metro Transit at www.kingcounty.gov.

Access and parking: Take exit 17 off I-90 and head south to Gilman Boulevard; turn right onto Gilman. Just past the visitor information center, take the first left, onto Northwest Juniper Street, and then turn left immediately onto Rainier Boulevard North. The trail starts at the southern end of Rainier Boulevard North. GPS: N47 32.37' / W122 02.34'

Consider parking at the visitor center.

K SOUTH SHIP CANAL TRAIL

This flat, paved trail runs through a peaceful park setting between the Fremont Bridge and beyond Seattle Pacific University on the south side of the ship canal. The benches on the grassy waterfront, the shade of the willow trees, the boats slowly passing by, and the occasional rising of the bridge provide a relaxing stroll or skate. To the west the trail passes through an industrial area. Bicyclists use the trail as a connector between city hike routes.

Activities:

Location: Seattle, in King County

Length: 1.25 miles of the less industrial segment

Surface: Asphalt

Wheelchair access: The entire paved eastern section of the trail is wheelchair-accessible.

Difficulty: Easy

Food: Try the Fremont eateries and breweries across the bridge.

Restrooms: There are no restrooms along this trail.

Seasons: The trail can be used year-round.

Rentals: See appendix A for a list of rentals in Western Washington.

Contacts: Seattle Parks and Recreation Department (206) 684-4075, www. seattle.gov; Washington Trails Association, www.wta.org

Bus routes: For more information, check out Metro Transit at www.king-county.gov, or call them at (206) 553-3000.

Access and parking: Park at the eastern end, located on the east side of the Fremont Bridge. Go to West Lake Avenue North; turn at Morrison's North Star Marina and follow the Cheshiahud Lake Union Loop access road downhill to the parking lot by the trail. GPS: N47 38.80' / W122 20.97'
    Another option is to park at Ewing Ming Park on 3rd Avenue West, a few blocks north of West Nickerson Street; or you can park on Nickerson Street and head east toward the Fremont Bridge for the pleasant part of the trail.

L SNOQUALMIE CENTENNIAL TRAIL–CORRI-DOR TRAIL

The Northwest Railroad Museum is the highlight of this trail. Pass old steam engines on the tracks, visit the museum, and take a train ride to the ledge above the famous Snoqualmie Falls in summer or during the Christmas holidays. Visit the elegant Salish Lodge just beyond the trail.

Activities:

Location: Snoqualmie, in King County

Length: 0.6 mile

Surface: Asphalt, dirt

Wheelchair access: The entire trail is wheelchair-accessible.

Difficulty: Easy

Food: You'll find restaurants in the town of Snoqualmie.

Restrooms: There are restrooms in town and at the museum.

Seasons: The trail can be used year-round.

Rentals: See appendix A for a list of rentals in the Puget Sound area.

Contacts: City of Snoqualmie, Parks and Public Works, (425) 831-5784, www.snoqualmiewa.gov

Bus routes: For more information visit Metro Transit at www.kingcounty. gov, or call (206) 553-3000.

Access and parking: Take I-90 to exit 31. Head north and follow WA 202 through North Bend and on to the town of Snoqualmie, where the highway becomes Railroad Avenue Southeast. You can park on the street near the Northwest Railroad Museum or at the public parking area near the trailhead, 2 blocks farther on Railroad Avenue Southeast between Southeast Northern Street and Southeast Fir Street. GPS: N47 31.91' / W121 49.68'

Trail users pass over a trestle along the ROW River Trail in western Oregon.

OREGON

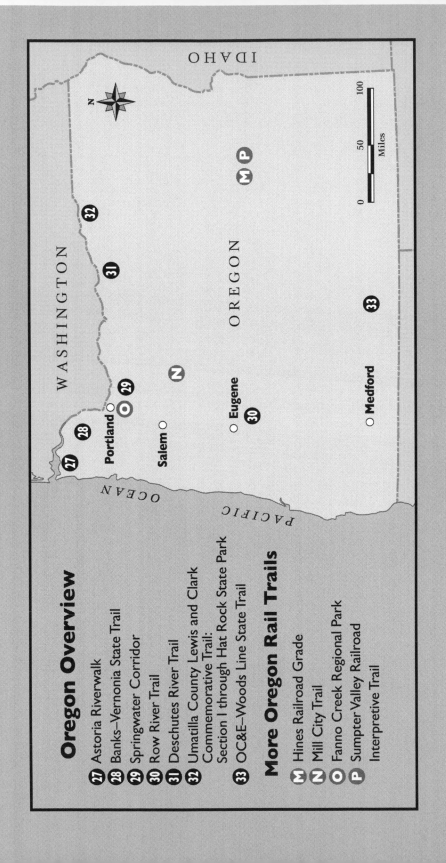

Oregon Overview

27 Astoria Riverwalk
28 Banks–Vernonia State Trail
29 Springwater Corridor
30 Row River Trail
31 Deschutes River Trail
32 Umatilla County Lewis and Clark Commemorative Trail: Section I through Hat Rock State Park
33 OC&E–Woods Line State Trail

More Oregon Rail Trails

M Hines Railroad Grade
N Mill City Trail
O Fanno Creek Regional Park
P Sumpter Valley Railroad Interpretive Trail

Oregon's rail trails run the gamut of terrain, scenery, and travel options. Some draw you to the state's most stunning sites; others combine with impressive light-rail and bus service to provide a commuter pathway. Tour forested foothills, riverside farmland, covered bridges, reservoirs, and miles of trail through mountains and river valleys. Pick a rural desert perch above the Columbia River, enjoy an oceanfront town, or follow the Deschutes River into a desert canyon. Travel beside towns buried underwater when dams were built.

Lewis and Clark reached Astoria in 1805, making this town the oldest settlement in the West. This beach resort town of the early 1900s sits on the northwestern tip of Oregon, where the Columbia River empties into the Pacific. A civilized trail here entices you to stroll, ride, dine, and explore history. Meanwhile, the Banks–Vernonia State Trail, also west of Portland, is quite a contrast: It's a forested pathway in the hills near tall trestles and railroad remnants between the tiny towns of Banks and Vernonia.

Springwater Corridor is part of a network of trails around Portland and outlying areas. Combined with light-rail and bus service, this route provides a great leisure trip to Gresham and a commuter route with convenient, more passive options for the return trip. Botanical gardens and wildlife refuges near the trail replace the amusement parks that rallied railroad riders in the early 1900s.

The rich agriculture of the Willamette River Valley, from Portland south, drew the railroads up from California as early as 1870. Try the Row River Trail and enjoy the wildflowers, wildlife, and covered bridges as you travel alongside the river and the lake created by the dam.

In eastern Oregon the desert trails traverse above rivers and beside basalt rock walls. The rural Umatilla County Lewis and Clark Commemorative Trail sits high above the Columbia River, near the McNary Dam, and ends in riverfront parks. The Deschutes River Trail starts near the Columbia River Gorge and leads miles into a desert canyon with ever-changing rock formations, high above the Deschutes River. In the Malheur National Forest, a trail leads you through timbered terrain, and an interpretive nature trail showcases the highest point of the Sumpter Valley Railway.

Near the border of California, the OC&E–Woods Line State Trail passes through small towns and climbs the old railroad switchbacks as it traverses 108 miles of diverse scenery and terrain.

Travel through history, natural beauty, and urban amenities on the rail trails of Oregon. These trails are gifts that allow us to tour the state while we walk, skate, ski, or ride bikes and horses. Take advantage of them!

27 ASTORIA RIVERWALK

Portland's beach resort town of the early 1900s sits on the northwestern tip of Oregon, where the Columbia River empties into the Pacific Ocean. Lewis and Clark's 8,000-mile trek in search of the Northwest Passage brought them here in 1805, making this town the West's oldest American settlement and a National Historic District. Later the Spokane, Portland & Seattle Railway brought city folk to the beach on Friday night for a weekend on the coast. Today bridges and boardwalks, canneries and cafes, docks and decks, galleries, and espresso shops decorate the riverfront with history, views, and tourist delights.

Activities:

Location: Portway Street at Smith Point to 53rd Street (Alderbrook Lagoon), Astoria, in Clatsop County

Length: 6.4 miles

Surface: Paved and planked trestles

Wheelchair access: The trail is wheelchair-accessible.

Difficulty: Easy. Use caution on the wooded trestles if using bicycles, skates, or wheelchairs.

Food: You'll find things to eat in downtown Astoria.

Restrooms: Facilities are at the foot of 39th Street, the Dough Boy Monument, city public buildings, and between 12th and 13th Streets on Exchange Street.

Seasons: The trail can be used year-round.

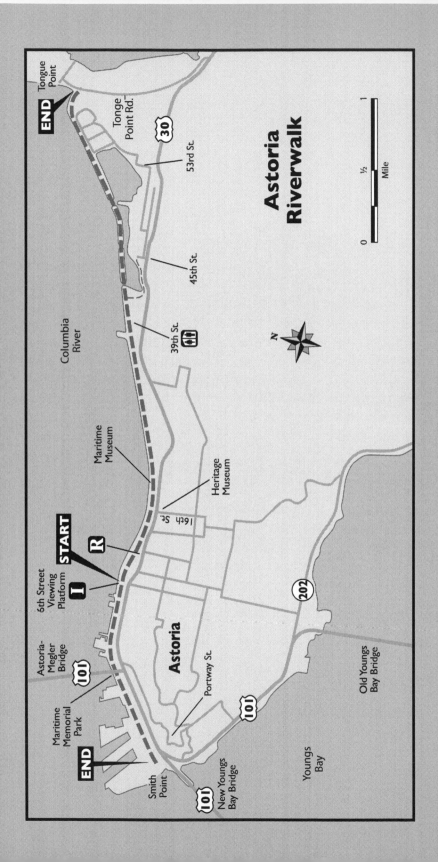

Astoria
Riverwalk

Columbia
River

Tongue
Point

Tonge
Point Rd.

30

53rd St.

45th St.

39th St.

Maritime
Museum

Heritage
Museum

16th St.

6th Street
Viewing
Platform

START

R

I

END

Astoria-
Megler
Bridge

101

Maritime
Memorial
Park

Astoria

Portway St

101

101

New Youngs
Bay Bridge

Smith
Point

Youngs
Bay

Old Youngs
Bay Bridge

202

END

N

0   ½   1

Mile

Rentals: Bikes and Beyond, 125 9th Street, Astoria, (503) 325-2961, www.bikesandbeyond.com

Contacts: City of Astoria Parks and Recreation Department, (503) 325-7027, www.astoriaparks.com; Astoria-Warrenton Chamber of Commerce, (503) 325-6311; www.travelastoria.com

Bus routes: A restored city trolley runs about 3 miles from the western trail terminus near Smith Point to 39th Street. Astoria Trolley's schedule varies by season. You can flag it down at any point. The trolley cannot take bicycles; however, the City Bus does allow bicycles.

Access and parking: To reach the trail, drive US 101 to Astoria. From I-5 in Washington, exit at Longview, cross the Columbia River, and head west on US 30. From Portland take US 30 West. From the south, take US 101 North. The trail is easily accessed anywhere along its length. Any numbered street from 6th to 39th ends at the river's edge and the trail. Park on the street. Consider starting at the 6th Street Riverwalk viewing platform. GPS: N46 11.47' / W123 50.19'

The Astoria Riverwalk Trail invites you to savor the sights, sounds, and tastes of a fun town while the historic buildings, fort, and monuments paint a picture of the earliest days of pioneering on the West Coast. US 101, the coastal highway, is a busy street loaded with commercial activity. Using the Riverwalk lets you avoid this main drag and explore on foot, on a bike, or quite easily in a wheelchair. You can access this trail from almost anywhere and design a tour of your own.

Astoria's downtown section, from 6th to 17th Streets, is more formal, with benches, lighting, and interpretive kiosks. It meanders along the riverfront with easy access to shops, restaurants, and museums. From 15th to 41st Streets you'll find a 10-foot-wide paved trail with fewer shops and restaurants. Use extreme caution on the trestles; the open ties here can capture a foot or bike tire. If you head west from 6th Street, you'll encounter industrial aspects of the waterfront.

Though Astoria has an impressive list of claims to fame, its most amazing sight may be the view of the Columbia River disappearing into the ocean. A 4.1-mile drive to Washington over the Astoria-Megler Bridge offers inspiring views from this continuous three-span through-truss bridge. The shore is one of ten locations between Alaska and Mexico where thousands of birds may gather at one time. Try a visit during fall migration.

For a unique tourist attraction, watch a bar pilot and a river pilot leap between a tug and freighter to pilot the ship up and down the Columbia River. The river bar that separates the Columbia from the Pacific is considered one of the most dangerous in the world. It is said to have claimed 233 ships that now lie at the bottom of the "Graveyard of the Pacific."

If you hear a chorus of sea lions, look down to see them below the trestles. The area offers kayaking, canoeing, surfing, fishing, clamming, and boat tours. When you're done recreating, stop at the Astoria Brewing Company on 11th Street and sample local beer, seafood, and creative homemade desserts. Or try the Rogue Ale Public House on 39th Street. Several local breweries and the distillery offer tours.

Nearby Attractions

Climb the 164 steps to the observation deck of the Astoria Column for a panoramic view of the region. The neighboring town of Warrenton has a waterfront trail. Nearby scenic locations include Long Beach Peninsula (famous for cranberries) and Seaside on the Oregon coast. Nearby rail trails include Washington's Willapa Hills Trail: Raymond to South Bend Riverfront Trail (Trail 20) to the north and the Banks–Vernonia State Trail (Trail 28) toward Portland.

Walk up the 6th Street Riverwalk viewing platform for an elevated view of Astoria.

28 BANKS–VERNONIA STATE TRAIL

The paved Banks–Vernonia State Trail stretches through the foothills on the east side of the Oregon Coast Range, 35 miles west of Portland and 52 miles east of the coastal town of Seaside. At the north and south ends you'll travel near the highway. As you approach the middle third of the trail, it leaves the road, climbs into the forested hills, and enters a different world. Miles of side trails in L. L. "Stub" Stewart State Park create additional options. While on the main trail, look up at two 90-foot-high, 680-foot-long wooden train trestles. Enjoy views of the Oregon Coast Range. Listen for an owl. You might see a fox, an elk, a deer, or a great blue heron.

Activities:

Location: The towns of Banks and Vernonia, in Columbia and Washington Counties

Length: 21 miles

Surface: Paved, with a horse trail on the side of the pavement. Horses occasionally are required to travel on the paved trail in some sections.

Wheelchair access: Wheelchair access is at the Vernonia and Banks Trailheads, and at L. L. "Stub" Stewart State Park.

Difficulty: Easy to moderate, with a 2 to 5 percent grade. The short, steep 11 percent grade descending to the highway near the Tophill Trailhead requires extreme caution.

Food: The small towns of Vernonia and Banks have food. The town of Manning just east of the junction of US 26 and OR 47 has a market and a restaurant.

Restrooms: Banks Trailhead offers flush toilets and drinking fountains. There are vault or chemical toilets at all the other trailheads.

Seasons: The trail can be used year-round.

Rentals: Banks Bicycle Repair & Rentals, 14175 NW Sellers Road, Banks, (503) 680-3269, www.banksbikes.com

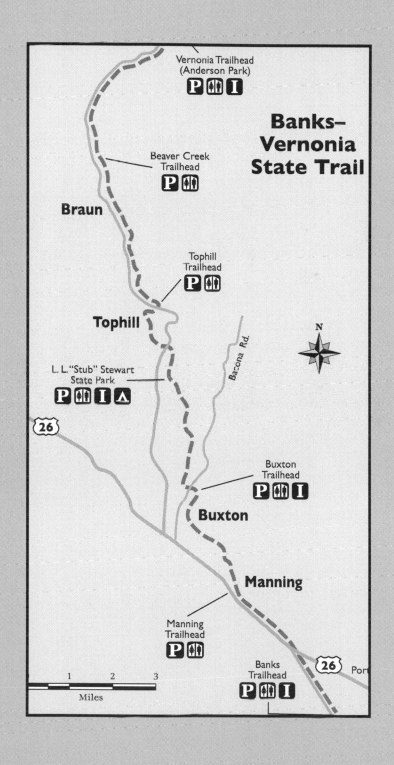

Banks–
Vernonia
State Trail

Vernonia Trailhead
(Anderson Park)

Beaver Creek
Trailhead

Braun

Tophill
Trailhead

Tophill

Bacona Rd.

N

L. L. "Stub" Stewart
State Park

26

Buxton
Trailhead

Buxton

Manning

Manning
Trailhead

Banks
Trailhead

26   Port

1   2   3
Miles

Contacts: L. L. "Stub" Stewart State Park, (503) 324-0606, https://stateparks. oregon.gov/

Bus routes: None

Access and parking: Trailheads are clearly marked along OR 47. To start in Vernonia, take US 26 from Seaside or from Portland to OR 47. If you're coming from Portland west on US 26, go north 15 miles on OR 47. Turn south at the railroad engine on Adams Street in Vernonia. Park on the streets near Anderson Park or in the gravel lot off Weed Avenue. There's an information kiosk at this northern terminus of the trail near Jefferson Avenue. GPS: N45 51.38' / W123 11.64'

The Beaver Creek Trailhead is located on OR 47, just over 4 miles south of Anderson Park. The Tophill Trailhead (with hitching posts), also on OR 47, is about 8 miles south. You'll have to make a steep uphill climb whether you start here or just pass through this part of the trail. To access the trail at L. L. "Stub" Stewart State Park, continue south on OR 47 past the Tophill Trailhead. Turn left into the park. The trail crosses over the entrance road. Look for trail access signs. There is no specified parking for the Banks–Vernonia State Trail in the park, though day-use parking is located 0.75 mile up a steep grade from the trail crossing at the Hilltop day-use area within the state park.

Only twenty-five Oregon parks charge a daily parking fee. To park here you'll need a pass. Find information on the Oregon Parks website at https://stateparks.oregon.gov/. Purchase options include one-day passes and annual passes, available online, at trailheads, at state park offices, or at specified local vendors.

To reach the Buxton Trailhead, turn north on Fisher Road from US 26, 0.5 mile east of the intersection with OR 47. Follow signs to the park. The Manning Trailhead is also on US 26, 1 mile east of OR 47. Banks Trailhead, the southern terminus, is on the east side of Nehalem Highway (OR 47), on the corner of Northwest Banks and Northwest Sellers Roads.

||||||||||||||||||||||||||||||||||||||||||||||||||||||||||||||||||||||||||||||||||||||||||

The Spokane, Portland & Seattle Railway built the Gales Creek & Wilson River line in 1922. Other railroads refused to build a line expressly for hauling lumber, so this one was created to move timber products from northwestern Oregon, in particular from the Oregon-American lumber mill in Vernonia. The trains also carried freight and passengers from Keasey to Portland. The line ceased operation when the mill closed in 1957. The Vernonia South Park & Sunset Railroad leased the line and operated a steam sightseeing train from 1960 to 1965. Abandoned in 1973, the rails were salvaged and the right-of-way sold to the state highway department. In 1990 it became the first linear state park in Oregon.

Seven trailheads allow for easy access and trips of various lengths on the paved or the gravel / bark dust path for horses. When you choose your starting point, keep in mind that the Tophill Trailhead is on top of the hill and it is a 2 to 5 percent grade down to Vernonia (a 300-foot elevation decline from Tophill) and to Banks (a 700-foot decline from Tophill). Bicyclists are asked to ride on one side, equestrians on the other. The grade may tempt you to cruise downhill on a bike; if so, pay attention to avoid collisions. Bicyclists must yield to all users, and hikers must yield to horses.

Deep forest provides shade along the Banks–Vernonia State Trail near L. L. "Stub" Stewart State Park.

This description takes you from Anderson Park in Vernonia southward. Trail mile markers descend from 21 in the north to 0 at the southern terminus. In Vernonia, the Banks–Vernonia Trail connects to the paved loop around Vernonia Lake, creating a lakeside trailhead alternative. After you leave the west end of the park at mile marker 21, the trail parallels OR 47 and the Nehalem River until shrubs and fir trees separate you from the highway.

The trail leaves open areas lined with blackberry bushes and deciduous trees at mile 14 and climbs into a Douglas fir forest. As you approach the Tophill Trailhead near mile marker 12, prepare for a steep 11 percent descent to OR 47, where the burned Horseshoe Trestle forces trail users to cross the highway. Use caution here.

A short climb returns you to the original grade. The 90-foot-high Horseshoe Trestle was 680 feet long before the other end fell victim to a fire. Indeed, fires plagued the construction of this portion of railway from the very start.

Cross the highway south of the trail after mile marker 11. Shortly you will enter L. L. "Stub" Stewart State Park. Once you cross the steel bridge over OR 47, you are in the state park. For 3.5 miles the park surrounds the Banks–Vernonia State Trail. Various multiuse and natural surface trails connect to a variety of facilities in the state park. The trail crosses the entrance road to the park near milepost 10.5. Campsites, RV sites, hike-in campsites, a horse camp, rustic cabin rentals, disc golf courses, mountain bike–specific trails, and a day-use area provide a convenient and interesting overnight spot for trail users. Reservations are highly recommended.

Continuing south on the main trail, you will encounter a variety of trails for side trips. The state park has nearly 30 miles of multiuse trails. Due to weather conditions and maintenance schedules, trail conditions may vary.

Arrive at Buxton Trailhead at mile 7.0. Enjoy the grassy area and the pond full of newts, turtles, and frogs. This water source is a fire retention pond for forest fire fighting. The second largest trestle on the trail, the Buxton Trestle over Mendenhall Creek, is south of the parking lot. Hikers and bicyclists cross the trestle; equestrians use a short bypass from the parking lot, rejoining the trail south of the trestle.

Near milepost 5, cross Pongratz Road. Manning Trailhead is just ahead past mile 4.0. Continuing southeast, the trail ends in Banks.

Once you've explored the trail to your heart's content, turn around and return the way you came. If you're on a rail trail roll, check out the Astoria Riverwalk (Trail 27) or Portland's Springwater Corridor (Trail 29).

29 SPRINGWATER CORRIDOR

The Springwater Corridor is the major southeast section of a system of nature trails encircling Portland. Ride, walk, or skate the trail to enjoy parks, botanical gardens, and wetlands—not to mention herons, coyotes, and deer—as you travel through industrial, suburban, and rural areas. August is blackberry month; don't hesitate to savor your way down this Hall of Fame rail trail.

Activities:

Location: Portland to Boring, in Multnomah and Clackamas Counties

Length: 21.5 miles

Surface: Asphalt

Wheelchair access: The trail is wheelchair-accessible at several points.

Difficulty: Easy

Food: You'll find several restaurants along the trail and in downtown Gresham.

Restrooms: There are restrooms at Gresham Main City Park, at the trailhead next to Tideman Johnson Natural Area, along the trail east of milepost 13, and at Boring Station Trailhead Park.

Seasons: The trail can be used year-round.

Rentals: Everybody's Bike Rentals and Tours, 305 NE Wygant Street, Portland, (503) 358-0152, www.pdxbikerentals.com

Contacts: Portland Parks and Recreation, (503) 823-PLAY (7529), www.portland.gov; Portland Visitor Center, (877) 678-5263, www.travelportland.com; Gresham Visitor Center, (503) 665-1131, www.greshamchamber.org; Clackamas County Parks, (503) 742-4414, www.clackamas.us/parks/

Bus routes: See sidebar in this chapter for information on the light-rail system and bus routes.

Access and parking: To start at the northern terminus of the trail, park along Southeast Fourth Avenue between Southeast Ivon and Southeast Caruthers Streets just east of the Willamette River near the Ross Island Bridge in Portland. GPS: N45 30.24' / W122 39.71'

The trail numbering starts in the northwest and increases as you head south and east.

Another western starting point is next to Tideman Johnson Natural Area, at the parking lot at Southeast Johnson Creek Boulevard near Southeast 45th Street.

At the trail's southeastern terminus, you can leave your car 5 miles from the east end of the trail by parking near Gresham Main City Park on US 26 and South Main Avenue or at the trailhead at Hogan Avenue, south of 19th Street in Gresham. For the eastern terminus, park at Boring Station Trailhead Park, in Boring off OR 212.

|||||||||||||||||||||||||||||||||||||||||||||||||||||||||||||||||||||||||||||||||||||||||||||||||||||

The Springwater Corridor covers 21.5 miles and is the major southeast section of the planned 40-Mile Loop around the greater Portland area, a path first conceived in 1903 to serve as a nature trail encircling the city and connecting park sites. Though the forefathers lived in a city of woodlands and meadows, they had the foresight to plan a trail system. The original name, 40-Mile Loop, is a bit confusing, since the loop consists of 100-plus miles of trails along with a regional trail system covering more than 200 miles of interconnected trails. Portland's regional trail system will ultimately connect the Columbia River, Willamette River, Columbia Slough, and Johnson Creek, along with parks and communities.

The Springwater Division Line of 1903 reached peak usage in 1906. Portland General Electric and the Portland Railway Light & Power Companies had six electric plants and 161 miles of rail, carrying 16,000 passengers each year and hauling farm produce to Portland markets. Towns popped up along the line; the railroad rallied ridership further by building amusement parks. Thousands of weekend passengers rode the rail to such destinations as the Oaks Amusement Park on the Willamette River. Passenger service continued until 1958. The city took over in 1990, and the Portland trail segment opened in 1996.

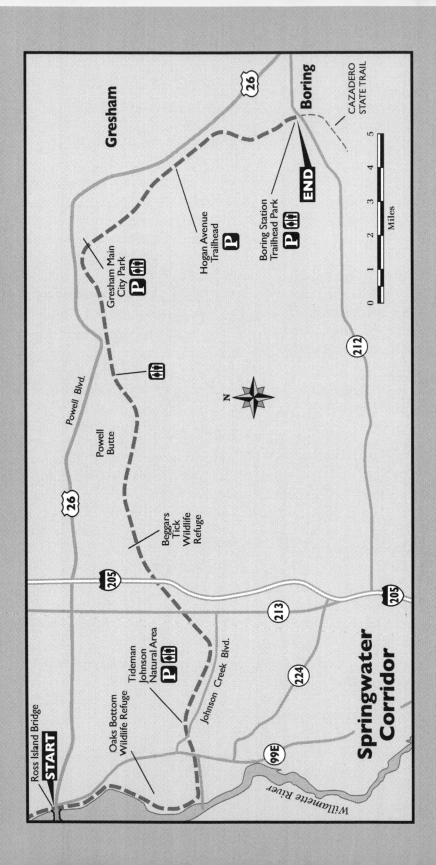

The trail passes through an industrial area near SE Ivon Street and SE Fourth Avenue in Portland.

There are several spots from which to access the trail. This description takes you from the trail's starting point at SE Ivon Street and SE Fourth Avenue, just east of the Willamette River near the Ross Island Bridge. (The trail numbering starts in the northwest and increases as you head south and east.) Shortly you will pass alongside the Oaks Bottom Wildlife Refuge, comprising more than 170 acres of preserved wetlands, meadows, and woodlands. Residential and migrating birds frequent the area. Take a 1-mile detour on one of the side trails.

After passing the southern end of the refuge at mile 4.0, you will come to a gap in the trail between 7th and 19th Avenues, locally dubbed the Sellwood Gap. Many people take Umatilla Street. Directions are posted on the trail to guide you through the detour and back onto the trail, which resumes at Southeast Ochoco Street and 19th Avenue. Watch for bridges over Johnson Creek, McLoughlin Boulevard, and the railroad tracks as you head to Tideman Johnson Natural Area, located near trail mile marker 6.5. Take the side trail down to the creek; it loops back to the main trail. From the park the trail runs east beside roads in a mildly industrial neighborhood. Cross to the north side of Johnson Creek Boulevard at Southeast Bell Avenue for a brief respite from road noise.

Find Beggars Tick Wildlife Refuge on the left at milepost 11.0, at Southeast 111th Avenue. Take a break to wander the wetlands and watch the wood ducks, teals, and mergansers.

Take a right at Southeast 122nd Avenue for several blocks to explore 5 acres and 1,500 species of native plants at the Leach Botanical Garden. Mile 12.5 places you adjacent to a 630-foot-high volcanic rise called Powell

Taking the MAX

Another result of Portland's prowess for planning is the city's light-rail system, the MAX. This system allows you to bike, roll, or stroll the Springwater Corridor as far east as Gresham and then return easily via bus or rail. Bikes can ride on the regular fare. For more information on the light-rail system and buses, visit www.trimet.org, or call (503) 238-RIDE (7433).

Butte Nature Park, with an access trail to the butte. Stop for views of the city and the mountains; a hike among the orchards, meadows, and forest; or a picnic. There are restrooms and an interpretive center on the opposite side of the hill.

Hills begin to appear and civilization disappears (for a while) as you head toward the mountains. Cross a peaceful creek at mile 13.5. Pass beside Powell Boulevard and under Southwest Eastman Parkway on your way to Main City Park in Gresham. To explore the eateries of historic Gresham on a pedestrian walkway or catch the bus or MAX back to Portland, exit the trail at the park and go through the park to Main Street. It's fun to arrive for an evening out. To get to the MAX, cross US 26 (Powell Boulevard) and continue on Main to 10th. Cross the tracks to the transit center.

To complete the trail, continue for another 5.5 miles to Boring Station Trailhead Park in Boring. Boring Junction is the last remaining ticketing station of the Springwater Corridor. Consider extending your journey for 3 miles on another rail trail. The Cazadero State Trail starts on the south side of OR 212 and is administered by Oregon State Parks.

Portland is a great destination, blessed with such amenities as a rose garden, a paved waterfront trail, and great food. Take some extra time and explore this vibrant city.

30 ROW RIVER TRAIL

This abandoned railroad line left five Howe truss bridges and twenty-three pile trestles to cross. Ospreys and eagles, a small town, covered bridges, and prairie wildflowers will delight you as you tour the scenic right-of-way. With more than twenty covered bridges, Lane County has more of these scenic spans than any other county west of the Appalachians.

Activities:

Location: Cottage Grove, 25 miles south of Eugene, in Lane County

Length: 16 miles

Surface: Asphalt and adjacent 0.25-inch gravel for horses

Wheelchair access: This trail is wheelchair-accessible.

Difficulty: Easy, although there's 1 mile of hills that may be tough for beginner skaters.

Food: You'll find things to eat in the towns of Dorena and Cottage Grove.

Restrooms: There are vault toilets at the Mosby Creek Trailhead, Dorena Dam access, Harms Park, Bake Stewart Park, Dorena between trail mile posts 12 and 13, and Culp Creek.

Seasons: The trail can be used year-round.

Rentals: Rainy Peak Bicycles, (541) 942-8712, 533 East Main Street, Cottage Grove, www.rainypeak.com

Contacts: Bureau of Land Management, Eugene District Office, Springfield, (541) 683-6600, https://www.blm.gov/visit/row-river-trail; City Cottage Grove, (541) 942-5501, www.cottagegrove.org; Cottage Grove Chamber of Commerce, (541) 942-2411, www.cgchamber.com

Bus routes: #98, Lane Transit District, (541) 687-5555, www.ltd.org

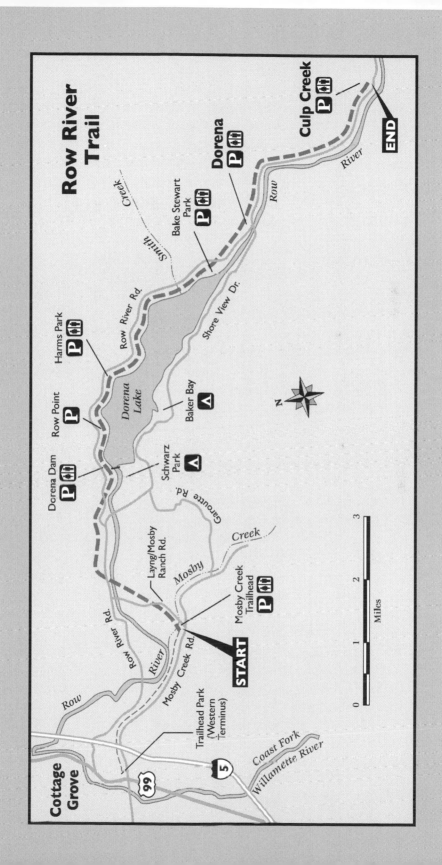

Row River Trail

Cottage Grove

Culp Creek

P 🚻

END

Dorena

P 🚻

Bake Stewart Park

P 🚻

Smith Creek

Row River Rd.

Shore View Dr.

Row River

Harms Park

P 🚻

Row Point

P

Dorena Lake

Baker Bay

⚑

Dorena Dam

P 🚻

Schwarz Park

⚑

Garoutte Rd.

Layng/Mosby Ranch Rd.

Mosby Creek

Mosby Creek Trailhead

P 🚻

Row River Rd.

Row River

Mosby Creek Rd.

START

Trailhead Park (Western terminus)

99

5

Coast Fork Willamette River

N

0   1   2   3
Miles

Access and parking: To reach the western trail terminus in Cottage Grove, take exit 174 off I-5 at Row River Road in Cottage Grove. Park downtown on Main Street or on 10th Street by Bohemia Park. To reach the Mosby Creek Trailhead, go southeast from Cottage Grove on Row River Road and drive 2.5 miles southeast to the Currin Covered Bridge next to Layng / Mosby Ranch Road. Turn right, crossing Mosby Creek. Continue on Layng / Mosby Ranch Road to the trailhead parking, on the right. GPS: N43 46.62' / W123 00.48'

R ow River Trail originates in Cottage Grove, passes by the Dorena Dam, and runs beside Dorena Lake as it follows the Row River. The river (pronounced to rhyme with *cow*) was named for a fatal brawl over grazing rights in the 1850s. The Willamette Valley was one of the great farming areas in the 1880s, along with the Palouse and Walla Walla Valleys. These eastern areas of the state were already building railroads for their farm products, as the West needed to move its goods.

In 1883 the Oregon & California Railroad constructed a line through Salem, and in 1902 the "Old Slow and Easy" main line of the Oregon & South Eastern Railroad Company was built. It ran ore from the Bohemia mining district as well as logs, supplies, mail, and passengers from Cottage Grove to Disston, in the Umpqua National Forest. In 1914 the Oregon, Pacific & Eastern took over. Though regular passenger service ended in July 1930, the *Goose* hauled summer tourists in the 1970s. A handful of runs served the Culp Creek lumber mill into the late 1980s. The Bureau of Land Management (BLM) acquired the right-of-way in 1993, and paved it in 1996. The remaining 3 miles, through the city of Cottage Grove, were paved in the early 2000s and repaved years later.

Although you can access the trail from several points, including the 3-mile segment through Cottage Grove along Mosby Creek Road, this description takes you on the most scenic section, from the Mosby Creek Trailhead's convenient parking area and eastward. The trail parallels Row River Road most of the way, and trail marker numbering increases as you head easterly. You'll arrive at Dorena Dam, and the lake it created, near trail mile 6.5. Before the dam was built, the river repeatedly flooded towns

A rail trestle spans Mosby Creek at the Mosby Creek Trailhead.

downstream. In addition to flood control, the dam provides irrigation, recreation, and improved navigation.

Look for a spring shout of color from the delicate plants at Row Point,
remnants of the native prairie community. Please leave them to be enjoyed
by others on the trail. At about mile marker 8.0, see if you recognize the
trestle at Harms Park, immortalized in the movies *Stand by Me, Emperor of
the North*, with Ernest Borgnine, and Buster Keaton's *The General*.

Smith Creek is an area of streams, marshes, and canary grass fields.
Ospreys, herons, ducks, and geese are commonly seen. A keen eye may
also catch a bald eagle, a deer, or the occasional black bear.

Bake Stewart Park is named for two lilies—one edible and one poi-
sonous. The bulb of the blue-flowering lily was once dug up in early spring
and baked in earth ovens for winter storage, while the white, or "death,"
camas lilies were carefully avoided. A paved trail connects the Row River
Trail and the park. Arrive at the post-dam town of Dorena at mile 12.5.
Established in 1899, the original townsite included a church, dancehall,

Enjoy a rest along the Row River Trail on the north side of Dorena Lake.

post office, store, blacksmith shop, and grocery, all located near the center of the present reservoir. To prepare for the dam, a portion of the railway and some buildings were moved. Others were burned prior to the filling of the reservoir in the 1940s. Culp Creek, the eastern terminus of the trail, was one of twenty mill towns along the railway. Before the railroad, logs went to mill via "river rats." These fellows made quite a wage riding the logs downriver to the mills. The railroad put an end to these wild and risky rides. The last mill disappeared decades ago.

Whenever you're ready, turn around and return the way you came. While in the area, take a Cottage Grove Covered Bridge Tour. Drive, road bike, or call the chamber of commerce for tour information on the "Covered Bridge Capital of Oregon." Alternately, bicycle the 38-mile Covered Bridges Scenic Bikeway—a loop around the lake via roads and the Row River Trail.

31 DESCHUTES RIVER TRAIL

Take a scenic desert tour in a canyon above the Deschutes River. It's a fairly flat trail that offers a slight downhill grade on the return. Nifty features along the way include a constant view of the river and trailside fishing access. The canyon is hot, somewhat rocky, and occasionally sandy. A visit to the surrounding area, including the Columbia Gorge, Hood River, Goldendale, and The Dalles, offers an aesthetic, tasty, and interesting weekend.

Activities:

Location: Deschutes River State Recreation Area at the Columbia River, Wasco, in Sherman County

Length: 16 miles

Surface: Dirt and gravel

Wheelchair access: The trail is not wheelchair-accessible.

Difficulty: Easy, although in several spots the gravel may challenge bicycle riders.

Food: The nearby town of Biggs has full services.

Restrooms: Public restrooms are at the park and along the trail at 4.0, 6.0, 8.0, and 10.0 miles.

Seasons: The trail is open year-round for hikers and bikers; open Mar 1 through June 30 for equestrians, by reservation only. Carry extra water during the hot summer season.

Rentals: There are no rentals available near the trail.

Contacts: Deschutes River State Recreation Area, (541) 739-2322; Oregon State Parks Information Center, (800) 551-6949, https://stateparks.oregon.gov/. Make camping reservations at Oregon State Parks Reservation Center, (800) 452-5687.

Bus routes: None

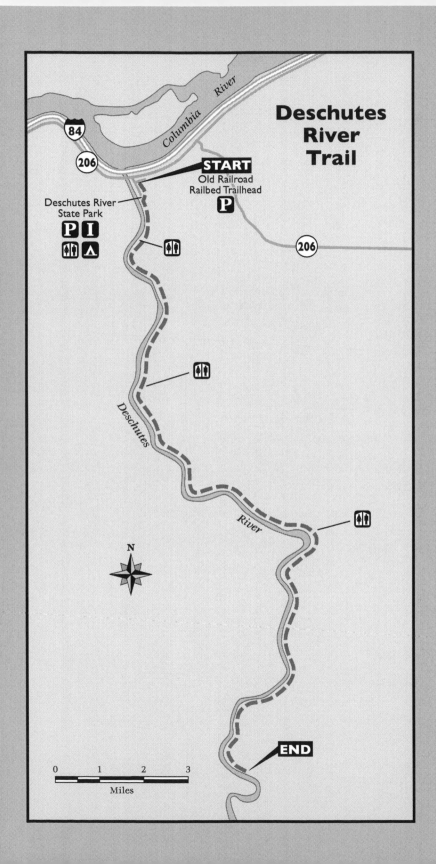

Deschutes
River
Trail

84

206

Columbia River

START
Old Railroad
Railbed Trailhead
P

Deschutes River
State Park
P **I**

Deschutes

River

206

N

0   1   2   3
Miles

END

Access and parking: Take exit 104 off I-84; park signs point you south of the highway. Turn right (west) at the stop sign at the frontage road in the corner town of Biggs. Turn left into Deschutes River State Recreation Area at just under 5 miles. Park at the Old Railbed Trailhead parking area at the state park entrance and head uphill. GPS: N45 38.04' / W120 54.49'

O n the Deschutes River Trail, you're in the desert. You'll have hot, dry weather and little shade most of the year. There are no roads and no water beyond the park (except the river). Oregon State Parks provides a few outhouses. To have a great day here, bring a hefty supply of water in insulated containers, heavy-duty sunscreen, and snacks. Try the trail in spring when lupine and other wildflowers are blooming, the weather is moderate, the pale hair of bighorn sheep stands out against the green, and folks from west of the Cascades are ready for relief from the winter soak. Also check out autumn, when the cooler temperatures paint plants in tints of red, yellow, and light green.

Note that the trail Is dotted with an invasive weed called puncture vine, or goat head, whose three-thorned seeds can flatten bike tires. Use bicycle tubes coated on the interior with a product called "slime." Bring an extra tube and a patch kit. If you get a flat, check your tire carefully for additional seeds waiting to injure your tubes. The Department of Fish and Wildlife sprays the area and provides habitat for birds, deer, and bighorn sheep along the trail and on the ridgetops. You may see western meadowlarks, doves, ospreys, and golden eagles.

In addition to the main, upper trail, two lower walking trails run closer to the river for 2 miles. Anglers bicycle or walk to the lower trail and fish for steelhead from the banks of the Deschutes. Several paths along the main trail lead down to the river. The first 2 miles of the Deschutes River Trail are in the state park; the other miles are in Fish and Wildlife lands. The trail ends at a washout, which marks the start of Bureau of Land Management land.

From your perch on the trail, the canyon displays various rock formations and views of the river. Magpies swoop, showing their striking

Interpretive signs near the start of the trail add a glimpse into the area's history.
Dave Lindsay

black-on-white feathers. Small birds and butterflies disperse as you disrupt the occasional drinking puddle.

You may see a train heading for Bend on the active line across the river. This western line and the right-of-way you'll travel were built by fierce competition. After receiving approval in 1906, two railroad companies—Hill's Oregon Trunk (OT) and Harriman's Des Chutes Railroad Company—went head to head in 1908 in a violent and political battle. The Oregon Trunk was a subsidiary of the Seattle, Portland & Spokane Railway, which was itself a subsidiary of the Northern Pacific and the Great Northern. Harriman's project was a subsidiary of the Oregon-Washington Railroad & Navigation Company, a Union Pacific company. The battle ended in Bend on October 5, 1911, when 73-year-old James Hill drove home the golden spike in two blows. Des Chutes Railroad, where the trail runs, built 95 miles of track into Metolius. It used the Oregon Trunk trackage for routes from Metolius to Bend. The 156 miles of OT track is still used.

Trail mileage on the rail trail is well marked. The terrain drops into the river from the trail, presenting a dramatic view. At mile 3.5, near Colorado Rapid, a dirt road provides access to the river and an outhouse. Also located at 3.5 miles is a rock wall built by Chinese railroad workers. Uphill from the trail, natural springs irrigate a cluster of shade trees. Cross a bridge built over a washout near mile 4.5. At mile 5.5 a side trail leads to another outhouse. View the old pilings of "Free Bridge," a non-toll bridge, at mile 7.0. For a swim, some shade, or a visit to an outhouse, drop down to the river at mile 8.0.

From here the canyon widens and flattens. You might see a lonely cow grazing across the river, or whitewater rafters floating downriver. At 10.0 miles the trail approaches the Deschutes at a spot where towering rock formations jut out across the water. At mile 11.0, out of the barren hills, occasionally some golden wheat and barley fields emerge, followed by the old Harris homestead. The Department of Fish and Wildlife sometimes plants grains here to provide upland bird habitat (pheasant, quail, chukar) and deer and elk forage. It also plants cottonwood trees for shade and for the birds—but no sooner are the trees planted than the beavers arrive to chow down. **Beware:** Grasses hide rattlers, bull snakes, and nestling fawns.

Most travelers turn around at the Harris Ranch, because the trail beyond it is more remote. Washouts from the floods of 1995, 1996, and New Year's Eve 2005 have been repaired with bridges covered by heavy gravel. Most of these are beyond mile 11.0. Washouts make the trail impassable beyond mile 16.0. When you're ready, turn around and return the way you came.

32 UMATILLA COUNTY LEWIS AND CLARK COMMEMORATIVE TRAIL: SECTION 1 THROUGH HAT ROCK STATE PARK

Umatilla, Oregon, is a rural desert community at the southern tip of the I-82 bridge across the Columbia River. This area provides easy access from Oregon to Washington's Yakima Valley wine country. The historic trail begins and ends at riverside parks. Section 1 of the Umatilla County Lewis and Clark Commemorative Trail is a nonmotorized diverse-use trail. The Commemorative Trail comprises four sections, with equestrian access on Sections 1 and 4.

Activities:

Location: Umatilla County, 3 miles from the town of Umatilla

Length: 7.6 miles

Surface: Sand/gravel

Wheelchair access: The trail is not wheelchair-accessible.

Difficulty: Easy to difficult. Most of the trail is easy, although its middle section has some hills.

Food: You'll find a convenience store and a cafe at the Hat Rock RV Park next to Hat Rock State Park. There are minimarts 1.1 miles west of McNary Beach Park. The town of Umatilla is 3 miles from McNary Beach Park.

Restrooms: There are flush toilets and drinking water at McNary Beach and Hat Rock State Parks Apr through Oct; a vault toilet is available year-round at McNary Beach Park, Warehouse Beach Recreation Area, and the boat ramp at Hat Rock State Park.

Seasons: The trail can be used year-round.

Rentals: No rentals are available along this trail.

Contacts: McNary Lock and Dam Park Ranger Office, (541) 922-2268, https://www.nww.usace.army.mil/Missions/Recreation/McNary-Dam-and-Lake-Wallula/Lewis-Clark-Commemorative-Trail/; Hat Rock State Park,

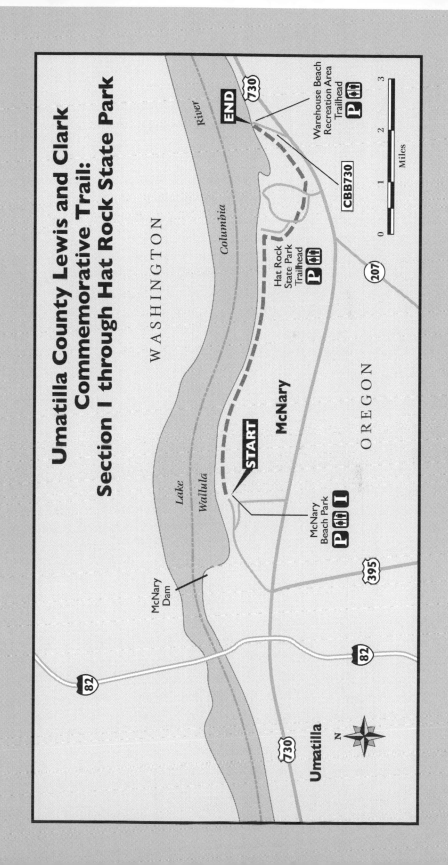

(541) 567-5032, https://stateparks.oregon.gov/; Hat Rock Campground Good Sam Park, (541) 567-4188, www.hatrockcampground.com

Bus routes: None

Access and parking: To begin at the western trailhead, drive about 4 miles east of Umatilla on US 730 to the McNary Beach Park sign. Turn left (north) onto Beach Access Road; drive about 0.75 mile to the McNary Beach Park Recreation Area entrance and turn right into the park. Continue to the trailhead parking lot at the eastern edge of the park. GPS: N45 55.86' / W119 16.06'

The entrance to Hat Rock State Park is 8.2 miles east of Umatilla on US 730. The eastern starting point is at Warehouse Beach Recreation Area and is the primary staging area for equestrians, accessed by turning north off US 730, 1 mile east of Hat Rock State Park; follow the Warehouse Beach signs.

||||||||||||||||||||||||||||||||||||||||||||||||||||||||||||||||||||||||||||||||||||||||||||||||||||||

This trail description covers the area from McNary Beach Recreation Area Park east through Hat Rock State Park, ending at the trailhead at Warehouse Beach Recreation Area. Previously known as the Lake Wallula River Hiking Trail–Hat Rock Corridor, it was absorbed into a longer trail system developed to celebrate the Lewis and Clark Expedition's travels through the area more than 200 years ago.

Located along the Columbia River in the Oregon desert, the rugged terrain is stunningly beautiful in its simplicity. Ride or walk this trail on a sunny day—and most days here are sunny—and you'll think you're in heaven. The trail is unshaded, so in summer bring water, serious sunscreen, and a hat. In winter wear warm clothing for protection against chilling winds.

McNary Beach, on the western end of Section 1 of the Commemorative Trail, lies adjacent to the dam that in 1953 flooded miles of Oregon-Washington Railroad & Navigation Company (OWR&N) line and several towns upriver. McNary Dam was built to produce hydroelectric power and to relieve the problems of navigating the Columbia. Inland waterways were critical to trade, and the Umatilla rapids caused more grief and delay to barge lines than any other obstacle on the Columbia River. The dam flooded the main-line railroad from Cold Springs to Attalia and Wallula. The 35-mile backflow, along the Yakima line to the Kalan Bridge, was called Lake Wallula.

Following dam construction, the towns and rail yards were moved to their new location and the railroad rebuilt. This boosted the success of the OWR&N, an operating segment of the Union Pacific Railroad. Though the waterways could now compete with the rails, government funding allowed the railroad to improve the tracks that had been so hastily blasted through basalt cliffs in 1880. Sharp curves, rockfalls, and avalanches had for decades caused delays and derailments, shoving engines over the banks and into the river. The last steam-powered train ran these tracks in 1955.

Now you can walk 7.6 miles of the route beside the chunk of history that lies under Lake Wallula. To the west, paved access to the trail starts to the left off the McNary Beach Park road before you reach any of the parking lots. It quickly becomes dirt and gravel at the information kiosk, where the trail cuts into the basalt cliffs and through the sagebrush at the eastern end of the eastern parking lot by a grassy riverfront with picnic tables. The first mile is easy. Then the trail climbs up onto a steeper riverbank with great views. Choose the uphill fork where a side trail heads down to a pump plant. The path seems to end at a washout 2 miles down the trail; however, it was improved in 2005 and is passable. Still, use caution. If you find it too risky, explore the east end of the trail from Hat Rock State Park to Warehouse Beach Recreation Area, a 2-mile stretch.

As you approach Hat Rock State Park from the west, the trail becomes relatively flat. The view becomes more interesting as homes, inlets, and rock formations appear. During the sunny summer, the wide river looks blue in color. Sagebrush dots the trail varying in color from a subtle green in spring to a faded yellow in late summer. Boats cruise by, and locals walk their dogs on the trail. Listen for the metallic rustle of cheatgrass and bunchgrass moved by the wind.

Arriving at Hat Rock State Park is like entering the Emerald City. Everything takes on color and texture and life. Desert browns and yellows turn into bright green during summer. An array of yellow, orange, and red greets visitors in autumn. Ducks and geese create ripples on a pond as they fetch gifts of food. Anglers wait on the banks of the inlet and pond

Visitors to Hat Rock State Park pursue water sports.

for steelhead, bass, or catfish. Canoeists and kayakers launch for a scenic paddle. A little bridge across the inlet leads to open desert trails. Hat Rock towers above the park looking like . . . you guessed it, a huge hat.

Continue through Hat Rock State Park on the trail until it rejoins the river's shoreline. Hat Rock was a land feature sighted by Lewis and Clark and recorded in personal journals written during their expedition. Travelers today can pass the rock and follow the old railroad bed for 2 miles to Warehouse Beach Recreation Area, a day-use area with restrooms, picnic shelters, and a swimming beach. This is the primary access point for equestrians as well as mountain bikers and hikers.

Experience other sections of the Commemorative Trail by heading west from the western side of Section 1. The trail drops down to the McNary Lock and Dam, passes by the McNary Wildlife Nature Area, enters the city of Umatilla, and then returns to the Columbia River. Consider visiting the Deschutes River Trail (Trail 31) farther west near the Columbia River Gorge.

33 OC&E–WOODS LINE STATE TRAIL

Explore the 108-mile OC&E–Woods Line State Trail for its solitude and panoramic views. Walkers, joggers, bicyclists, equestrians, and other nonmotorized travelers have one thing in common on this great pathway—they're all welcome!

Activities:

Location: OC&E Main Line: Klamath Falls to Bly, in Klamath County; Woods Line: Beatty to the Silver Lake, in Lake County

Length: 108 miles open to the public (68 miles on the OC&E Main Line Trail; 40 miles on the Woods Line Trail)

Surface: The trail is paved for 8 miles out of Klamath Falls to Olene. The trail is graded and rolled in the late spring from the Olene Trailhead to the Switchback Trailhead.

Wheelchair access: Only the paved section is wheelchair-accessible.

Difficulty: Easy to moderate

Food: Klamath Falls has all services. There are convenience stores in Olene, Sprague River, Beatty, and Bly; cafes in Dairy, Sprague River, and Bly.

Restrooms: There are restrooms at Wiard Junction, Route 39, Switchbacks, and Reeder Road Trailheads and at Horse Glade and Silver Creek Marsh Campgrounds.

Seasons: The trail can be used year-round. The paved section is plowed in winter to clear the trail for bicycling; trailheads are not plowed.

Rentals: Zack's Bikes, 831 Main Street, Klamath Falls, (541) 851-9200, www.zacksbikes.com

Contacts: Collier Memorial State Park, (541) 783-2471; Klamath Rails-to-Trails Group, http://klamathrailstotrailsgroup.org/; Oregon State Parks and Recreation Department, Salem office, (503) 986-0707, https://stateparks.oregon.gov/; Fremont–Winema National Forest, Silver Lake Ranger District, (541) 576-7500, https://www.fs.usda.gov/detail/fremont-winema/about-forest/offices

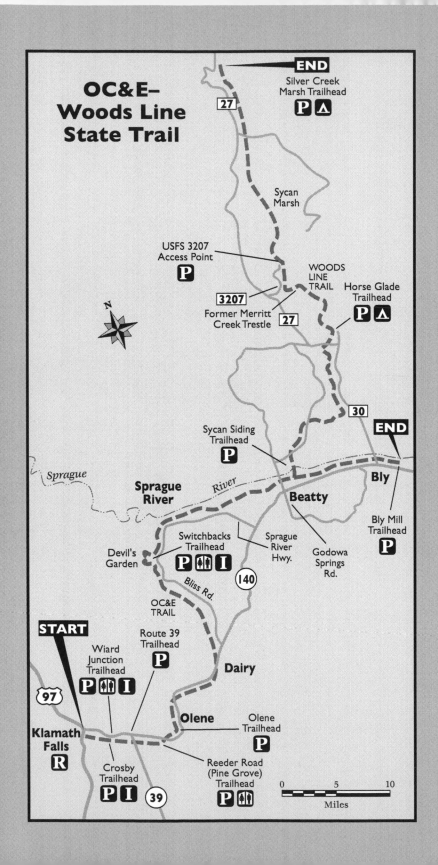

Bus routes: None

Access and parking: Reach Klamath Falls from US 97 or OR 66 to OR 140. For the Main OC&E Trailhead, drive 0.25 mile east of Washburn Way on Crosby Avenue. Turn left between the self-storage facility and lumber facility and drive to the parking lot next to the trail. GPS: N42 12.44' / W121 45.11'

- Bly Mill Trailhead: Take OR 140 east from the intersection of OR 140 and South 6th Street. Travel approximately 35 miles to Beatty. From Beatty, continue 12 miles to a small stone block building located on the left. The trailhead entrance is on the left just past the building.

- Sycan Siding Trailhead: This trailhead lies at the intersection of the OC&E Trail and the Woods Line Trail. Take OR 140 east to Beatty. For Sycan Siding, turn left onto Godowa Springs Road. After 2.1 miles, turn right onto Sycan Road. Turn right when the paved road turns to dirt and park.

- Silver Creek Marsh Campground Trailhead: This is the last trailhead on the Woods Line segment. From the turn for FR 3207, continue about 15 miles on FR 27 to the intersection with FR 3142. Stay to the left on FR 27 and go about 7 more miles to Silver Creek Campground and the trailhead.

At the turn of the twentieth century, railroads were leading the growth of the West. Robert Strahorn had a dream of connecting central and eastern Oregon with rail lines by linking Klamath Falls to Lakeview via Sprague River, and Bend and Burns via Sprague River and Silver Lake. The first step in this grand plan was the OC&E (Oregon, California and Eastern Railroad), also known as the Klamath Municipal Railway. Groundbreaking occurred near 3rd Street and Klamath Avenue in Klamath Falls on July 3, 1917.

Quickly a ribbon of steel stretched out toward Sprague River. Soon mills and branch lines sprang up along this new railway. The line was declared open on September 16, 1923. In 1927 the line was extended to Bly, but that would be the end of the line for Strahorn's dream.

Southern Pacific and Great Northern (later, Burlington Northern) jointly operated the OC&E from 1925 until 1974. One railroad would manage the line for five years and then pass responsibility to the other for five years. Weyerhaeuser took over the entire line in 1974, but by the end of the 1980s, the line was no longer a cost-effective way to move logs. The line was rail-banked and handed over to Oregon Parks and Recreation in 1992.

The trail is actually two trails—the original OC&E and the old Weyerhaeuser Woods Line that heads from Beatty to north of the Sycan Marsh at Silver Creek Marsh Campground. Woods Line heads uphill from south to north and is forested, with sagebrush meadows. On the main-line trail you'll travel through ranchland and desert, with one hilly section. Future plans are to connect to the Lake Ewauna Trail via an East Main Street Extension in Klamath Falls and develop hiker/biker camps along the trail.

If you're a cross-country ski enthusiast, in winter you'll find snow in the switchback area and on the upper 10 through 40 miles of the Woods Line. Trailheads are not cleared of snow for parking.

OC&E Main Line Trail, 68 miles

The first 8 miles of the OC&E Trail are paved, starting at the main OC&E Trailhead off Washburn Way in Klamath Falls and ending at Olene on OR 140. Pass by local shopping areas and through residential neighborhoods in Klamath Falls. This section receives the most use, but there's much more to explore as the trail heads east.

The trail continues on to agricultural areas with wonderful views of surrounding mountains, including Mount Shasta to the south. As you enter Olene, look for the big yellow rail snowplow and old grange building. In Olene the trail crosses OR 140 and pushes on through juniper and sagebrush and then the Poe Valley. To your right spreads a panoramic view of the Poe Valley and the Lost River.

Continue on to Swede's Cut, the spot where Swedish workers carved a pass through solid rock to gain access to Pine Flat. The job required great skill at using drills and black powder—and more than a bit of bravado.

Emerge from Pine Flat at the town of Dairy, about 10 trail miles from Olene. To visit the cafe in town, continue to the Dairy Siding just east of town. Bear right. Go to the T intersection with OR 140 and turn right; Dairy

Trail users can rest on a bench after crossing the trestle west of the Wiard Junction Trailhead.

is 0.8 mile away. This is your last chance for food or water until the town of Sprague River, 20 miles farther. The valleys around Dairy and Bonanza saw violent conflicts between Native Americans and settlers during the Modoc Indian War in 1872.

From Dairy the trail heads north to skirt Bly Mountain via Switchback Hill. Just past Hildebrand the forested trail gains 600 feet in 9 miles at a 2 percent grade. Climb up Switchback Hill on a large horseshoe turn—so sharp that the end of the train saw the lead cars passing directly above. The switchback allowed the heavy trains laden with timber and some cattle to make the 600-foot climb. Passengers rode the line only in the 1920s. The tracks zigzag over the steep hillside, forming a double switchback. From the top look to the southeast for a great view of the Devil's Garden. Take a 7.0-mile (roundtrip) side expedition to this extinct volcano on old logging roads.

The trail descends to the river and the town of Sprague River, about 5.5 miles from the Switchbacks Trailhead. Here in the Sprague River Valley, you'll find a country store and vistas of surrounding mountains, forests, and ranches. Your next stop is Beatty, about 12 miles ahead. To reach this town, take Godowa Springs Road about a mile south to OR 140.

Just east of Beatty, the Woods Line branches north. To continue on the OC&E Main Line Trail, head east through pastures of grazing cattle, marshes, and open-water areas. Sandhill cranes, eagles, red-tailed hawks, egrets, great blue herons, ducks and geese, swarms of red-winged black-birds, beavers, deer, and other wildlife can be seen along the Sprague River. The trail ends in Bly near the South Fork of the Sprague River and just southwest of the Gearhart Wilderness Area, at mile 68.0.

Woods Line Trail, 40 miles

To take the Woods Line Trail, head northeast from Beatty on a steady uphill climb. The trail crosses over the Sprague River and passes the Sycan Siding (former maintenance yard for the Woods Line).The trestle at mile 9.0 was abandoned once the ravine was filled in. At mile 10.0 you'll reach Five-Mile Creek and trout fishing; for the next 6 miles, this creek will be your com-panion. Arrive at Horse Glade Trailhead at mile 19.0; you'll find camping here. Pass through second-growth forest; at mile 27.0 you'll encounter a reroute across Merritt Creek. In 2021, forest fires burned the most spec-tacular structure on the trail: the Merritt Creek Trestle, which spanned 400 feet and stood 50 feet above the ground. A temporary reroute uses the low water drainage crossing via a dirt road on the north side of the trail to regain the Woods Line Trail. Plans include a redesign of the area. Check with Forest Service trail managers for updated information on trail and forest usability.

At present the trail ends north of the Sycan Marsh at Silver Creek Marsh Campground.

More Rail Trails

M HINES RAILROAD GRADE

The Malheur National Forest sits in the Blue Mountains of eastern Oregon and is currently home to the original Hines Railroad Grade. This old railbed serves dual purposes now. It is incorporated into mountain biking trails in summer and into snowmobile, cross-country skiing, and snowshoeing trails in winter. Its grade is mostly moderate, with occasional challenging sections. Enjoy views of Logan Valley and the Strawberry Mountain Wilderness on this trail.

Activities:

Location: Malheur National Forest, John Day, in Grant County

Length: Three mountain biking / hiking routes incorporating segments of the rail trail with forest roads, ranging from a 17.2-mile out-and-back section to a 6.1-mile or 7.9-mile loop option

Surface: Gravel, dirt, and forest roads

Wheelchair access: The trail is not wheelchair-accessible.

Difficulty: Moderate to difficult

Food: No food is available along this trail.

Restrooms: There are restrooms and drinking water at the Big Creek Campground on FR 815 off FR 16.

Seasons: The trail can be used year-round. It serves as a groomed snowmobile trail Dec to Apr.

Rentals: No rentals are available along this trail.

Contacts: USDA Forest Service, Prairie City Ranger District, (541) 820-3800, www.fs.usda.gov/recarea/malheur/recreation

Bus routes: None

Access and parking: From Prairie City take CR 62 for 19 miles to Summit Prairie. From here, travel west on paved FR 16 for approximately 6 miles, near mile marker 19.0. Turn right onto FR 815. Travel 1 mile to Big Creek Campground and the trailhead and kiosk with route descriptions. GPS: N44 11.21' / W118 36.94'

In winter when Big Creek Campground is inaccessible, you can park at the Summit Prairie snowmobile parking area.

N MILL CITY TRAIL

The trail passes over a refurbished railroad bridge that crosses the salmon-filled pool created by Mill City Falls. It parallels the North Santiam River for a while and offers several scenic points. While you're in town, take a whitewater rafting or kayaking trip. Future plans include upgrading the trail.

Activities:

Location: Mill City, Linn County

Length: 2.0 miles

Surface: Asphalt

Wheelchair access: The trail is wheelchair-accessible.

Difficulty: Easy

Food: There are restaurants near the start of the trail in Mill City.

Restrooms: Mill City Falls Park offers flush toilets.

Seasons: Year-round

Rentals: No rentals are available along this trail.

Contacts: City of Mill City, (503) 897-2302, www.ci.mill-city.or.us

Bus routes: Take Route 30X through the Cherriots Regional system, (503) 588-2877, http://cherriots.org.

Access and parking: Go east on OR 22 to Mill City. Turn right toward City Center onto North 1st Avenue, then turn left at the intersection with Northwest Alder Street and continue downhill on North 1st Avenue toward the North Santiam River. You'll see the railroad bridge on your right, near the small Hammond city park. GPS: N44 45.32' / W122 28.64'

Park at the nearby Mill City Falls Park paved lot along North East Wall Street, west of North 1st Avenue. This area is approximately the center of this 2-mile trail. A 1-mile option is to head west across the rail bridge toward Wayside Memorial. Alternately, there is an approximately 0.25-mile street route eastward from the bridge on Northeast Wall Street to Santiam Pointe Loop Northeast, where the paved trail continues for approximately 0.75 mile along the river.

FANNO CREEK REGIONAL TRAIL

This trail originates from the Oregon Electric ROW. It connects two parks in a rural section of Beaverton and is part of a master plan to link Beaverton's 2,240 park acres, 90 parks, and 70 miles of trails.

Activities:

Location: Beaverton, in Washington County

Length: 0.8-mile section between two parks, plus a 3.7-mile extension beyond Vista Brook Park

Surface: Asphalt

Wheelchair access: The entire trail is wheelchair-accessible.

Difficulty: Easy

Food: Near the trailhead across the street from Garden Home Recreation Center

Restrooms: Find restrooms at Garden Home Recreation Center, Vista Brook Park, and Greenway Park.

Seasons: The trail can be used year-round.

Rentals: No rentals are available along this trail.

Contacts: Tualatin Hills Park and Recreation District, (503) 645-6433, www. thprd.org

Bus routes: For information visit www.trimet.org, or call (503) 238-RIDE (7433).

Access and parking: Take Sunset Highway (US 26) west to OR 217. Turn south, drive to Allen Boulevard, then turn east and cross over Scholls Ferry Road. Turn south onto 92nd Avenue and continue until 92nd Avenue becomes Garden Home Road. Follow this road 1 mile to Oleson Road; turn left into Garden Home Recreation Center on Oleson Road and park at the north end of the parking lot. GPS: N45 28.03' / W122 45.12'

SUMPTER VALLEY RAILROAD INTERPRETIVE TRAIL

This noteworthy interpretive trail marks the highest point of the Sumpter Valley Railway: 5,277 feet. It overlooks switchbacks into the John Day Valley. Learn about the historic railway and why the route was abandoned.

Activities:

Location: Malheur National Forest, John Day, in Grant County

Length: 0.5 mile

Surface: Asphalt and packed gravel

Wheelchair access: The trail is not wheelchair-accessible, due to a few steep sections and a section of packed gravel.

Difficulty: Moderate

Food: No food is available along this trail.

Restrooms: There is a vault toilet at the trailhead.

Seasons: While the trail can be used year-round, the lot adjacent to the highway isn't plowed; expect snow Nov through Apr.

Rentals: No rentals are available along this trail.

Contacts: Malheur National Forest, (541) 820-3800, www.fs.usda.gov/recarea/malheur/recreation

Bus routes: None

Access and parking: From Prairie City take US 26 east for 8 miles. The trail is located on the right, before Dixie Summit. GPS: N44 32.07' / W118 36.54'

Long tunnels and tall trestles thrill bicyclists on the Route of the Hiawatha Rail Trail in northern Idaho.

Idaho

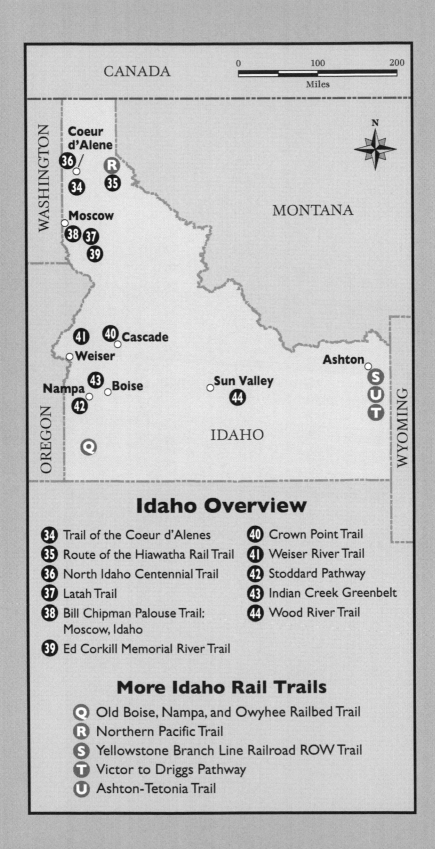

Idaho Overview

- **34** Trail of the Coeur d'Alenes
- **35** Route of the Hiawatha Rail Trail
- **36** North Idaho Centennial Trail
- **37** Latah Trail
- **38** Bill Chipman Palouse Trail: Moscow, Idaho
- **39** Ed Corkill Memorial River Trail
- **40** Crown Point Trail
- **41** Weiser River Trail
- **42** Stoddard Pathway
- **43** Indian Creek Greenbelt
- **44** Wood River Trail

More Idaho Rail Trails

- **Q** Old Boise, Nampa, and Owyhee Railbed Trail
- **R** Northern Pacific Trail
- **S** Yellowstone Branch Line Railroad ROW Trail
- **T** Victor to Driggs Pathway
- **U** Ashton-Tetonia Trail

Rail trails in Idaho are constantly emerging as part of a statewide and regional effort to expand and interconnect trails. Current trails are on, or near, past railroad main lines and spurs that once carried timber, silver, copper, gold, grains, fruits, and passengers through the region.

Northern Idaho rail trails go through rural timber and mining towns, through remote forests, and along clean rivers and lakes. In southern Idaho, rail trails run past rural farms, basalt rock canyons, and forested passages, and through park-studded greenbelts along creeks and rivers.

If you're looking for long, nonmotorized, paved rail trails, head to northern Idaho. The Trail of the Coeur d'Alenes runs for 73 smooth miles; the North Idaho Centennial Trail boasts 24 miles. For a ride through timbered wilderness on a compacted-gravel rail trail that heads downhill through tunnels and across trestles, try the Route of the Hiawatha, also in northern Idaho.

Spring is an ideal time to visit rail trails in Latah County in northern Idaho. Shamrock-green grain fields glisten in the sunshine, meadowlarks chirp, and a cool breeze blows. Three paved trails, each unique in its own way, are within a short drive of Moscow. The Ed Corkill Memorial River Trail runs from Juliaetta to Kendrick and is a stroll through railroad history in rural towns, while the Latah Trail from Troy to Moscow is a rigorous rolling pathway through forest and farms. The latter connects directly with the Idaho section of the Bill Chipman Palouse Trail, which starts at the University of Idaho campus in Moscow and runs to Pullman, Washington, and features detailed interpretive signs providing railroad tidbits and local history.

In the southern part of the state, the short Crown Point Trail attracts winter sports enthusiasts. For the longest rail trail in the state, visit the Weiser River Trail, which runs for 86 miles. Urban trails in southern Idaho with nearby attractions and amenities include the Stoddard Pathway and the Indian Creek Greenbelt. Or travel on the Wood River Trail in Wood River Valley, where the railroad helped to build the famous Sun Valley Resort.

While in eastern Idaho, take in the rural trails with views of rivers and famous snowcapped mountains. Wherever you travel in Idaho, enjoy the diversity that the state's rail trails offer.

34 | TRAIL OF THE COEUR D'ALENES

If you're looking for one of the longer paved trails in the country, visit the Trail of the Coeur d'Alenes, located in the northern panhandle of Idaho. It runs for 73 smooth, flat miles, offering a diverse mixture of timber and mining towns against a backdrop of wetlands, rivers, lakes, and mountains. Toss in wildlife viewing and food stops. The result is an endless opportunity for admiring the region's lush scenery and rail history.

Activities:

Location: Coeur d'Alene tribal lands and the towns of Plummer, Harrison, Enaville, Pinehurst, Kellogg, Osburn, Wallace, and Mullan, in Benewah, Kootenai, and Shoshone Counties

Length: 73 miles (agency trail maps indicate 71.4 miles at the eastern terminus)

Surface: Asphalt

Wheelchair access: The entire trail is wheelchair-accessible.

Difficulty: Easy, with a moderate uphill grade heading into Plummer

Food: Restaurants are located in the small towns along the trail, such as the Snake Pit Bar and Restaurant in Enaville.

Restrooms: Public facilities are available at numerous trailheads and along remote sections of the trail at rest-stop waysides. Trailhead restrooms include Hn'ya)pqi'nn ("Gathering Place") near Plummer, Hntsaqaqn ("Stopping Place"), Hnpetptqwe'n ("Place for Racing"), Plummer Point, Chatcolet,

Hndarep ("Canoe Landing"), Sqwe'mu'lmkhw ("A Familiar Place"), Harrison Marina, Springston, Medimont, Lane, Bull Run, River Bend, Cataldo, Enaville, Kellogg Depot, Restless Rapids, and Mullan.

Seasons: The trail can be used year-round. Snow is often in the northern reaches between Nov and May.

Rentals: The Cycle Haus, 100 North Coeur d'Alene Avenue, Harrison, (208) 689-3436, https://thecyclehaus.com; Silver Mountain Resort's Silver Mountain Sports Shop at 110 Morningstar Drive, Kellogg, (866) 344-2675, www.silvermt.com; Coeur d'Alene Bike Company at 21 Railroad Avenue, Kellogg, (208) 786-3751, www.cdabikeco.com; Coeur d'Alene Bike Company, 314 North 3rd Street, Coeur d'Alene, (208) 966-4022, www.cdabikeco.com. Near the eastern terminus off I-90 at exit 0, try Lookout Pass Ski and Recreation Area, (208) 744-1301, www.ridethehiawatha.com.

Contacts: Plummer to Harrison section: Coeur d'Alene Tribe Natural Resources Division, (208) 686-7045, www.cdatribe-nsn.gov; Harrison to Mullan section: trail headquarters, Coeur d'Alene's Old Mission State Park, (208) 682-3814; Heyburn State Park, (208) 686-1308; Idaho Department of Parks and Recreation, www.parksandrecreation.idaho.gov. For other trails in the region, visit the Friends of the Coeur d'Alene Trails website, www.friendsofcdatrails.org. For information about the Cataldo to Mullan area, contact Historic Silver Valley Chamber of Commerce, (208) 784-0821, www.silvervalleychamber.com. For shuttles contact Lou's Bicycle Shuttle Service in Harrison, (208) 818-2254, www.captain-lou.com.

Bus routes: City Link runs a free bus service between Coeur d'Alene and Plummer; call (877) 941-RIDE (7433) or Kootenai County Transit Services at (208) 446-2255, or visit https://www.kcgov.us/486/Transit-Services.

Access and parking: There are numerous trailheads with parking and, in many cases, restrooms. Because this trail is famous and well used, there is good trailhead signage along the major driving routes. Here are the easily accessible trailheads, starting with the western terminus, Hn'ya)pqi'nn ("Gathering Place"), near Plummer.

- Plummer Trailhead: The western terminus, also called Hn'ya)pqi'nn, is reached by taking US 95 north from Moscow or south from the town of Coeur d'Alene. Turn west onto Anne Antelope Road and then immediately left into the large, well-marked parking lot on the west side of the highway, on the north side of the town of Plummer. Pick up the trail just beyond the kiosk and restrooms. GPS: N47 20.44' / W116 53.39'

- Indian Cliffs Trailhead: Used mainly by hikers, take ID 5 east from the town of Plummer. Drive about 5 miles and turn left into Heyburn State Park on Chatcolet Road. Continue past the park headquarters building, on the right. Go about 1.2 miles and turn left to the Indian Cliffs Trailhead, which also says "Nature Trail." A per-vehicle day-use pass or annual state park pass is required to park here. An Idaho State Parks Passport is available for Idaho residents during their annual vehicle registration through the local Department of Motor Vehicles offices. For information on day-use and annual passes, go to www.parksandrecreation.idaho.gov.

- Chatcolet Trailhead: This is considered the main trailhead for bicyclists, though you can start at any of the trailheads. Continue past Indian Cliffs Trailhead for 0.8 mile to the V in the road. Take the right onto Chatcolet Lower Road and go 0.4 mile into the Chatcolet Trailhead parking lot, on the right. The trailhead parking lot is about 2.5 miles from the park headquarters building. A per-vehicle day-use fee or annual pass is required.

- Harrison Trailhead: Take ID 97 south from Coeur d'Alene, or north from its junction with ID 3, to the town of Harrison. Turn west off ID 97 into Harrison, onto Harrison Street. Go 1 block to Lakefront Avenue. Turn left onto Lakefront Avenue and then immediately right into the small trailhead parking area, next to One Shot Charlies. Walk or bike downhill 1 block to the official trailhead, next to the city beach and the parking areas for the local businesses.

- Medimont Trailhead: Follow ID 3 north from the junction of ID 97 and ID 3. After 9.3 miles, turn left off ID 3 onto Medimont Road and follow the road for about 1.5 miles. Turn left onto South Ruddy Duck Road. The trailhead is on the left, a few hundred feet ahead.

- Black Rock Trailhead: Travel 15.6 miles north on ID 3 from the junction of ID 97 and ID 3. Turn left to the trailhead parking area.

- Bull Run Lake Trailhead: Drive 18.7 miles north on ID 3 from the junction of ID 97 and ID 3. Turn right on South Bull Run Road and go 0.3 mile.

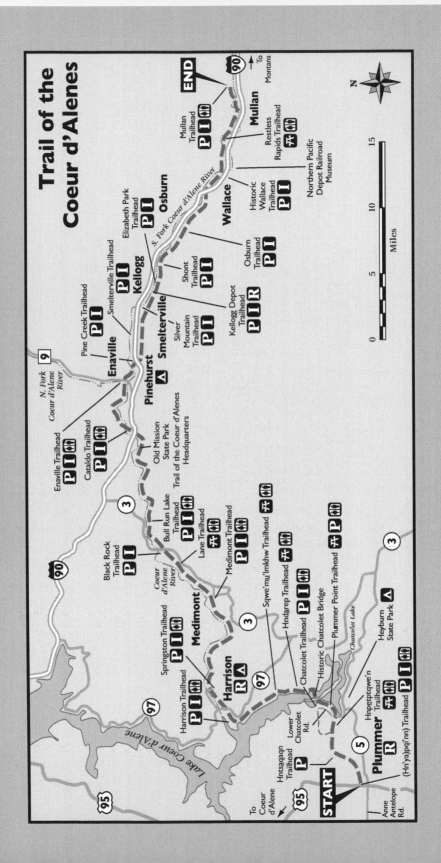

Trail of the Coeur d'Alenes

Turn right again to stay on South Bull Road. The trailhead is 0.2 mile ahead on the left.

- Cataldo Trailhead: ID 3 North arrives at I-90 at 21.9 miles from the junction of ID 97 and ID 3. Take I-90 east for 6.1 miles to exit 40, turn right off the exit toward Cataldo, and go 0.7 mile to the trailhead.

- Enaville Trailhead: Head east on I-90 from Cataldo. After 2.3 miles, take exit 43 (Kingston). Turn left off the ramp and drive north onto FR 9 for 1.8 miles through Kingston and on to Enaville. Park in Enaville at the trailside paved lot on the left off FR 9.

- Pine Creek Trailhead: Travel I-90 East to exit 45 at Pinehurst, turning left off the ramp. Drive 0.3 mile and turn left into the paved trailhead lot.

- Smelterville Trailhead: Drive I-90 East from Pinehurst to exit 48 into Smelterville, turning right off the exit. In less than 0.1 mile, turn left and then immediately right into the trailhead parking area.

- Silver Mountain Trailhead: Continue east on I-90 to exit 49. Turn right off the exit ramp onto Bunker Avenue. After 0.4 mile turn right to the trailhead, parking at the Silver Mountain parking lot. Pick up the trail on the south side of the lot, though you may see signs saying "Silver Valley Trail Route and Kellogg Greenbelt."

- Kellogg Depot Trailhead: There are two parking options near one another at this trailhead. Take exit 51, the Kellogg exit, off I-90. Turn right off the exit onto Division Street. Go 1 block and turn right onto Railroad Avenue and then left into the parking area next to Coeur d'Alene Bike Company, located near the Kellogg Depot Trailhead. Pick up the trail just off the parking lot. For the second option, turn left off Division Street onto Station Avenue, and then turn left again into the small parking lot area at the Passenger Depot Building, which serves as the Historic Silver Valley Chamber of Commerce. Pick up the trail on the north side of the parking lot.

- Shont Trailhead: Use exit 54 off I-90. Turn right off the exit and drive less than 0.1 mile, turning left into the trailhead parking area.

- Osburn Trailhead: Take I-90 to exit 57. Turn right off the ramp and then left at the stop sign onto Canyon Avenue. Drive 0.1 mile toward Osburn.

Turn left onto Mullan Avenue and then right onto South 6th Street. Cross the trail and turn right into the trailhead parking area.

- Historic Wallace 6th Street Trailhead: Take the second Wallace exit, number 62, off I-90. Turn right off the ramp at the stop sign and travel around the corner onto Bank Street. About 0.3 mile after turning right from the stop sign, turn right onto 6th Street. Go 4 blocks, passing the Northern Pacific Railroad Depot and Museum, on the right. Continue under the interstate overpass to the trailhead parking, on the right.

- Mullan Trailhead: Take exit 68 off I-90. The off-ramp becomes River Street and practically puts you at the trailhead. Travel on River Street, driving toward the town of Mullan, which is visible from the exit. Take a left off River Street onto 2nd Street and immediately turn right into the trail's eastern terminus parking lot.

||||||||||||||||||||||||||||||||||||||||||||||||||||||||||||||||||||||||||||||||||

Traveling the trail from the western starting point in the town of Plummer to the eastern terminus in rural Mullan near the Idaho–Montana border is an adventure not to be missed. You will travel on the original rail route for much of the trip, and can stay at one of the campgrounds near the trail.

Along the way you travel beside vacation homes, lakes, streams, rivers, wetlands, interstate highways, mining towns, and timber towns. Frequent interpretive signs along the trail keep visitors informed about nature, history, and nearby attractions. Colorful wildflowers grace the trail in spring and summer, while in autumn deciduous trees show their many colors against the deep green backdrop of the coniferous trees. En route it is common to spot moose, deer, ospreys, bald eagles, and other wildlife.

Winds usually move up the rivers and valleys by midday and calm down in the evenings. Some days they reach 10 to 15 miles per hour. Bicyclists may want to factor winds into their departure time and their direction of travel.

Taking the trail from east to west, starting at the eastern terminus in Mullan and heading to Plummer, gives one a sensation of gradually descending downhill. Along the trail, waterfalls and creeks flow into the South Fork of the Coeur d'Alene River, then into the main stem of the river, which passes through the lake district and finally into Coeur d'Alene Lake. The route crosses over thirty-six bridges and trestles.

This long trail is an environmental cleanup effort that has resulted in a smooth, seamless trail. In the late 1880s mining was growing in popularity in the Silver Valley near Kellogg. Rails were constructed to assist the mining and timber industry. Waste rocks and tailings from the mines were used to create the railbed. Unfortunately, they contain high levels of lead and heavy metals that leach into the soil and water sources.

General awareness of contamination hazards from lead has increased during the last couple of decades. Cleanup activities were a joint effort among the Union Pacific Railroad, numerous government agencies, and the Tribe of the Coeur d'Alenes. The rail tracks were removed, asphalt was put down, and gravel barriers were installed to restrain contaminants.

Today recreationists enjoy a smooth-as-silk surface that is one of the longest paved trails in the United States and guaranteed to stay intact forever. Due to the environmental cleanup resolution, the trail has to be seal-coated every five years and asphalted every twenty to twenty-five years. The seal-coating schedule takes place with a segment-rotation. Each segment of the trail has its own character. There are numerous developed trailheads accessing the trail. You could break your trip into sections as small as you desire and do an out-and-back. Or you could increase the distance for a one-way trip by hiring a shuttle from Lou's Bicycle Shuttle Service, based out of Harrison. Bicycle rentals and repair services are available near the trailheads in Harrison and Kellogg.

Plummer to Harrison, 16 Miles

Water dominates the scenery in this segment. From the trail's start at the Plummer Trailhead to the Harrison Trailhead, the route takes visitors along the Plummer Creek canyon, by Chatcolet Lake, across a 3,100-foot-long bridge trestle, and beside the wide-open Lake Coeur d'Alene.

After leaving the hustle and bustle of the large, paved western trailhead on US 95, called *Hn'ya)pqi'nn* ("The Gathering Place") in the language of the Coeur d'Alene tribe, you will pass a gravel pit and the backyards of Plummer residents. At about 1 mile from the trailhead, you travel through forested areas along the trail. The trail marker mileage is a bit off at the start of the trail, but it equalizes toward Chatcolet Lake. When the rail trail was first built, it followed the railroad's original mileage numbering system. Later, a short western section added by the Coeur d'Alene extended the trail to US 95, creating variances in the stated trail mileage ranging from 71.4 to 73 miles. This description's mileage corresponds with the trail maps at the trailheads.

Get ready for a roly-poly ride. Ponderosa pines along this section provide food and shelter for local birds like pileated woodpeckers and warblers. Between miles 2.0 and 5.0, there are two rest stops, one at a rail trestle crossing over Plummer Creek.

At about 5.2 miles the trail enters Heyburn State Park, the oldest park in Idaho. This spot also serves as a trailhead, with limited parking and no restrooms. For spectacular views of the area, take a quick hike on the dirt Civilian Conservation Corps (CCC) Nature Trail and Indian Cliffs Trail, just off the paved trail.

Return to the asphalt trail and continue to the larger Chatcolet Trailhead at 7.0 miles. Vistas open up, and the famous Historic Chatcolet Bridge appears in the distance, as does the marina located at the trailhead. This and Indian Cliffs Trailhead are fee-based parking sites along the trail, requiring a per-vehicle day-use fee or an annual state park pass. As you travel along Chatcolet Lake toward the trailhead, forested mountains blanket the scenery while ducks bob on the water and ospreys soar above.

Pass the Chatcolet Trailhead and proceed to the long bridge trestle. Mile 8.0 puts you at the east end of the bridge, where you will pass near lakeside cabins and many interpretive signs. Two more trailside picnic sites with restrooms are beside the trail between mile 8.0 and the Harrison Trailhead at 15.3 miles. O'Gara Bay and Shingle Bay lie between the Chatcolet and Harrison Trailheads. Be sure to wear sunscreen. You travel close enough to the lake to be exposed to reflected sunlight as well as the direct rays of the sun.

The area you are traveling through was once important for commerce. Mining started in the Silver Valley in the mid-1880s. Lumber, ore, and passengers were transported via boats on the waterways between 1880 and the 1920s. Rail lines started in 1888 to move timber and ore. After the rails arrived, boat use dropped off.

When you enter the Harrison area, you will receive your first exposure (pardon the pun) to information regarding the soil and sediments in this area and beyond. As previously noted, these materials still contain high levels of lead and other heavy metals, by-products of prior mining activity.

Information signs, starting at the Harrison Trailhead, provide guidance and advice on how to avoid contamination. Children and pregnant women are at higher risk. Basically, do not drink lake, stream, or river water. Refrain from eating plants from the trailside, such as those tempting wild berries. Wash your hands before eating, and avoid contact with the soil. Stay on the paved trail and in designated safe areas, such as picnic sites and restroom waysides. These guidelines will apply for the rest of your journey eastward.

That doesn't mean you can't venture into the trailside towns. At the Harrison Trailhead you can tent or RV camp or enjoy a meal at the Gateway Marina. Or go a block into this small town for a meal at any of a number of local restaurants.

Harrison to Pine Creek Trailhead at Pinehurst, 33 miles

The water theme continues as the trail leaves the Harrison Trailhead and glides along a glacial valley, past lakes and wetlands, and along the Coeur d'Alene River toward Pinehurst. Follow the trail as it heads north, then east, along Anderson Lake, which branches off from Lake Coeur d'Alene. Visitors are now entering the lake region, where a chain of twelve lakes along the Coeur d'Alene River blanket the area in glistening wetness, supporting wildlife in a moist environment. Sightings of deer, otters, beavers, ospreys, nesting eagles, and other wildlife are common experiences for the alert observer, especially during mornings and evenings.

After leaving the marina in Harrison, you will pass Anderson Lake Wayside at 16.6 miles and cross over a rail trestle. Nesting bald eagles are in this area in spring, as well as osprey nests. The Springston Trailhead appears at 18.3 miles, near the northeast edge of Anderson Lake. Beyond, the Cottonwood picnic site and Gray's Meadow Wayside enhance the next 2.0 miles with rest stop options. On the way you are enveloped in the vibrant green of the nearby hills, the distant mountains, and the wetlands. Beyond lies a 3.5-mile stretch of trail with the potential for sighting Canada geese, great blue herons, and even moose. After Cave Lake Picnic Spot at 24.2 miles, you reach the Medimont Trailhead on Cave Lake at 25.8 miles.

Continue on the trail toward the next picnic and restroom area at Lane, at 29.6 miles. Beyond is Black Rock Trailhead at 31.3 miles, with a parking area and interpretive signs at the Coeur d'Alene River Wildlife Management Area. Idaho Department of Fish and Game oversees about

5,000 acres in the area. The agency has identified more than 200 bird species and 300-plus species of wildlife in the management area.

Beyond the management area the trail passes marshlands. The highway traffic becomes audible as you travel toward the Bull Run Lake Trailhead and restrooms at 33.5 miles. After this trailhead users can access picnic areas at 34.9, 36.3, 38.5, 40.1, and 40.5 miles. Along the way, read about local floods and the river ecosystems that support trout and whitefish.

Be sure to take a break near the Latour Creek picnic area at 40.1 miles or the Old Mission Viewpoint at 40.5 miles, and gaze across the gently flowing Coeur d'Alene River for a view of the historic mission building at Coeur d' Alene's Old Mission State Park. Built during 1850 to 1853, it is acknowledged as one of the oldest buildings still standing in Idaho. The park serves as the trail's headquarters, though it is not accessible from the trail. The Cataldo Trailhead at 42 miles has no services, though I-90 crosses over the trail near this point. There is an RV campground along the trail near 42.0 miles, accessed off I-90.

Leave Cataldo, cross the bridge built over the river in 1902, and continue northeast away from I-90. Pass along the river through a forested stretch where you might see muddy animal prints on the trail. Next are picnic waysides at Pine Meadows at 43.6 miles, Gap Rock at 44.3 miles, and Backwater Bay at 45.6 miles. Meadows grace the trailside with yellow and white flowers in spring, while snow-topped mountains tower in the distance, adding color to the scenery along the trail.

After 45.6 miles the trail crosses the river via another bridge trestle, built in 1924. Shortly the trail moves into the outskirts of the small town of Enaville; the Enaville Trailhead is at 47.0 miles. Carefully cross the trail and highway; anticipate heavy motor vehicle traffic.

If you are hungry, hop off the trail for a bite to eat at the historic Snake Pit Bar and Restaurant in Enaville, off FR 9. They have been in business since 1880. Dine in the rustic timber building or out on the front porch.

Near Enaville, the South Fork and North Fork Coeur d'Alene River join to form the main stem of the Coeur d'Alene, which you have been following for many miles. Leaving Enaville, head up the south fork of the river toward the Pine Creek Trailhead at Pinehurst, at 48.7 miles. Though this paved trailhead does not have a restroom, the town of Pinehurst, a short 0.25 mile away, offers eateries, grocery stores, and a campground, all easily accessed off I-90.

Pine Creek Trailhead at Pinehurst to Mullan, 23 miles

Once the trail departs from the Pine Creek Trailhead, the character of the Trail of the Coeur d'Alenes changes dramatically. It morphs from a nature, water-based trail experience to a history-based journey that moves through numerous old timber and mining towns as it travels near, and right beside, busy I-90. This is not to say that it feels urban. Timbered mountains still surround visitors in a deep green cloak. The distance between restrooms increases along this section of trail, though you can jump off-trail and go into town for restaurants and restrooms.

Heading east from the Pine Creek Trailhead at 48.7 miles, you can keep an eye on I-90 as you approach the Smelterville Trailhead at 51.1 miles. Once there, the most convenient drive-through espresso hut sits right beside the trail, at the trailhead parking lot. A latte and a bagel with cream cheese is a perfect way to launch the forthcoming gentle uphill journey from the local elevation at about 2,100 feet to 3,300 feet in Mullan.

Continue through the industrial area along the trail to the Silver Mountain Trailhead at 53.1 miles, with trailside eateries. This is a busy recreation area year-round. In winter the ski area is in full swing. You can see the gondola passing overhead. Come summer, mountain recreation pursuits are popular, including hiking, mountain biking, and road bicycling.

The interstate shifts across the river at Silver Mountain as the trail picks up along the river. Stay on the trail as it passes through the town of Kellogg and by the Kellogg Depot Trailhead at 53.8 miles. There is a lot of mining history in the area, depicted on the interpretive signs. The best place to learn more about the area is at the Historic Silver Valley Chamber of Commerce visitor center, trailside in Kellogg. Just up the hill, the historic district of the town of Kellogg offers stores, eateries, and a hotel.

Silver Valley, in the Coeur d'Alene region, is about 4 miles wide and 20 miles long. For many years this area produced more silver than anywhere else in the world. Mining materials were carried by rail from the mines to Plummer.

While on this part of the trail, you will find that the bollards at Trail of the Coeur d'Alenes crossings appear a bit different than elsewhere on the route. The trail is merged here with the Silver Valley Trail Route and Kellogg Greenway. Keep following the trail eastward along the mild white water of the South Fork of the Coeur d'Alene River as it rushes west toward the lake region.

Nearby Attractions

A visit to the following sites will round out your visit to the trail:

- Heyburn State Park, (208) 686-1308, www.parksandrec-reation.idaho.gov. Located near Plummer at the western terminus, this is a pleasant park to enjoy hiking, camping, boating, and fishing.

- Coeur d'Alene's Old Mission State Park, (208) 682-3814, www.parksandrecreation.idaho.gov. This day-use park of historical significance is located off I-90, Cataldo exit 39.

- Northern Pacific Railroad Depot and Museum, 219 6th Street, (208) 752-0111, www.npdepot.org. Located in the eastern portion of the trail next to the Wallace Trailhead. Enjoy learning about the railroad and mining history of the area.

- Silver Streak Zipline Tours, (208) 556-1690, www.svrgas.com. Adrenaline seekers ride high above the historic Silver Valley on these tours. Meet at the office in Wallace.

- Sierra Silver Mine Tour, (208) 752-5151, www.silvermine-tour.org. Located in Wallace, this unique mining tour is led by actual miners who demonstrate operating mining equipment, giving the tour a realistic feel.

Elizabeth Park Trailhead is ahead at 55.2 miles. Beyond is a pretty stretch of trail along wooded hillsides near the river, with numerous side creeks contributing water. Milo Creek enters from the south, followed by Big Creek near the Shont Trailhead at 57.4 miles. On this segment you pass by forested mountains and abandoned lumber smelters and into small towns that were once active in lumber and mining industries. All are now within easy access of I-90.

Emerging from the forest, the trail enters the fringes of Osburn and the Osburn Trailhead at 60.4 miles. After leaving the outskirts of Osburn, the trail passes under I-90 and follows directly beside the interstate through another industrial area.

The town of Wallace is ahead, with a trailhead at 6th Street in downtown Wallace, at 64.6 miles. Visit the Northern Pacific Railroad Depot and

Museum just off the trail near the trailhead. In Wallace the trail literally travels under I-90 and along the South Fork of the Coeur d'Alene River, where local residents can walk on the trail out of the weather during rainy season. For a bird's-eye view of the forested historic valley, join a ride with Silver Streak Zipline Tours based out of historic Wallace. Hooked onto metal cables, you'll glide effortlessly from launching stations to landing stations 2,000 feet above the Silver Valley.

Railroads played an important role in this area by supporting the mining and timber industries. The first railroad built in Coeur d'Alene was the Coeur d'Alene Railroad and Navigation Company, which ran from the Old Mission to Wallace in the late 1880s.

Busting out of Wallace and into the woods again, the trail passes by Restless Rapids Wayside at 66.6 miles, and a restroom located near a scenic rapid. Golconda Wayside is just ahead, at 67.7 miles. Continue to the eastern terminus at Mullan at 71.4 miles, an old, still-inhabited mining town with a hotel and restaurant.

From Mullan you can return the way you came. While in the area, consider visiting the Route of the Hiawatha (Trail 35), the North Idaho Centennial Trail (Trail 36), and Northern Pacific Trail (Trail R).

Visit the Northern Pacific Railroad Depot and Museum near the Wallace Trailhead.

35 ROUTE OF THE HIAWATHA RAIL TRAIL

Opened to the public in 1998, the Route of the Hiawatha Rail Trail offers a spectacular amount of variety. It is famous for its tunnels, having the most rail-trail tunnels in the state and the longest tunnel in Idaho (1.66 miles long). Waterfalls, wildlife, seven high rail trestles, and ten tunnels—some in total darkness—await the 70,000 visitors who use the trail each year. One of the ten tunnels is closed to visitors. Dozens of informative interpretive signs enhance the experience by describing local mining, timber, and Milwaukee Road rail history.

Activities:

Location: Near the towns of Wallace, Mullan, and Avery, in Shoshone County

Length: 16.0 miles (Trail users travel 14.4 miles down, take the bus shuttle from Pearson up to Rolland, then bike or walk another 1.6 miles back through the St. Paul Pass Tunnel to their private vehicles at the trailhead.)

Surface: Compacted gravel

Wheelchair access: Motorized electric wheelchairs are allowed on the trail, with access points at all trailheads; however, trail managers advise that most do not have sufficient batteries or large-enough tires to withstand gravel-trail travel.

Difficulty: Easy to moderate

Food: Food is available at Lookout Pass Ski and Recreation Area, East Portal trailhead, and Pearson trailhead. Cash or credit cards accepted.

Restrooms: There are restrooms at Lookout Pass Ski and Recreation Area, East Portal Trailhead, Roland Trailhead, the halfway point at Adair, and Pearson Trailhead.

Seasons: The trail is open for bicycling and hiking seven days a week from Memorial Day weekend until mid-Sept, 8:30 a.m. to 5:00 p.m., Pacific Daylight Time. Opening and closing dates vary depending on snowpack. Peak season is July and Aug. Frequently updated information is available at www.ridethehiawatha.com.

Rentals: Rent mountain bikes, 400-lumen lights, and helmets near the northeastern terminus at Lookout Pass Ski and Recreation Area, (208) 744-1301, www.ridethehiawatha.com. See appendix A for additional bicycle rental options in northern Idaho.

Contacts: Lookout Pass Ski and Recreation Area, (208) 744-1301, www.ridethehiawatha.com, www.skilookout.com; Idaho Panhandle National Forests, St. Joe Ranger District, St. Maries Office, (208) 245-2531, www.fs.usda.gov/ipnf

Bus routes: Shuttle buses run continuously and pick up on a first-come, first-served basis. Possible wait time is up to 45 minutes on busy days. Shuttle buses carry riders and their bicycles from the Pearson Trailhead to the Roland Trailhead, at the west portal of the St. Paul Pass (Taft) Tunnel. Shuttles start at 11:00 a.m. Note the departure time of the last shuttle. On weekdays the last shuttle is at 4:15 p.m. During weekends in July and August, and holidays, it departs at 5:45 p.m. Ninety percent of trail users park their vehicles at the East Portal Trailhead. You will need to ride back through the tunnel to get to your vehicle. Or you can drive your own vehicle to the trailhead of your choice, though this is not recommended on most weekends due to heavy vehicle and camper traffic. For more exercise, ride the trail round-trip instead of one-way. For shuttle information, contact Lookout Pass Ski and Recreation Area, (208) 744-1301, www.ridethehiawatha.com.

Access and parking: The most commonly used access point is at the East Portal Trailhead at the northeast terminus. A smaller parking area for about 20 vehicles is at the Pearson Trailhead at the southwest terminus. Three other access points are also described. A trail-use fee is charged. Purchase passes online at www.ridethehiawatha, at Lookout Pass Ski and Recreation Area, or as a last resort, at the trailheads.

To access the downhill gradient from the northeast terminus, take I-90 east from Mullan toward Lookout Pass Ski and Recreation Area and into Montana toward Missoula. Take exit 5 (the Taft exit) in Montana. The East Portal Trailhead is 2 miles from the Taft exit on a gravel road. Turn right off the ramp, then left onto Rainey Creek Road. Cross a small wooden bridge on Rainey Creek Road and then continue to the right, onto FR 506. Many signs guide you to the East Portal Trailhead and parking areas near the St. Paul Pass (Taft) Tunnel 20. GPS: N47 23.80' / W115 38.09'

The southwest terminus at the Pearson Trailhead is accessed via a rough road about 20 miles from Wallace. Travel on I-90 and take exit 62 on the east side of Wallace. Turn onto Bank Street, heading south into the town of Wallace. Take Bank Street to King Street and turn left. King Street becomes FR 456, also called Moon Pass Road. Follow the rough and dusty dirt road past the intersection with FR 326 on the left, also called Loop Creek Road. Pearson Trailhead is just ahead, located south of the intersection with FR 326, on the east side of FR 456. Going through Wallace takes longer than driving I-90 into Montana, taking Taft at exit 5, and proceeding to the East Portal Trailhead.

To access the Pearson Trailhead from the east end of the town of Avery, drive about 9 miles north on FR 456. The trailhead is on the right, just before the intersection with FR 326. There are two approaches to access the smaller, less-used trailheads at Moss Creek and Roland, located between the East Portal and Pearson Trailheads. From the south, starting at the intersection of FR 456 and FR 326 (the latter of which is also called Loop Creek Road), drive about 3.5 miles on FR 326 to FR 506 and turn left. Follow the dirt road for about 1.5 miles to the 3-to 4-vehicle parking area at Moss Creek Trailhead. The next section of road is also the route of the Hiawatha Trail. Follow it for about 2.3 miles to the Roland Trailhead, with parking for 12 to 15 vehicles, which is near the west portal of the St. Paul Pass (Taft) Tunnel. From Roland Trailhead you can access the East Portal Trailhead by continuing on FR 506. It departs from the Hiawatha Trail at the Roland Trailhead. Drive for about 5 miles on FR 506, going up and over the St. Paul Tunnel and then turning right to get to the East Portal Trailhead in Montana. Watch for signs indicating the trailhead.

To access the southern trailheads from the East Portal Trailhead, leave the parking lot and turn left onto FR 506. Follow FR 506 for about 3.5 miles and turn left into the Roland Trailhead parking lot. For the 3-to 4-vehicle parking area at the Moss Creek Trailhead, continue about 2.3 miles on FR 506 and park on the left. There is additional parking at a third, lesser-used site at Adair, between Tunnels 25 and 26. Access Adair by taking FR 326 east from the intersection with FR 506. Go about 3 miles into the parking lot. For the southwest terminus at the Pearson Trailhead, continue on FR 506 to the intersection with FR 326 and turn right. Continue on FR 326, also called Loop Creek Road, to the intersection with FR 456. Turn left, go about 0.5 mile, and turn left again. Go 0.25 mile to the Pearson Trailhead.

|||||||||||||||||||||||||||||||||||||||||||||||||||||||||||||||||||||||||||||||||||||||

Travelers come from as far away as New Zealand, Australia, and Japan to enjoy this trail. If you want to take the quick, scenic route to the Pearson Trailhead and enjoy the downhill grade, allow 3 to 4 hours to complete the route if on a bicycle, and 30 minutes for the shuttle ride back to the Roland Trailhead. For the bicyclist desiring more of a physical challenge or wanting to avoid a shuttle, start at Pearson Trailhead and ride the uphill 2 percent grade to East Portal. Stop to read the interpretive signs along the way and catch your breath. At the trailhead at East Portal, turn around and relax during the downhill ride back to Pearson. You will have completed a 30-mile round-trip.

When you buy your trail pass at Lookout Pass Ski and Recreation Area or at a trailhead from a trail marshal, you will get a briefing. It is mandatory that each rider and hiker use a quality light (300–400 lumens minimum). Helmets and lights are mandatory for bicyclists. You can rent bicycles, helmets, and lights from Lookout Pass Ski and Recreation Area.

The railroad bed that you will be traveling on was originally built between 1906 and 1911. Known as the Pacific extension of the Chicago, Milwaukee & St. Paul Railroad, the line ran until it went bankrupt in 1977. This is a section of the abandoned Milwaukee Road, which went from Chicago to Seattle, crossing Montana and northern Idaho. Volunteers and government agencies converted the rails to a compacted recreation trail for bicyclists and hikers. Dogs, horses, and other pets are not allowed on the trail.

Along the route, you pass a variety of trees and plants, such as Douglas fir, white pine, maple, white ash, and huckleberries. Deer, elk, and moose roam freely on and off the trail. En route, water, restrooms, and picnic tables are provided for riders' comfort.

If starting at mile 0 at the East Portal Trailhead, you encounter the 1.66-mile-long St. Paul Pass (Taft) Tunnel, which crosses between Montana and Idaho. This is the most popular beginning point. The cold, wet, and

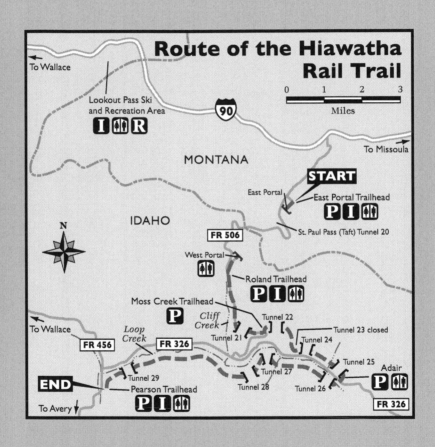

Route of the Hiawatha Rail Trail

To Wallace

Lookout Pass Ski and Recreation Area

I 👫 **R**

90

MONTANA

IDAHO

N

0   1   2   3
Miles

To Missoula

START

East Portal

East Portal Trailhead

P I 👫

St. Paul Pass (Taft) Tunnel 20

FR 506

West Portal

👫

Roland Trailhead

P I 👫

Moss Creek Trailhead

P

Cliff Creek

Tunnel 22

Tunnel 21

Tunnel 23 closed

Tunnel 24

To Wallace

Loop Creek

FR 456

FR 326

Tunnel 25

Adair

P 👫

Tunnel 27

Tunnel 29

END

Pearson Trailhead

Tunnel 28

Tunnel 26

FR 326

To Avery

P I 👫

A mountain biker reads an interpretive sign beside the St. Paul Pass (Taft) Tunnel 20 at the West Portal in Idaho. It is the longest tunnel on the trail.

totally dark tunnel is one of the many highlights on this trail. Be sure to have a good bike light or headlamp with you, not just any flashlight. Rent a bright light from the Lookout Pass Ski and Recreation Area if you need one. When you get deeper into this tunnel, all the light disappears; you will rely on your tiny light to see while bicycling or walking. The brighter the light, the better you will be able to see. It can be very disorienting in complete darkness. Some of the tunnels ahead have reflectors to help guide you through the dark. The average temperature in the various tunnels ranges from 46°F to 48°F, so you might need an extra layer of clothing, especially for this first tunnel.

As you pass through the St. Paul Pass (Taft) Tunnel, watch for the interpretive sign on the wall indicating the Montana–Idaho border. At the end of the tunnel, you emerge into what seems like the intensely bright light of day. You are now in Idaho and approaching the Roland Trailhead at 1.8 miles. Ultimately, you return to this trailhead via the shuttle service and retrace your route through the St. Paul Pass (Taft) Tunnel to the East Portal

Trailhead and your vehicle. If you're uncomfortable with this long tunnel and decide to avoid it, there is parking at the Roland Trailhead. Be aware that driving over Roland Summit is challenging; it lacks guardrails, and isn't recommended.

The many interpretive signs along the trail describe the history, culture, geology, and biology of the area. You will traverse nine tunnels, ranging from the 8,771-foot-long tunnel at the start to shorter, brighter tunnels of 178 feet. Additionally, you will pass over seven expansive, high trestles that afford wide-open views of the surrounding forests and valley.

Leave the Roland Trailhead, where FR 506 joins the trail for the next 2.3 miles, and head south toward Tunnel 21, located at 3.2 miles. Motor vehicles use Tunnel 21, so be sure your light is on and proceed cautiously. It is the only tunnel you will share with vehicles. If you hear a beeping sound, get off your bike and proceed behind the protective heavy jersey barriers. The beep signals a vehicle is passing slowly through the tunnel. After you exit Tunnel 21, stop at the scenic viewpoint on the west side to look down at the green panoramas of the Bitterroot Mountains in Idaho

Nearby Attractions

- Lookout Pass Ski and Recreation Area, (208) 744-1301, www.ridethehiawatha.com. Located just off I-90 at exit 0, the area serves as headquarters for the Route of the Hiawatha. Trail passes, shuttles, rentals, and food services are available. Trail passes are required for all users age 5 and older; children 4 and under go free. You can also purchase passes at trailheads from the trail marshals. Annual passes are available. Receive a 10 percent discount for groups of 15 or more registering together. There is a fee to ride the shuttle for all passengers age 5 and older. Sack lunches are available, as are bike helmet and light rentals.

- Get wet by whitewater rafting on the St. Joe, Moyie, and Lochsa Rivers with ROW Adventures, (800) 451-6034, www.rowadventures.com.

and Montana. You can see the route you are following and the steel trestles you will cross, nestled in the Idaho Panhandle National Forests.

The trail departs from the road at Moss Creek Trailhead before Tunnel
22. To avoid confusion between Tunnels 21 and 22, think as though you
were a train. Head straight toward Tunnel 22 so that you do not inadver-
tently follow FR 506 as it turns sharply downhill. At 4.1 miles you'll enter
Tunnel 22. This is the second-longest tunnel on the route. It is 1,516 feet
long, and you can see some daylight at the end of the tunnel. Within a
mile you will encounter a closed tunnel, number 23. Take the brief bypass
around it and head into a short tunnel, number 24, which runs for 377 feet.

When you arrive at 5.3 miles, you cross Trestle 216 at Small Creek. It is
515 feet long and 120 feet high. Immediately after this trestle you travel
over Trestle 218 at Barnes Creek, which is slightly smaller, at 507 feet long
and 117 feet high.

After negotiating the first two trestles, take a break at 5.8 miles and
read about the forest fire of 1910. Just ahead is Trestle 220 over Kelly
Creek, at 6.1 miles. Enjoy the passage; it Is the longest and tallest trestle
on the trail, measuring 850 feet long and 230 feet high. Continue downhill
toward the halfway point at Adair, at 6.9 miles and 3,707 feet elevation.
Trail users have moved steadily downhill from the 4,147-foot elevation at
the East Portal Trailhead.

At 7.0 miles you will encounter the 966-foot-long Tunnel 25, immediately followed by the 683-foot-long Tunnel 26. Between the two tunnels
you pass the Adair Trailhead, with the last restroom on the trail until the
Pearson Trailhead, and cross over the dirt FR 326.

Beyond Tunnel 26 are four trestles spread over 1.4 miles. If you are not
used to the heights yet, you will be soon. Cross over Turkey Creek, Russell/
No Name, Bear Creek, and Clear Creek, identified as Trestles 224, 226, 228,
and 230. They range from 281 feet to 760 feet long and from 96 feet to 220
feet high and provide a contrast to the back-to-back tunnels.

Trestles on the route have an interesting history. After the forest fire
of 1910, smaller wooden trestles were converted into earth-filled trestles
that could withstand a fire. Thus, there are many trestles that trail users
ride over that do not appear to be trestles. There are an estimated thirty
trestles of this nature on the trail.

Between 9.8 and 14.4 miles, the trail passes through three short tunnels, ranging in length from 178 to 470 feet long. At 10.6 miles the trail

passes near the historic mining towns of Falcon and Grand Forks, though no buildings remain.

At mile 14.4 you will pull in to the final trailhead at Pearson. Trail marshals bring 5-gallon containers of drinking water to the trailheads at Pearson, Moss Creek, Roland, East Portal, and Adair. If it is a hot day, they may have run out of water, so carry your own just in case. From the Pearson Trailhead you can pick up the shuttle back to the Roland Trailhead, or turn around and retrace the trail 14.4 miles back to the East Portal trailhead where you parked.

Future Plans

Plans are to extend the trail 31 miles on the western Montana side, with segments specifically designated for multiuse by hikers, mountain bikers, horses, all-terrain vehicles, snowmobiles, and passenger vehicles. Named the Route of the Olympian Rail Trail, the trail goes on the abandoned Milwaukee Railroad grade running from the existing Route of the Hiawatha's East Portal Trailhead from the back of the parking lot eastward to St. Regis, Montana. Currently, the Route of the Olympian Rail Trail supporters are striving to resolve challenges regarding a key trestle privately owned and in need of major repairs. If acquired, this trestle will help to connect St. Regis with the Route of the Hiawatha.

The Route of the Hiawatha is identified for inclusion in a connected loop of trails in the Idaho Panhandle, creating a large network of trails by joining existing rail trails. The Trail of the Coeur d'Alenes presently links with the Northern Pacific Trail in Mullan. Ultimately the Northern Pacific Trail will join the Route of the Hiawatha, which will then hook up with the Old Milwaukee Road and then the Trail of the Coeur d'Alenes near St. Maries.

While in the northern Panhandle, take in the Trail of the Coeur d'Alenes (Trail 34), the North Idaho Centennial Trail (Trail 36), and the Northern Pacific Trail (Trail R).

36 NORTH IDAHO CENTENNIAL TRAIL

A highlight of this trail is that it runs primarily along the Spokane River and Lake Coeur d'Alene. Trail users journey near I-90, pass through the conifers of northern Idaho, and go through the towns of Post Falls and Coeur d'Alene, ultimately finishing along the scenic Coeur d'Alene Lake Drive.

Activities:

Location: Post Falls and Coeur d'Alene, in Kootenai County in the northern Idaho Panhandle

Length: 24 miles (21.9-mile trail plus western terminus 2.1-mile spur)

Surface: Asphalt and public roads

Wheelchair access: The trail is wheelchair-accessible but slopes steeply near the Huetter Rest Area Trailhead, with 10 percent grades uphill and downhill.

Difficulty: Easy, with a few grades on the western and eastern ends

Food: There are many eateries just off the trail in Post Falls and Coeur d'Alene.

Restrooms: You'll find restrooms along the trail at the western trailhead (the I-90 Stateline rest area in Washington) and at the Huetter Rest Area, Seltice Way, Rutledge, and Higgens Point Trailheads. Additional restrooms and water are available at parks just off the trail on the western segment, including Corbin Park, Falls Park, and Coeur d'Alene City Park Beach. The eastern section along Coeur d'Alene Lake Drive between Rutledge Trailhead and Higgens Point has five wayside restrooms in a 4.5-mile stretch. All sites are wheelchair-accessible.

Seasons: The trail can be used year-round.

Rentals: Bicycles, cross-country skis, and snowshoes are available to rent at Vertical Earth, 1323 East Sherman Avenue, Coeur d'Alene, (208) 667-5503, www.verticalearth.com.

Contacts: North Idaho Centennial Trail Foundation, www.nictf.org; Idaho Department of Parks and Recreation-Farragut State Park, (208) 683-2425; Post Falls Chamber of Commerce, (800) 292-2553, www.visitpostfalls.org; Coeur d'Alene Chamber of Commerce, (208) 664-3194, www.cdachamber. com; City of Coeur d'Alene, www.cdaid.org

Bus routes: For information call City Link at (877) 941-RIDE (7433), or Kootenai County Transit Services at (208) 446-2255, or visit https://www. kcgov.us/486/Transit-Services.

Access and parking: There are many places to access the trail along I-90. This description begins from the western terminus, at the Idaho–Washington border in Washington: If coming from the east on I-90 from Post Falls, take exit 299 (Stateline) off I-90, just over the Idaho–Washington border in Washington. Turn right off the exit onto Spokane Bridge Road, then turn left into the interstate rest area located near Gateway Park. When coming from Washington, take exit 299 off I-90, turn left onto Spokane Bridge Road, and then left again into the rest area. Access the spur trail on the northeast side of the interstate rest area. GPS: N47 41.82' / W117 03.14'

Higgens Point Trailhead: This is the eastern terminus of the trail. From Rutledge Trailhead continue east for 4.5 miles on Coeur d'Alene Lake Drive to the large parking areas at the end of the road.

||||||||||||||||||||||||||||||||||||||||||||||||||||||||||||||||||||||||||||||||||||||||||||||||||||

Selected as Idaho's Millennium Legacy Trail, this route symbolizes a piece of Idaho's heritage. It offers a pleasing mix of urban settings against the backdrop of the Spokane River and Lake Coeur d'Alene. This trail allows for visits to local parks and an array of convenient food stops. Open year-round, the trail is nonmotorized, though parts of it are bike lanes or on local roads. The trail is managed by a partnership between Kootenai County, the Idaho Department of Transportation, the cities of Post Falls and Coeur d'Alene, and the North Idaho Centennial Trail Foundation. Frequent signage keeps trail users oriented.

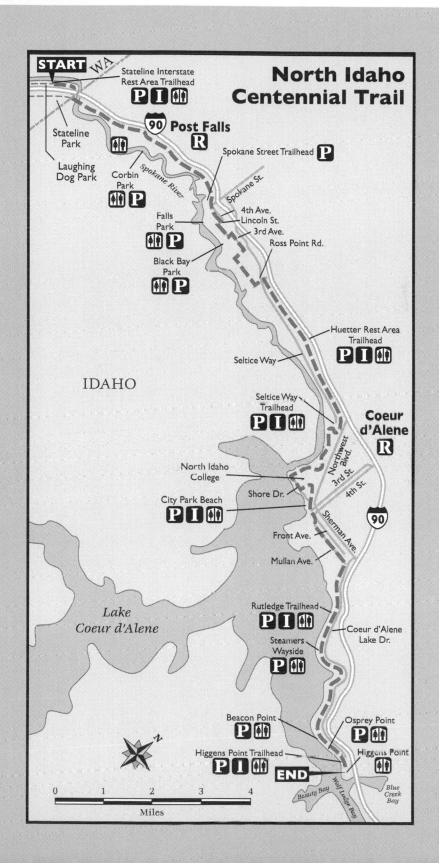

During your excursion, take in the overlook at Falls Park on the Spokane River near the town of Post Falls on the North Idaho Centennial Trail.

North Idaho Centennial Trail's western terminus is accessed at the interstate rest area in Washington just off I-90, near where the North Idaho Centennial Trail joins the Spokane River Centennial Trail. During your trail adventure you'll travel east along the Spokane River, through the towns of Post Falls and Coeur d' Alene, and along the shoreline of Lake Coeur d'Alene.

A trail realignment project at the Stateline rest area near Gateway Park moved the trail away from vehicle traffic. You can pick up the spur trail leading to the official start of the North Idaho Centennial from a variety of parking areas along the river on the north side of the Gateway Park, the interstate rest area, and the Patricia Simonet Laughing Dog Park.

The start of your journey involves a 1.2-mile U-shaped spur trail that leads to the North Idaho Centennial Trail and avoids road traffic. Follow the spur trail eastward as it passes between the river and East Appleway Avenue, then beneath the East Apple Avenue overpass. The trail then veers south, travels under the I-90 overpass, and heads west. Take a left turn off the spur and onto the North Idaho Centennial Trail's start on the south side of I-90.

North Idaho Centennial Trail mile markers described below begin at the Idaho–Washington border and ascend eastward. Shortly after passing the Idaho–Washington border you'll cross a rail bridge over the Spokane River. About 0.2 mile from the border, you will be at Idaho's Stateline Park, accessible only by trail.

Continue east with I-90 to your left. The Greyhound Park and Events Center comes into view. After 2 miles there is a busy road intersection. At this point the trail crosses diagonally to the left, resuming beside the Sleep Inn. An educational sign trailside describes the Pleasant View Road Railroad Trestle and Pleasant View Bridge. After you pass this area, the trail becomes a bit more rural and crosses small streets.

At about 3.2 miles, read about McGuires Junction, which served as a major intersection on the Milwaukee Road rail line. Two rails formed the junction. The Coeur d'Alene branch, formerly called the Coeur d'Alene Electric Line, headed east. The Metaline Falls branch, previously the Idaho & Washington Northern Railroad, traveled north.

Trail scenery gets even better at trail mile marker 4.0, where the river comes into view again and you can see the waterfalls in the distance. An interpretive sign describes a community member, D. C. Corbin, who built many of the railroads in this area.

Beyond the viewpoint the trail crosses a small road and runs along an active rail track. At this location Post Falls is easily accessed, as are restaurants just off the trail. Just before 5.0 miles, trail users cross five-lane Spokane Street. If you want a close-up view of the falls, turn right on Spokane Street and go about 0.2 mile into Falls Park. Stroll near the top of the waterfalls, and enjoy the mist of the Spokane River as it plunges 40 feet over rocks. Return to the intersection of the trail and Spokane Street.

To continue east on the trail, cross the rail tracks and follow the well-signed path along the tracks. The trail turns right onto a bike lane on Lincoln Street. Continue to a stop sign and turn left onto 3rd Avenue. Continue along the bike lane for 0.5 mile, still following the encouraging Centennial Trail signs. At about 6.0 miles the trail starts again on the left. Black Bay Park is to the right on a side trail. It offers restrooms, nature trails, shade trees, and a beach.

After the 6.0-mile mark, the trail moves more deeply into Post Falls, a city that was founded by Frederick Post. It's easy to jump off-trail and grab a bite to eat at one of the many nearby eateries. Between miles 7.0 and 8.0 the trail becomes a road path through a residential area. It resumes as a trail at the intersection of Ross Point Road and Seltice Way, at about 8.5 miles.

Cross the big intersection and join the trail as it climbs to run parallel with I-90 again, through a tree-shaded area. Grades in the range of 6, 8, and 10 percent greet trail users as they approach a major trailhead at the Huetter Rest Area, at 10.0 miles. Take in the shade, the visitor center, and the restrooms before continuing east on the trail.

After you leave the rest stop, you travel above the Spokane River valley and along I-90. Mountains that serve as a backdrop harbor native conifers, including Douglas fir, Engelmann spruce, western red cedar, ponderosa pine, western larch, and many other species.

Near 12.0 miles, enjoy the downhill grade as you approach the valley. North Idaho College and extension campuses of the University of Idaho, Boise State University, and Lewis and Clark College are located nearby. A few street detours, following Centennial Trail signs, will take you past the Seltice Way Trailhead at 13.0 miles, then across a big intersection and through an industrial area. Watch for the educational signs describing the extensive timber and rail history in this area. Between miles 14.0 and 16.0, the trail winds along the Spokane River, through the North Idaho College campus, and onto Shore Drive. Once on Shore Drive, the trail is along the lake. Soon you'll pass through Coeur d'Alene City Park Beach, by Coeur d'Alene Plaza, and past the city's marina facilities.

A quick visit to downtown Coeur d'Alene and its restaurants is convenient at this point. The fee parking lot is at 16.0 miles. Watch for Centennial Trail signs as the trail winds through residential areas after mile 16.0.

The trail follows Mullan Avenue and turns right at about 17.25 miles, hooking up with Coeur d'Alene Lake Drive and a distinct, separate trail route. At this point the trail changes out of its city mode and into a linear state park managed by Farragut State Park and the Idaho Department of Parks and Recreation. This linear park offers 1,000 feet of shoreline, a mile-long fitness trail, scenic overlooks, wide-open views of the lake, and glimpses of wildlife.

Rutledge Trailhead, at about 18.5 miles, is the formal start of this pleasant section. Even though the trail runs parallel to Coeur d'Alene Lake Drive, it feels relaxed and rural. Bird sightings are common in the area. Watch for great blue herons, ospreys, bald eagles, common mergansers, and American tree sparrows.

As you head to Higgens Point, the eastern terminus, ponder the fact that Lake Coeur d'Alene is 23 miles long and offers 109 miles of shoreline. The Spokane River is the western outlet of the lake.

Heading east there are plenty of waysides at which you can picnic, rest, use the restroom, and enjoy the peaceful scenery. You will pass Steamers Wayside at about 19.25 miles. Booth Park is just past 21.0 miles. Beacon Point, Osprey Point, and finally, the eastern terminus trailhead, are between miles 22.0 and 23.0.

Marina parking is at the end of the road and requires a day-use fee, or park for free at the end of the road. The paved trail continues about 0.25 mile more, uphill to Higgens Point, where a park sits at the top of the knoll. On the side of the trail before you climb up the final hill, there are two viewing scopes. These are great for bird watching and gazing at the boating activity on the lake. At the flat top of Higgens Point, take in the panoramic view of Blue Creek Bay, Wolf Lodge Bay, and Beauty Bay. Foot trails lead off the point, down to the beach, and back to the paved trail. When you are done, return the way you came. Along the trail between Higgens Point, Rutledge Trailhead, and eastern Coeur d'Alene are various eateries.

While in the area, consider visiting the Spokane River Centennial Trail (Trail 25), the Trail of the Coeur d'Alenes (Trail 34), or the Route of the Hiawatha Rail Trail (Trail 35).

37 LATAH TRAIL

This is a rail trail with an adventurous feel. Visitors pass through forested areas and open grain fields and travel near ID 8 as it heads from the rural town of Troy to the university town of Moscow in the Palouse region of north-central Idaho.

Activities:

Location: Troy and Moscow, in Latah County

Length: 11.0 miles, plus a 3.3-mile trail option westward to the University of Idaho campus and the Bill Chipman Palouse Trail, and a 4.5-mile trail option southeast from Troy

Surface: Asphalt

Wheelchair access: This trail is wheelchair-accessible.

Difficulty: Easy to moderate

Food: Restaurants, grocery stores, and gas stations are in each town.

Restrooms: Public restrooms are located at the Troy City Park, near the trail summit off Dutch Flat Road along the trail, at the trailhead located approximately 4 miles from Troy on ID 8, at the parking area near Carmichael Road, and the Berman Creekside Park on the Paradise Path in Moscow.

Seasons: The trail can be used year-round.

Rentals: For bicycle rentals and repairs in Moscow, try Paradise Creek Bicycles, 513 South Main Street, (208) 882-0703. You can rent snowshoes and cross-country skis in Moscow from the University of Idaho's Outdoor Program at their Outdoor Rental Center in the Student Recreation Center, 1000 Paradise Creek Street, (208) 885-6170, https://www.uidaho.edu/current-students/recwell/outdoor-program/rental-center.

Contacts: Latah Trail Foundation, (208) 874-3860, www.latahtrailfoundation.org; Moscow Parks and Recreation Department, (208) 883-7085, www.ci.moscow.id.us; Outdoor Program, University of Idaho, (208) 885-6810, https://www.uidaho.edu/current-students/recwell/outdoor-program;

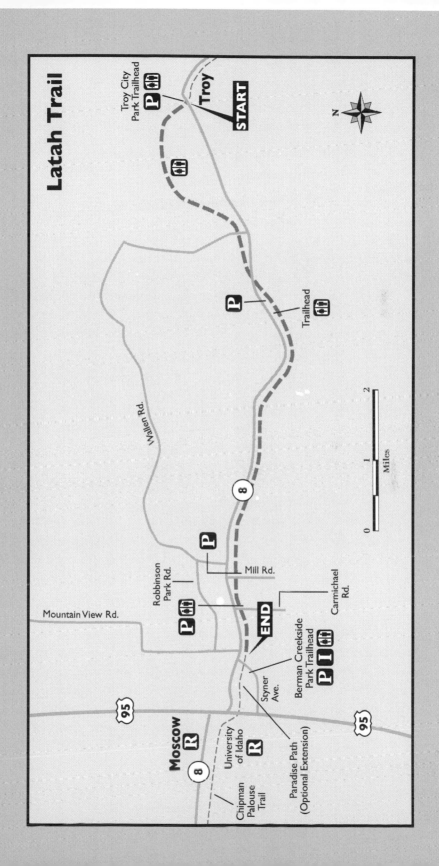

Moscow Chamber of Commerce, (208) 882-1800, www.moscowchamber. com; Moscow Area Mountain Bike Association, www.mambatrails.org

Bus routes: Smart Transit runs in Moscow Mon through Fri. Call (208) 883-7747 or visit www.smarttransit.org/.

Access and parking: There are several access points along ID 8. To reach the trailhead in Troy, take ID 8 east from the intersection of US 95 and ID 8 in Moscow. Drive 12.1 miles to Troy, turning left into Troy City Park. The trailhead begins on the west side of the park's parking lot. GPS: N46 44.20' / W116 46.54'

To park near the trail's western terminus, use the trailhead located on the southeast side of Carmichael Road off ID 8. There is another parking spot 11.8 miles out of Troy at the junction of US 95 and ID 8.

Troy to Moscow, 11 miles

Whatever season you visit the Latah Trail, you are in for a treat. During spring, shamrock-green grain fields glisten in the sunshine while meadowlarks chirp and a cool breeze blows. In late summer and autumn, miles of fields of ripe yellow grain ripple in the wind. When winter arrives, snow-covered trails encourage snowshoers and cross-country skiers to journey between Troy and Moscow.

The Latah Trail is a rolling pathway along the former Moscow–Arrow Rail Line. It passes through stands of timber and farmland, and along ID 8. Ultimately it connects with the Bill Chipman Palouse Trail, which travels from Moscow to the Idaho–Washington border and to Pullman, Washington.

As you travel between the two cities on the Latah Trail, the mile-marker numbers ascend based on your direction of travel. Either direction you go, you start at zero. Start in a forested area in the small town of Troy at the trailhead at Troy City Park, at trail mile marker 0. The first 2 miles you will swing away from the highway and up an incline, with glimpses of open meadows and distant forested hilltops. By 2.2 miles you will see a trail sign declaring "Summit." Take a break at the bench for a well-earned rest.

Continue through farmland to 3.5 miles, where ID 8 comes back into view. At 3.6 miles you reach a refurbished railroad trestle over Wallen Road.

The overpass tunnel under ID 8 serves as a place to get out of the sun, wind, or rain while traveling the Latah Trail between Troy and Moscow.

By 3.7 miles you will be traveling near the highway, a bit of a surprise after the remote portion at the start of the trail. From 4.4 miles the trail moves smoothly through an underpass, keeping trail users safe from the rigors of ID 8. It's a good place to stop and get out of the sun, wind, or rain for a break. Note the parts of the old stone overpass bridge repurposed into benches.

Given the rural nature of the trail, birders are usually in luck. Meadowlarks, ospreys, and Canada geese are no strangers to this trail. At 4.9 miles you will come to a trailhead with paved parking and restrooms, located on ID 8. From that point the trail moves downhill for over 1 mile to Katsam Crossing, at 6.1 miles. Grain silos and elevators soon loom into view. Continue heading through the rural countryside toward Moscow.

Between miles 9.0 and 9.2, the trail takes a sharp left turn and traverses uphill through cultivated fields until it reaches a knoll. The trail levels out a bit, with intermittent roads crossing over the trail as you approach the urban area of Moscow.

The strong winds that blow along this stretch can either help or hinder you. The posted suggested speed limit is 15 mph on all the trails, and you are wise to follow it, due to the intermittent farm and construction equipment crossings on the western end of the trail.

At about 10.0 miles you'll see the golf course along the highway. A "Welcome to Moscow, Home of the University of Idaho" sign turns up at 10.6 miles. If you continue on the trail, a cemetery can be spotted across the highway. By 12.0 miles you will find restaurants, a grocery store, and shops at the Eastside Marketplace, just off the trail.

The official end of the Latah Trail is the county line near Carmichael Road off ID 8. For an additional 3.3-mile ride, take the Paradise Path west to the eastern edge of the University of Idaho campus, then continue through the campus and to the eastern terminus of the Bill Chipman Palouse Trail.

You can extend your visit on the Latah Trail from Troy City Park by crossing ID 8 and picking up a 1-mile paved trail the county owns and maintains. It runs eastward behind the lumber yard and crosses ID 99. The Latah Trail continues southward as a 3.5-mile paved trail through Bear Creek Canyon, heading toward Kendrick.

Optional Extension: Latah Trail to Paradise Path to Bill Chipman Palouse Trail, 3.3 miles

To pick up the Bill Chipman Palouse Trail, continue past Carmichael Road and Mountain View Road. The trail connects smoothly with the Paradise Path, which in turn connects with the Bill Chipman Palouse Trail. The Paradise Path winds through parts of Moscow and the University of Idaho campus before hooking up with the well-marked Bill Chipman Palouse Trail.

If you are continuing from Troy, at about 12.5 miles the trail briefly sweeps off the original railbed for a detour into a neighborhood park, Berman Creekside Park. It's an excellent place to use as a trailhead, with a wheelchair-accessible toilet, water fountains, and paved parking. Additionally, interpretive signs describe butterflies, wetlands, and riparian zones. Continue toward the right along the creek when the trail splits, and meet up with the original railbed again.

At about 12.8 miles grain elevators come into sight, and, shortly after, the University of Idaho campus. Cross US 95 to get on the Paradise Path

Nearby Attractions

- Colter's Creek Winery, 215 South Main Street, Moscow, (208) 301-5125, www.colterscreek.com.

- The Alehouse, 226 West 6th Street, Moscow, (208) 882-BREW (2739). Consider refreshing yourself here after a trip on the local trails.

paved trail at the university. Once on the edge of the campus, follow the signs for the Paradise Path along the creek on the edge of the campus and across an assortment of campus roads. On the way, at about 13.4 miles, you'll cross another campus entrance at 6th Street. The trail continues, passing by the Student Recreation Center, which houses the University of Idaho Outdoor Program. You can rent cross-country skis or snowshoes here during winter.

Continue on the campus trail past soccer and baseball fields, and finally reach the Bill Chipman Palouse Trail on the west side of campus at the intersection of ID 8 and Perimeter Drive, across from the Palouse Mall.

When you are ready, turn around and return to the Latah Trail and Troy. As you travel on the Latah Trail from Moscow to Troy, the mile-marker numbers ascend in number, just as they did on your trip from Troy to Moscow.

While you are in the Moscow area, experience the Bill Chipman Palouse Trail (Trail 38) and the Ed Corkill Memorial River Trail (Trail 39). Additionally, there are miles of excellent singletrack mountain bike trails on Moscow Mountain.

Future Plans

There are plans to further develop the old gravel railbed through the beautiful and remote Bear Creek Canyon from the town of Troy, near the intersection of ID 99 and ID 8, to Kendrick. Once finished, the trail would connect with the Ed Corkill Memorial River Trail, completing an uninterrupted trail system from Pullman, Washington, through Moscow to Juliaetta.

38 BILL CHIPMAN PALOUSE TRAIL: MOSCOW, IDAHO

Running from one university town to another, this trail is a well-used urban commuter option featuring detailed interpretive signs about railroad lore and local history.

Activities:

Location: City of Moscow, Latah County, in north-central Idaho; city of Pullman, Whitman County, in eastern Washington

Length: 1.0 mile in Idaho; 6.0 miles in Washington

Surface: Asphalt

Wheelchair access: The wheelchair-accessible trailheads include the Sunshine Trailhead and the terminuses at Moscow, Idaho, and Pullman, Washington.

Difficulty: Easy

Food: Eateries, gas stations, and grocery stores are near the trailheads in Moscow, Idaho, and Pullman, Washington.

Restrooms: Emergency phones and restrooms are located near trail miles 1.5, 4.0, and 5.0 as measured from the western terminus in Pullman.

Seasons: The trail can be used year-round.

Rentals: In Moscow, bicycles can be rented at Paradise Creek Bicycles, 513 South Main Street, (208) 882-0703, https://paradisecreekbicycles.com/. Snowshoes and cross-country skis can be rented from the University of Idaho's Outdoor Program at their Outdoor Rental Center in the Student Recreation Center, 1000 Paradise Creek Street, (208) 885-6170, https://www.uidaho.edu/current-students/recwell/outdoor-program/rental-center.

Contacts: Pullman Civic Trust, https://www.pullmancivictrust.org/trails; University of Idaho, Outdoor Program, (208) 885-6810, https://www.uidaho.edu/current-students/recwell/outdoor-program; Whitman County Parks and Recreation in Washington, (509) 397-6238, https://whitman-county.org/362/County-Parks

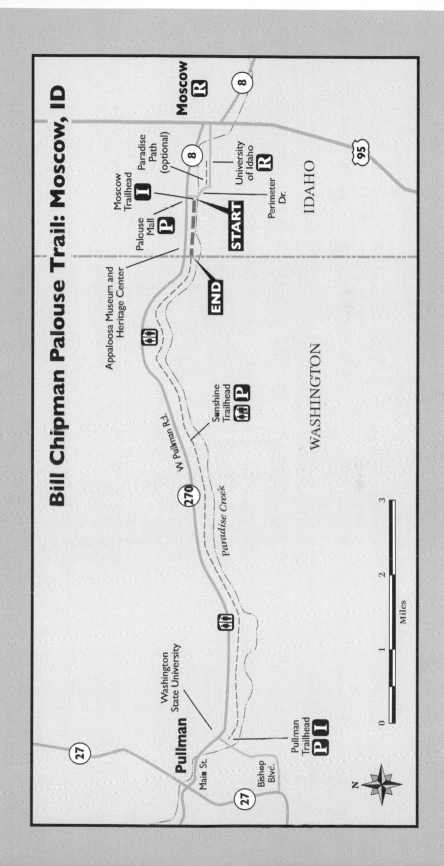

Bill Chipman Palouse Trail: Moscow, ID

Bus routes: For Moscow routes, contact SMART Transit, (208) 883-7747, www.smarttransit.org. For the Moscow-to-Pullman route, contact Star Line Luxury Coaches / Wheatland Express, (509) 334-2200, www.wheat-landexpress.com.

Access and parking: To start in Moscow at the eastern terminus of the trail, take ID 8 west from the junction of US 95 and ID 8, which becomes ID 270 at Perimeter Drive. (ID 270 is locally called West Pullman Road.) Turn right into the Palouse Mall shopping center at the intersection of Perimeter Drive and ID 270. Park on the eastern edge of the mall, cross ID 270, and start on the trail at the replica of a railroad station shelter and the kiosk. GPS: N46 43.94' / W117 01.52'

You can find free parking on the University of Idaho campus on weekends and evenings. Visitor parking permits are available for a fee at the parking office on campus at 1006 Railroad Street. Call (208) 885-6424 or visit https://aims.parking.uidaho.edu. Metered parking spots also are available.

E ven though only 1 mile is on the Idaho side, this 7-mile trail is worth a visit for all the rail history you can learn along the way. A jaunt for the whole distance into Pullman, Washington, extends the trip. You will be counting trail mile markers from the start at 7.0 miles, descending to 0 mile at the western terminus in Pullman, Washington.

Begin your journey on this popular trail by reading the kiosk information at the rail station replica that stands as the eastern terminus. Frequent benches, portable toilets, and emergency phones smooth the way for visitors. Educational signs along the way inform trail users about railroad lingo and other Palouse region tidbits. For example, *station* is a train stop; a *depot* is similar, but always with a smaller building. Another interesting fact is that the area produces the majority of peas and lentils grown in the United States. This is due to the Palouse region's warm, dry summers and rich soils.

Dedicated in 1998, the trail is part of the federal rails-to-trails program. It is jointly managed by the cities of Moscow and Pullman, the University of Idaho, Washington State University, and Whitman County, Washington.

The eastern terminus of the Bill Chipman Palouse Trail is located in Moscow, Idaho.

The trail was named in honor of Bill Chipman, an important community member who was killed in a vehicle accident in 1996.

In 1885 the first railroad cars arrived in Moscow, having traveled from the Snake River. Five years later, in 1890, the Northern Pacific Railway completed a parallel line that linked Moscow to Pullman and Spokane. Between 1919 and the 1950s, the train line carried students to the University of Idaho from all over the state. It was called the Silver and Gold Student Special.

The trail quickly leaves Moscow, traveling alongside ID 270. Within 1 mile of the trailhead, you cross the border between Idaho and Washington. Your options are to continue on the Bill Chipman Palouse Trail (Trail 26), 6 miles farther into Pullman, Washington, or return to Moscow. Consider visiting the Appaloosa Museum before you leave Idaho. It is easily accessed off the trail by crossing the highway at the state border.

Paradise Path in Moscow and spur trails in Pullman connect to the Bill Chipman Palouse Trail.

While you are in Latah County, try the Latah Trail (Trail 37), which starts on the east side of the University of Idaho campus in east Moscow, and the Ed Corkill Memorial River Trail (Trail 39), southeast of Moscow.

Nearby Attractions

Appaloosa Museum, 2720 West Pullman Road, Moscow; Appaloosa Horse Club / Appaloosa phone at (208) 882-5578, www.appaloosamuseum.com. Visit the live Appaloosa horse exhibit in summer.

39 ED CORKILL MEMORIAL RIVER TRAIL

Rural in nature, this trail winds beside two small towns as it runs along the Potlatch River and amid lush vegetation. It follows the original Northern Pacific / Burlington Northern Moscow–Arrow rail line in west-central Idaho.

Activities:

Location: In the towns of Juliaetta and Kendrick, in Latah County

Length: 5.3 miles

Surface: Asphalt

Wheelchair access: The trail is wheelchair-accessible.

Difficulty: Easy

Food: There is a gas station, plus grocery stores and restaurants near the trail in the rural towns of Juliaetta and Kendrick.

Restrooms: There are restrooms at the eastern trailhead at the Juliaetta Centennial Park in Juliaetta and at the Kendrick City RV Park next to the trail at 805 Railroad Street.

Seasons: The trail can be used year-round.

Rentals: None in this rural area. See appendix A for bike rentals in Latah County.

Contacts: Kendrick City Hall, (208) 289-5157, www.cityofkendrick.com; Juliaetta City Hall, (208) 276-7791; Kendrick–Juliaetta and the 7 Ridges, www.Kendrick-Juliaetta.org

Bus routes: None

Access and parking: Take US 95 north from Lewiston, exiting onto US 12. Travel east to ID 3; turn left and go 8.2 miles to the southern terminus trailhead, located on the right at the Juliaetta Centennial Park in Juliaetta. GPS: N46 34.01' / W116 42.65'

You can continue a total of 13.5 miles from the junction of US 12 and ID 3 to the northern terminus trailhead in Kendrick, passing through Juliaetta on the way. In the town of Kendrick, ID 3 becomes West Main Street,

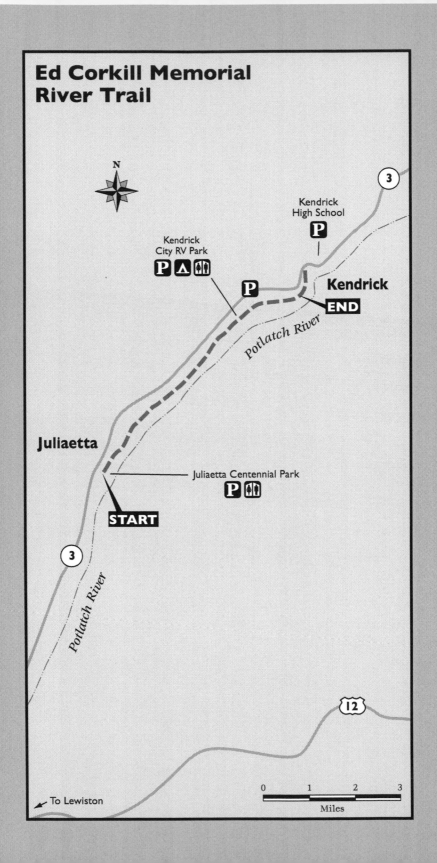

then East Main Street. Continue across the bridge and turn left into the
Kendrick High School parking lot to access the Kendrick Trailhead. The trail
heading toward Juliaetta starts from the front of the school property. Cross
back over the bridge and go across East Main Street. Turn left onto the trail.

An alternative parking spot is located in Kendrick, 13 miles from the
intersection of US 12 and ID 3. Turn right into an RV dumping station in
Kendrick. Cross over Railroad Street. The paved trail is just off the gravel
lot, putting you 5 miles from Juliaetta via the trail. You can also park near
the Kendrick City RV Park next to the trail at 805 Railroad Street.

The Ed Corkill Memorial River Trail was dedicated in 2004. The Idaho
Department of Transportation awarded more than $336,000 to the
Juliaetta–Kendrick Recreation District as an Enhancement Award to
develop the rail trail. On the trail visitors learn about locomotive whistle
signals (described on interpretive signs) and pass grain elevators towering above the trail near Juliaetta and Kendrick. While in Kendrick, take a
self-guided history tour.

Starting at the trailhead at Juliaetta Centennial Park, near open canyons of basalt rock and green lawns, the trail heads toward the town of
Juliaetta. During spring and summer, lush berry bushes, white syringa
flowers, and cattails line portions of the trail.

During the first 0.5 mile, the trail passes an old ranch along the river
and a telephone pole log manufacturer on the north side of the trail. Soon
after, the Juliaetta silo and grain elevator dominates the scenery as you
travel between the river and the town of Juliaetta.

From the late 1800s to the late 1950s, the Northern Pacific and Idaho
Railroad had tracks between these two towns, which were the end of the
branch line from near Spokane. Timber, livestock, fruits, grains, and vegetables were transported on the rails, making the Potlatch River Valley an
important trading post. The Juliaetta depot was closed in 1958.

Interpretive signs along the trail at mile 0.8 describe rail post signage,
including mileposts, speed restrictions, and other signs. Continue along
the river, crossing a trestle at 1.2 miles. If you need a rest, settle in on one
of the many benches along the way.

Between miles 2.0 and 3.5, you'll travel away from ID 3, with small
ranches appearing trailside. Once you reach 3.5 miles, the Kendrick city

The Juliaetta grain elevator is a striking feature along the Ed Corkill Memorial River Trail.

limits begin and the town's silo and grain elevator come into view. Soon the trail runs behind houses, past the grain elevator and silo, and beside the river. At 4.5 miles you can read about locomotive whistle signals that were used before modern forms of communication were developed. Often the train engineer and the train crew could not see each other, so whistle signals became the standard to indicate train maneuvers when stopping, backing up, and releasing brakes.

At 5.0 miles, read more about Kendrick's train history. To reach the northern terminus trailhead at 5.3 miles, go to the end of the paved trail, turn right onto East Main Street, cross the bridge, and then turn left into the Kendrick High School parking lot. Return to Juliaetta the way you came.

If you have the time while you're in the area, visit the Latah Trail (Trail 37) and the Bill Chipman Palouse Trail in Idaho (Trail 38).

Future Plans

Near the trailhead at Kendrick High School, you can see the closed portion of the old railbed. Future plans include continuing the trail from Kendrick and up the canyon to Troy, where rail trail enthusiasts can connect with the Latah Trail (Trail 37) and then continue to Moscow and connect with the Bill Chipman Palouse Trail (Trail 38) at the Idaho–Washington border.

40 CROWN POINT TRAIL

Views of West Mountain, on the far shore of Lake Cascade, add beauty to this trail. In the winter snow blankets the area, while in the spring and early summer, snow-covered mountains add contrast to the glittering lake.

Activities:

Location: Cascade, in Valley County

Length: 3.0 miles

Surface: Sand and dirt

Wheelchair access: This trail is not wheelchair-accessible.

Difficulty: Easy

Food: Restaurants, gas stations, and a grocery store are in the town of Cascade.

Restrooms: Restrooms are available at the free public parking lot on Vista Point Boulevard and at the campground fee area at Lake Cascades State Park's Crown Point Unit.

Seasons: The trail can be used year-round. Skiers, snowshoers, and snow-mobilers are allowed to travel on the trail when the snow is at least 4 inches deep.

Rentals: See appendix A for rental options in the town of McCall, located 22 miles north of Cascade, in Valley County.

Contacts: Idaho Department of Parks and Recreation, Lake Cascade State Park, (208) 382-6544, www.parksandrecreation.idaho.gov; Valley County Pathways, www.valleycountypathways.org; Cascade Chamber of Commerce, (208) 382-3833, www.cascadechamber.com

Bus routes: Mountain Community Transit has a Green Line connecting the towns of Cascade and McCall. Contact the administrative office in Nampa (Treasure Valley Transit) at (208) 463-9111.

Access and parking: For the main trailhead at Lake Cascade State Park's Crown Point Unit, take ID 55 north out of the town of Cascade. Cross the bridge over the North Fork of the Payette River. From the north side of the bridge, drive 0.5 mile to Vista Point Boulevard and turn left. Stay on the dirt road for 1 mile to the intersection with Crown Point Parkway.

There are three parking area options at this trailhead. One free option is to turn left at the intersection and then immediately left into a free public paved parking lot. Another free option is to go straight through the intersection to the gate at the trailhead and park on the side of the entrance, but not blocking the gate. The third option is to turn left into the Lake Cascade State Park's Crown Point Campground and pay the per-vehicle day-use fee, or use an annual pass. Idaho residents can use the Idaho State Park Passport, available for a fee with their annual Idaho license plate renewal at a local Department of Motor Vehicles office. For information on day-use and annual passes, go to https://parksandrecreation.idaho.gov/.

Access the trail just as you enter the state park. GPS: N44 31.56' / W116 03.31'

Pine trees, sagebrush, and a combination of basalt rocks and decomposing granite line the Crown Point Trail. Strategically placed benches afford stunning views of Lake Cascade, the fourth-largest lake in Idaho. When full of snowmelt water in spring, the lake sits at 4,828 feet in elevation. As water is released for irrigation purposes downstream, over 86 miles of shoreline are exposed.

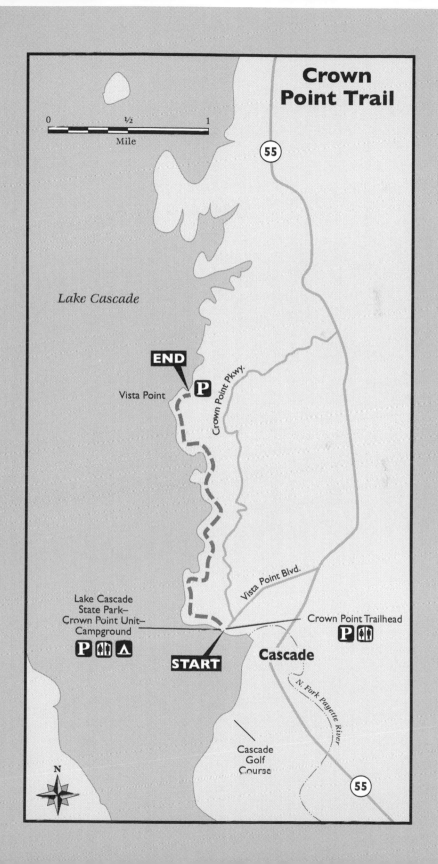

Crown Point Trail

0   ½   1
Mile

55

Lake Cascade

END

Vista Point

P

Crown Point Pkwy.

Lake Cascade
State Park–
Crown Point Unit–
Campground

P 🚻 ⛺

Vista Point Blvd.

Crown Point Trailhead

P 🚻

START

Cascade

N. Fork Payette River

Cascade
Golf
Course

55

N

In winter Crown Point Trail is used for snow sports.

Fishing for rainbow trout, perch, and bass is a popular pursuit. During winter cross-country skiers, snowshoers, skijorers, and dogsledders use the trail.

The town of Cascade served as a depot for the railroads when the rails were built in Long Valley between 1912 and 1914. The Oregon Short Line Railroad (Union Pacific) placed tracks from Smith's Ferry to McCall to move supplies up and down the mountainous valley.

During the late 1940s a reservoir was built next to the town of Cascade, and the train tracks along the north fork of the Payette River had to be rerouted. The tracks were moved from their original location near the waterfalls on the north end of Cascade to the eastern shoreline of Lake Cascade. Crown Point Trail is on the rerouted railbed.

Railroad use in the area continued for decades after the 1940s, until the Boise Cascade lumber mill shut down in McCall. Rail tracks were removed in 1980, with the land reverting to the adjacent property owners.

Nearby Attractions

Take in Kelly's Whitewater Park in Cascade, where you can ride an inner tube, glide on a standup paddleboard, or float in a raft through the whitewater park. For information visit www.kellyswhitewaterpark.com. Rent river equipment on-site from River Gear, (208) 382-6580, www.rivergearcascade.com. Visit www.kellyswhitewaterpark.com.

You can follow the sandy railbed, which runs for 1 mile along the lake, with easy access to the shoreline. It then shifts slightly inland away from the lake among the ponderosa pine trees.

The squawks of ospreys and the *tap-tap-tap* of woodpeckers can be heard. Foxes also live in the area, and you might be treated to their calls. Soft sand on the trail serves as a perfect medium for local wildlife to leave their paw prints. Wolves, cougars, deer, raccoons, badgers, and black bears travel this rail trail. Interpretive signs along the trail describe the area's flora and fauna.

Intermittently the trail returns to the lake, where wide-open views of the long valley are possible. At 0.9 mile the trail enters a small basalt canyon. At 1.3 and 1.7 miles from the trailhead, you enter small canyons of decomposing granite rocks. It's easy to imagine the train chugging through these narrow passageways.

On the latter half of the trail, many small bays appear and the grade gently increases. During early spring and late summer, coarse-sand beaches and boulder gardens emerge due to the lowering of reservoir water levels for irrigation purposes downstream.

Continue on the trail past some homes to 3.0 miles, where the trail currently ends at the tiny neighborhood trailhead parking area at Vista Point Loop off of 4 Seasons Drive.

When you are ready, return the way you came and enjoy the scenery. West Mountain dominates the landscape on the west side of the lake. Sweeping views of the Cascade Golf Course and other Lake Cascade campgrounds come into view at 0.25 mile from the border of the Crown Point Campground and the trailhead.

Future Plans

Valley County Pathways' long-range plan includes creating over 70 miles of pedestrian pathways between Cascade and New Meadows, plus connecting mountain resorts and state parks around Lake Cascade and Payette Lake. Part of the plan involves development of the old rail line that traversed Long Valley as land negotiations are completed. Plans include extending the Crown Point Trail to Sugar Loaf boat launch and campground.

41 WEISER RIVER TRAIL

At 86 continuous miles, the Weiser River Trail is the longest non-motorized multiuse rail trail in Idaho and a designated National Recreation Trail. It travels on the original railbed beside the Weiser River and through rural towns of southwestern Idaho. Along the way it passes by farmland, basalt canyons, riparian zones, and the alpine setting of the Payette National Forest.

Activities:

Location: Weiser, Midvale, Cambridge, Council, and Rubicon near New Meadows, in Washington and Adams Counties

Length: 86 miles

Surface: Primarily original ballast material that has been graded and rolled. There are also dirt and gravel sections and short paved segments in the towns of Weiser, Midvale, Cambridge, and Council. Horses use the entire trail.

Wheelchair access: The trailheads at Weiser, Midvale, Cambridge, and Council are wheelchair-accessible.

Difficulty: Easy on the paved sections; intermediate on the remote segments

Food: Restaurants, grocery stores, and gas stations can be found in Weiser, Cambridge, Council, and New Meadows. Midvale offers restaurants and a grocery store.

Restrooms: Portable toilets are available Apr 1 to Oct 31 at the Cambridge, Mesa Siding, Council, and Starkey Trailheads. There are vault toilets at the Weiser, Midvale, and Presley Trailheads year-round and seasonally at the Wye Trailhead and Evergreen Campground.

Seasons: The trail can be used year-round. The southern segment is free of snow by March; the northern section is generally free of snow May to Oct.

Rentals: See appendix A for mountain bike, cross-country ski, and snow-shoe rental options in the town of McCall, located about 20 miles north-east of the northern trailheads.

Contacts: For information on current trail conditions, or to purchase the comprehensive trail guidebook, *The Weiser River Trail,* written by Margaret Fuller and Anita Van Grunsven, visit www.weiserrivertrail.org.

Bus routes: None

Access and parking: There are several established trailheads and a number of small roadside spots that you can use to access this long trail. Trailhead information is provided for the termini of each segment, starting with the southern trailhead in Weiser.

- Weiser Trailhead: From I-84 take US 95 north to Weiser. After crossing the Weiser River and entering the town of Weiser, continue about 0.1 mile and turn right on East Main Street. Go 0.6 mile to the trailhead parking lot on the left. This is not the official starting point of the trail; however, it serves as the main south-end trailhead. The trail is paved west for about 0.5 mile to 4th Street (the southern starting trail mileage marker at 0.22 mile), located 3 blocks west of US 95. Take the trail going east to access the full length of the trail. GPS: N44 14.74' / W116 56.68'

- Midvale Trailhead: Take US 95 north from Weiser 20 miles to Midvale. The trailhead is near highway mile marker 104, on the east side of the road in a paved lot off Bridge Street, near the Midvale Community Park.

- Cambridge Trailhead: From Weiser take US 95 north about 41 miles into Cambridge. US 95 turns sharply east at an intersection. Continue east to the trailhead kiosk, on the east side of the highway by the Washington County Fairgrounds.

- Council Trailhead: From the Mesa Siding access point, follow US 95 north 3.4 miles into Council. US 95 becomes Michigan Avenue. At the curve in the road, turn left onto Moser Avenue and follow it a few blocks to Railroad Street; turn right. Wind through a residential area for 0.2 mile and turn left onto Hornet Creek Road. The trailhead is immediately on the left; the trail is beside the parking lot.

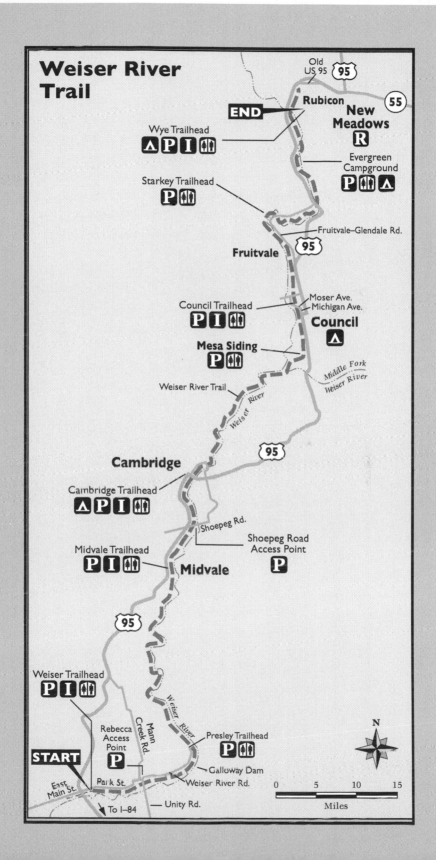

- Wye Trailhead: Continue north on US 95 past the Tamarack Lumber Mill. Watch for the "Wye Trailhead ½ mile" sign and turn right onto Rim Road. Follow Rim Road to Tamarack View Drive and turn right. It's about 0.5 mile to the trailhead and RV camp from US 95. If coming south from New Meadows, the trailhead turnoff will be about 6 miles south of New Meadows. This is a good parking option, since the West Pine Trailhead is no longer available for use. The trail runs beside US 95 to the official end of the trail at Rubicon, north of Wye trailhead.

Weiser, Midvale, and Cambridge form the southern portion of the Weiser River Trail. Cambridge, Council, and Rubicon, near New Meadows, form the northern portion. Both segments are on the original railbed almost the entire length. This trail description mileage begins at mile 0.7 in Weiser, west of where US 95 crosses the Weiser River near the terminus of the original railbed.

Since the trail passes through four rural communities and two counties, originally there wasn't one single organization able to oversee the vast miles of the trail. The Friends of the Weiser River Trail (FWRT) stepped in to fill the gap and develop the trail. This nonprofit volunteer group formed in 1996 to coordinate trail efforts by preserving and improving the rail corridor. In 1997 the former railbed was converted into a recreational multiuse trail, and now the Weiser River Trail is unique in that very few rail trails in the country are owned and managed by a volunteer organization and its members. In 2010 the Weiser River Trail received status as a National Recreation Trail.

Historically the Weiser-to-New Meadows rail system was in operation under various owners from as early as 1895 until 1995, when the rails were abandoned. The Oregon Short Line, the Pacific & Northern Railway, and, more recently, the Union Pacific were involved over the years. Rails moved timber, livestock, and farming supplies. They also transported passengers as the populations of Adams and Washington Counties grew.

From its humble start as an abandoned Union Pacific Railroad corridor that was first converted to 7 miles of nonmotorized rail trail, the trail is a labor of love in constant motion. Thanks to the Friends of the Weiser River Trail, the trail distance and quality have steadily improved over the years.

When renovation began, rails were removed and the surface smoothed. In many years the FWRT receive matching grants from the Recreational Trails Program, administered through the Idaho Department of Parks and Recreation and from other sources.

The continual support, dedication, and volunteer work of many individuals and the FWRT keep this lengthy trail growing and improving. Trestles were improved by adding side rails for safety and planking to the surface for smooth crossings. Small segments of the trail were paved near the towns. An information kiosk, a small paved parking lot, and a trailhead were constructed at the Weiser city limits, serving as an ideal launching spot for northward travel on the trail. A ten-unit RV camp was completed near the northern terminus at the Wye Trailhead. As funds become available, trailheads, parking, access points, and interpretive signs are continually improving.

Bicyclists, hikers, and horseback riders traverse various segments of the route. Other outdoor activities near the trail include canoeing, kayaking, rafting, and fishing on the Weiser River. Birding and wildlife photography opportunities also abound. Cross-country skiers and snowshoers travel the trail in winter, especially along its northern sections.

The Weiser Trailhead sits near the southern end of the Weiser River Trail.

Stretches of the trail are desolate, so carry drinking water, snacks, and perhaps a cell phone, although there will be sections of the trail where cell service may not be available. Due to the rugged nature of the trail, if bicycling, a mountain bike with shock absorbers will make the journey more pleasant.

Weiser to Midvale, 31.3 miles

There are a number of access points in and near Weiser. Visitors can travel short segments of the trail and then head into this town of over 5,000 to enjoy the history and amenities. Check out Weiser's historic buildings, including a train station, courthouse, church, and various homes.

Spring is the best time of year to experience this section. Green fields, chirping birds, cool weather, and the absence of weeds that can puncture bicycle tires make for ideal traveling on the trail. However, the trail can be wet and muddy in spring; contact the Friends of the Weiser River Trail for current conditions.

If beginning at the Weiser Trailhead, you will be starting near mile 0.7, on a paved section of the trail. When heading east and then north from Weiser, the trail mile markers ascend, indicating the distance from the original site of the Weiser Depot, located just west of US 95 in Weiser. For a brief jaunt on the western paved portion, you can head west for about 0.5 mile to 4th Street. Across the US 95 bridge lies the undeveloped southwestern end of the old railbed, managed by the FWRT. Return to the Weiser Trailhead for your adventure east and then north.

Shortly after leaving the Weiser Trailhead heading east, the pavement turns to dirt and gravel; it will remain so until a small portion in Midvale. The farther you go from Weiser, the more rural the trail becomes. Along the way you cross trestles near 2.5 miles and after 5.0 miles. Just before 6.0 miles you cross Unity Road.

From here the trail continues through agriculture fields. Though you cannot see the river yet, you will meet up with it soon. Notice the mile markers as you travel the trail. They are made of old railroad spikes and ascend in number as you head east.

When you arrive at mile 10.0, you will see Galloway Dam. This is a good boating and fishing access spot, though boaters should consider a portage around the low head dam. After leaving the dam you enter a remote canyon. Just ahead is the Presley Trailhead and a restroom at mile 11.4.

The trail from Weiser to beyond Galloway Dam has noticeably shifted from a small rural town to ranchlands and into a canyon, where you may even see a herd of deer. Ring-necked pheasants, killdeers, hawks, chukars, and ospreys are but a few of the birds that trail users can see or hear. Bring a flower identification guide if visiting in spring or summer; the wildflowers are prolific along the trail.

There is hardly any shade on the trail from Weiser to Midvale, so use sunscreen and protective clothing. During summer, consider traveling in the early morning before it gets hot.

After leaving Presley Trailhead you enter a remote area, cross over a trestle, view trailside cliffs, and travel through an area without any signs of residents. At 14.5 miles you can see a concrete structure on the hill that once was used to load grain into railroad cars.

You'll travel near the Weiser River and cross another trestle over a creek after 18.0 miles. From here you enter a narrow canyon and pass a rocky slope at 21.0 miles. Just ahead is a lengthy high trestle at Thousand Springs Creek, before 22.0 miles. Another trestle is at 23.5 miles at Sheep Creek.

Continue on the trail, where you interact frequently with the river and small creeks. Basalt rocks are visible in the surrounding canyons, and the environment is a mix of desert grasses, sagebrush, and riparian vegetation, such as poison ivy.

Eventually trail adventurers heading east and then north from Weiser see the upcoming mountains, which appear at about 28.0 miles, when the scenery opens and affords views of the valley. The trail crosses the Sage Creek trestle at 30.0 miles. Farm fields and the town of Midvale materialize shortly after. Midvale is a small town of several hundred residents. It was known as the wool capital of the United States in the 1900s. The Pacific & Idaho Northern Railway reached the town in 1899. There is a grocery store, a coffeehouse, a bed-and-breakfast, and a park with an outdoor swimming pool. All amenities are within a block or two of the trailhead in Midvale.

Midvale to Cambridge, 8.7 miles

From the Midvale Trailhead, about 8 miles of trail pass intermittently along the Weiser River and US 95. The dirt and gravel trail is generally level, with slight inclines and declines.

Many views of the river, and in spring of the distant snowcapped mountains, are available on the Midvale-to-Cambridge section. The scent of green alfalfa fields, the tweets of meadowlarks, and glimpses of red-winged blackbirds are but a few of the many experiences along the trail.

You'll come to the Shoepeg Road Bridge over the Weiser River at about 36.0 miles. There is parking near the bridge. Enjoy a view of Cuddy Mountain before continuing north on the trail along the river, entering a canyon along US 95. At about 39.0 miles you can see the dirt road that once served as the old highway and crossed the river. In 1997 Silver Bridge was swept away in high water. Now the site serves as a fishing access and has limited parking.

Head on to the town of Cambridge. At 40.5 miles you will reach the Cambridge Trailhead, passing the Washington County Fairgrounds along the way. Within 2 blocks of the trail, you will encounter a grocery store, motels, and restaurants.

Cambridge to Council, 19.7 miles

Late spring, summer, and autumn are fine times to travel the cooler alpine northern section that passes through ponderosa pine trees and along the Weiser River from its source in the mountains north of Council.

From riparian areas along the Weiser River to the mountainous terrain in the Payette National Forest, the northern segment of the Weiser River Trail offers a variety of ecosystems. Going north from Cambridge, a slight uphill grade runs on packed dirt and gravel.

The trail is paved a short distance in Cambridge. After the pavement ends, the gravel trail moves through fields and into another canyon. You'll find Mundo Hot Springs about 2.0 miles out of Cambridge. Exit the trail at the intersection with Mill Road and head east to Goodrich Road. Mundo Hot Springs is on the left side of Goodrich Road, about 0.5 miles from the trail. Visitors enjoy the on-site hot springs, lodging, camping, and bistro.

Vegetation increases as you reconnect with the river. At about 46.0 miles the trail crosses over a trestle at Grizzly Creek. Continue through this secluded segment, along the river and hills. Sunflowers, willows, and cottonwoods grow along the trail. Deer, yellow warblers, and wild turkeys dart in and out of view.

Autumn is a pleasant season for a stroll north of Cambridge.
Dave Lindsay

Travel over the trestles that cross Cottonwood and Goodrich Creeks. Pass over Cow Creek on a small trestle at 47.5 miles, then the Goodrich Creek trestle at 49.5 miles. Goodrich Road reaches the trail before 50.0 miles. It serves as an access point with limited parking. Goodrich was once a small town on the rail line.

At 51.5 miles you cross a bridge over the river, and at about 54.0 miles you travel over a trestle that crosses the Middle Fork of the Weiser River. Near 56.5 miles the trail returns to the highway, 4.0 miles south of Council near Mesa Siding. Fruit growing was popular in this area in the early 1900s. In the autumn, trail users graze on the ripe fallen apples.

Between Mesa Siding and Council, the trail runs beside US 95 in the open area of the valley from 56.5 miles to 60.0 miles. The trail is paved in Council from Cool Creek, near 58.0 miles, to Airport Road, which is north of town. Take a break at the Council Trailhead at 60.2 miles and read local history at the railroad-themed kiosk shelter.

Council to Wye Trailhead, 26 miles

After checking out the historical interpretative area—including the railroad side car and the Old Council Depot, relocated to the trailhead—follow the trail as it leaves the drier climate. You'll enter a lush forest containing

Nearby Attractions

Annual events in the area include:

- The FWRT spring Bike Ride, spring four-day Weiser River Wagon Train Ride, spring 50k Ultra and Relay, and October Trek two-day bicycle ride. These events introduce outdoor enthusiasts to the Weiser River Trail and raise trail funds. Contact the FWRT at (888) My-Trail (698-7245) or www.weiserrivertrail.org.

- Cambridge's Hells Canyon Days, first week in June; www. cambridgeidaho.com.

Douglas fir and ponderosa pine. Much of the trail can be viewed from Fruitvale–Glendale Road and, later, US 95. There are a few small access sites along the way.

As the trail flows north from Council, it merges into a mixture of meadows and timbered areas near the highway bypass between Council and Fruitvale. You will encounter the old town of Fruitvale at 66.0 miles. Fruitvale had a depot building until 1915, when it was moved to Council to serve as the depot there. Continue on the trail as it passes along Fruitvale–Glendale Road and continues near residences in the forest and onto a narrow bridge crossing, beyond 67.0 miles. Near 69.5 miles you will find the Starkey Trailhead and a restroom.

From this point the trail travels through deep forest and out to an open valley. You will cruise by the old rail-line town of Glendale at 72.0 miles. Continue to 73.0 miles, where you can see a narrow canyon and US 95. Get ready to cross the river on a trestle as it passes under the US 95 bridge at about 74.0 miles. Two more trestle crossings are ahead, followed by some homes and a long trestle near 76.0 miles.

Continue on the trail as it travels above the river. Near 76.5 miles the small settlement of Evergreen existed near the tracks in the early 1900s. Travel toward mile 77.0, where a footpath accesses the rail trail from the Evergreen Campground. The USDA Forest Service campground was built in the early 1920s. This is a good place to hop off the trail and use the restrooms and refill your water containers. The lush green forest may entice you to camp overnight in this pleasant spot.

Follow the trail as it goes uphill and through the forest to the flats of the upper valley, exiting the timbered area and traveling next to US 95, at about 78.5 miles. The trail crosses a trestle at about 79.0 miles. Near 81.0 miles you can see the road to Lost Valley Reservoir as it departs from US 95; you can also see a restaurant at the intersection.

The next few miles run along US 95 and include a detour off the original railbed. The present-day Tamarack Lumber Mill, owned by Evergreen Forest Products, sits atop the original railbed. Take the gravel road between miles 81.0 and 82.5 that detours you around the mill. It heads uphill and then downhill to rejoin the original railbed. Near mile 83.0 you'll encounter the turnoff for the Wye Trailhead, where you'll find the terminus trailhead, horse camping, and RV/tent camping, located about 0.5 mile off the Weiser River Trail. The Y in the tracks was originally used to turn trains around. Rubicon, which is now just a name on the map, is located at 84.5 miles. It was the end of the tracks after the rails were abandoned, and is considered the current Weiser River Trail northern terminus. The trail continues north to mile 85.7, near the retired West Pine Trailhead, though you are likely parked at the Wye trailhead.

Consider taking advantage of the gentle downhill gradient by traveling the trail from north to south. Between Rubicon and Council the trail loses more than 1,200 feet of elevation. Another 275 feet of elevation are lost from Council to Cambridge, and 527 feet of elevation between Cambridge and Weiser.

Future Plans

There are many plans for improvements along the trail. FWRT's next long-term goal is to extend the northern portion of the trail from the West Pine area near Rubicon to the New Meadows train depot, built in 1911—a distance of about 5.0 miles.

42 STODDARD PATHWAY

A reprieve from the hustle and bustle of Nampa's suburban life, this trail offers a restful path along grasslands and trees, through a neighborhood park, and near open fields and houses. It serves as a reminder of southwest Idaho's rural personality.

Activities:

Location: City of Nampa, in Canyon County

Length: 2.7 miles

Surface: Asphalt

Wheelchair access: The trail is wheelchair-accessible.

Difficulty: Easy

Food: There are nearby convenience stores and plenty of eateries in Nampa.

Restrooms: There are portable toilets at the Maple Wood Park and Locust Lane trailheads.

Seasons: The trail can be used year-round from dawn to dusk.

Rentals: None in Nampa. See appendix A for Treasure Valley rentals.

Contacts: City of Nampa Parks and Forestry Department, (208) 468-5890, www.nampaparksandrecreation.org

Bus routes: None

Access and parking: There are three trailheads for this trail. The La Rita Schandorff Trailhead on Murray Street serves as the northern starting point for this trail description.

Head west on I-84 from Boise. Take exit 38 and turn left onto Garrity Boulevard. Go 1.3 miles and turn left onto Kings Road. Drive 1.7 miles and turn right onto Amity Avenue. Continue 0.6 mile more and turn right onto Murray Street. Go a few hundred yards past the La Rita Schandorff Trailhead's one-way exit and turn left into the trailhead parking area. The trail

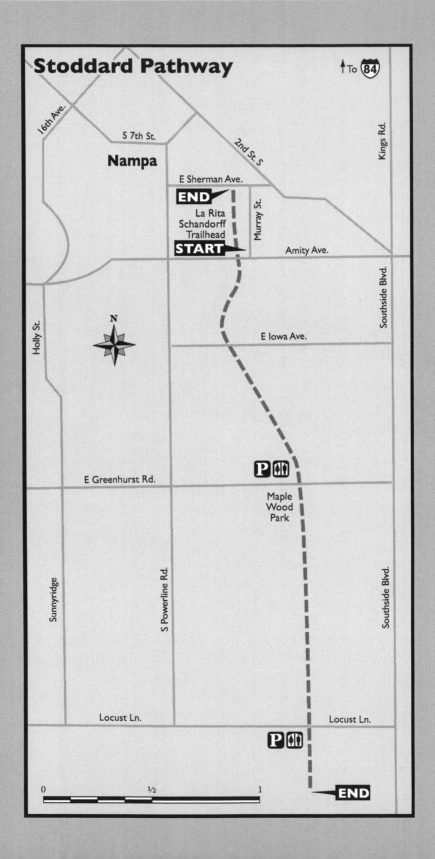

starts at the southern end of the parking area at Amity Avenue. GPS: N43 33.70' / W116 32.88'

The trail's southern terminus is just beyond the trailhead at Locust Lane. Find another trailhead at the Maple Wood Park off East Greenhurst Road.

||||||||||||||||||||||||||||||||||||||||||||||||||||||||||||||||||||||||||||||||||||||||||||||

City trails are becoming more important and increasingly available as population growth continues in the western Treasure Valley. Nampa offers citizens and visitors alike this rail trail for escaping the city pace and spending time with nature.

Originally the rail tracks ran from Nampa to Melba, and on to Silver City in the Owyhee Mountains. When the Union Pacific Railroad closed the rails in this area, the city agreed to take over the Stoddard line as a trail. During the mid-1990s the trail was an undeveloped dirt path, which the city of Nampa re-created as a paved multiuse rails-to-trails conversion trail.

Stoddard Pathway provides exercise opportunities in a rural setting.

Start on the trail by crossing over Amity Avenue. Go south through a natural-grass corridor between homes and an industrial property. At the crossing at East Iowa Avenue at 0.5 mile, continue south. The trail travels another 0.5 mile to the trailhead across from Maple Wood Park, passing through a grass-and tree-studded corridor between homes. The City of Nampa Forestry Department planted trees in 2004. Interpretive signs describe the English oak, Austrian pine, and other trees in the area. To visit the rest of the trail, cross over East Greenhurst Road and continue on the paved trail as it passes through the Maple Wood neighborhood park. Vegetation along the trail shields users from some of the developing urban sprawl.

The corridor widens and feels more rural through this last 1.5 miles of trail on this southern segment, between East Greenhurst Road and the terminus, just past the Locust Lane trailhead. Retrace the trail you just traveled on, ending back at the northern terminus off Amity Avenue. Another option is to continue 0.2 mile on the northern trail section to Sherman Avenue, then return to the La Rita Schandorff Trailhead. While you are in the area, consider visiting the Indian Creek Greenbelt (Trail 43).

43 INDIAN CREEK GREENBELT

This short trail runs parallel to an active railroad track located on the other side of the creek's bank. During the irrigation season, typically April through September, the waterway along the trail glitters in the sunshine and expands activity options to include fishing, tubing, canoeing, and kayaking. After a jaunt on the trail, you can readily access a restaurant for a quick bite to eat.

Activities:

Location: Kuna, in Ada County

Length: 0.8 mile westward

Surface: Asphalt for the first 0.7 mile, followed by a 0.1-mile dirt trail to a BMX bike area

Wheelchair access: Wheelchair-accessible from the parking lot at the trailhead onto the paved portions of the trail

Difficulty: Easy on the paved portion; moderate on the dirt BMX segment

Food: There are eateries along the trail and a few short blocks into the town of Kuna.

Restrooms: You can find restrooms seasonally at the Indian Creek Greenbelt Park Trailhead, a Kuna city park.

Seasons: The trail can be used year-round from dawn to dusk.

Rentals: None in Kuna. See appendix A for rentals in the Treasure Valley.

Contacts: City of Kuna, (208) 922-5546, http://kunacity.id.gov

Bus routes: None

Access and parking: From Boise take I-84 west to exit 44 (Meridian/Kuna). At the end of the off-ramp, reset the trip meter and turn left (south) on ID 69 South (Western Heritage Historic Byway). Continue for about 7 miles, staying right when the road curves to the right and becomes North Kuna / Meridian Road. At 7.7 miles the road name changes to East Avalon Street

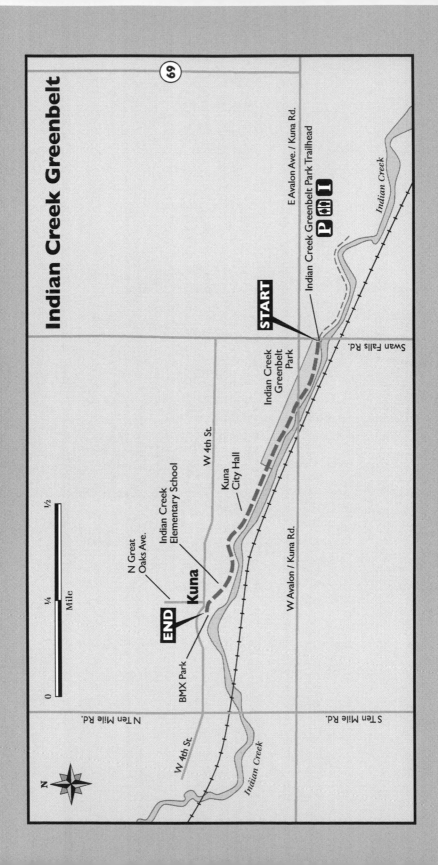

/ Kuna Road. At 8.1 miles turn left onto South Swan Falls Road and then immediately right into the parking area at Indian Creek Greenbelt Park. The trail segment described starts on the east end of the parking lot, near the road bridge over Indian Creek. GPS: N43 29.27' / W116 24.84'

K una (pronounced *Q-nuh*) is a rural town of 28,000. It hosts the Indian Creek Greenbelt and is the place to head if you want to admire sparkling Indian Creek when it runs during irrigation season or to partake in the variety of other recreation activities available year-round.

Visitors and residents enjoy walking, biking, fishing, picnicking, and birding. There are bike repair stations, BMX bicycle parks, and an 18-hole disc golf course along the trail. An active Union Pacific rail track is on the other side of the creek, lending atmosphere.

The best access point is at the parking lot, with restrooms and wheelchair accessibility to the trail. Start at the Indian Creek Greenbelt Park, near the visitor information kiosk.

The greenbelt passes along Indian Creek, offering refreshing resting spots.

The segment described consists of paved asphalt and brief dirt detour to a BMX park, for a 0.8-mile westward jaunt. Pass through the tree-shaded park offering recreational activities popular with youth and families. Avoid road crossings by taking the left side of Y intersections and travel beside the creek. Pass behind the elementary school near 0.5 mile. Around 0.7 mile the trail comes to the last Y intersection. The right side enters the dirt parking area off West 4th Street at North Great Oakes Avenue, and the left branch crosses a metal footbridge onto the 0.1-mile dirt path to a BMX bicycle area at the current western end of the trail. Return the way you came, perhaps taking a break trailside to enjoy views of the creek. Other trailside options include a number of restaurants in town just off the trail.

For an extension to your journey, return to the trailhead at South Swan Falls Road. Cross the road and head east on the paved trail another 0.3 mile to the Kuna Parks and Recreation headquarters and the current eastside trail terminus. Pass close to the disc-golfers on the way back to the trailhead along Swan Falls Road.

Immediate plans include extending the trail eastward from the Parks and Recreation headquarters. The long-term goal is expansion westward.

Nearby Attractions

Kuna is considered the gateway to the Morley Nelson Snake River Birds of Prey National Conservation Area (NCA) and the 40-mile Western Heritage Historic Byway. Stock up on food and gas before heading into the desert to explore these areas, as you'll be traveling through undeveloped countryside. View the scenic highway map kiosk by the trailhead.

- Morley Nelson Snake River Birds of Prey National Conservation Area, https://www.blm.gov/programs/national-conservation-lands/idaho/morley-nelson-snake-river-birds-of-prey

- Western Heritage Historic Byway, www.fhwa.dot.gov/byways/byways/2593

44 WOOD RIVER TRAIL

Originating close to the rugged Smoky and Boulder Mountains south of the Sawtooth National Recreation Area in central Idaho, this trail passes through the Wood River Valley. Following on or next to the original railbed, the trail goes by the town of Ketchum near the famous Sun Valley Resort. The valley widens as the trail heads south through the towns of Hailey and Bellevue.

Activities:

Location: Towns of Ketchum, Hailey, and Bellevue, in Blaine County

Length: 20 miles

Surface: Asphalt

Wheelchair access: Due to the dirt and gravel parking lots, the path is not accessible from designated parking sites; however, the trail is wheelchair-accessible from street access and neighborhood intersections.

Difficulty: Easy, except for a few moderate hills at the beginning of the trail and at the bridges near trail mile 9.0

Food: Eateries, grocery stores, and gas stations are just a few blocks from the trail in the towns of Ketchum, Hailey, and Bellevue, and at Sun Valley Resort's River Run Lodge.

Restrooms: You can find restrooms at the Sun Peak Picnic Area trailside between mile 0 and mile 1.0 and at the East Fork Road Trailhead.

Seasons: The trail can be used year-round; from Dec to Mar the trails are groomed for cross-country skiing.

Rentals: In Ketchum you can rent cross-country skis, and snowshoes at Backwoods Mountain Sports, 711 North Main Street, (208) 726-8818, www.backwoodsmountainsports.com. Rent bicycles, cross-country skis, and snowshoes at The Elephant's Perch, 280 East Avenue, (208) 726-3497, www.elephantsperch.com; or Sturtevants, 340 North Main Street, (208) 726-4512, www.sturtevants-sv.com; or Sturtevants, Limelight Hotel 151

South Main Street, (208) 726-0898, www.sturtevants-sv.com. At the Sun Valley Resort you can rent bicycles at Peter Lane's Mountain Sports at Sun Valley Village, 1 Sun Valley Road, (208) 622-2279, www.sunvalley.com; and at Peter Lane's Mountain Sports, River Run Plaza, 520 Serenade Lane, Ketchum, (208) 622-6123, www.sunvalley.com. In Hailey, you can rent bikes, cross-country skis, and snowshoes at Sturtevants, 1 West Carbonate Street, (208) 788-7847, www.sturtevants-sv.com.

Contacts: Blaine County Recreation District, (208) 578-2273, www.bcrd. org

Bus routes: Contact Mountain Rides at (208) 788-7433 or www.mountainrides.org.

Access and parking: This description starts from the northern terminus at Hulen Meadows and heads south. Hulen Meadows: Take ID 75 north from Bellevue and Hailey into the town of Ketchum, where ID 75 becomes Main Street. Continue north past the turn for Sun Valley. From the stoplight at the intersection of Main Street / ID 75 and Saddle Road, continue north 1.9 miles to Hulen Meadows Road; turn left, then immediately left again into the large dirt trailhead parking lot. The trail starts on the west side of the lot. GPS: N43 43.10' / W114 22.69'

Gannett Road–Bellevue southern terminus: From ID 75 and Fox Acres Road in south Hailey, head south to Bellevue. Travel 4.5 miles to highway mile marker 111, in the southern part of Bellevue. Turn left onto Gannett Road and find a parking spot along the road in the industrial area. The trail starts to the northeast.

||||||||||||||||||||||||||||||||||||||||||||||||||||||||||||||||||||||||||||||||||||||||

From the trail's start in the upper reaches of the valley, with eye-popping views of snowcapped mountains, to the open terrain with feeder canyons at the southern end of the trail, visitors move through a segment of Idaho's rich history. Following the Wood River and ID 75, the trail is dotted with educational signs that identify points of interest and nature-related information on the local wetlands, geology, and plants.

Popular year-round, the trail experiences a steady flow of visitors. During winter the rail trail is groomed for cross-country skiing, with snow

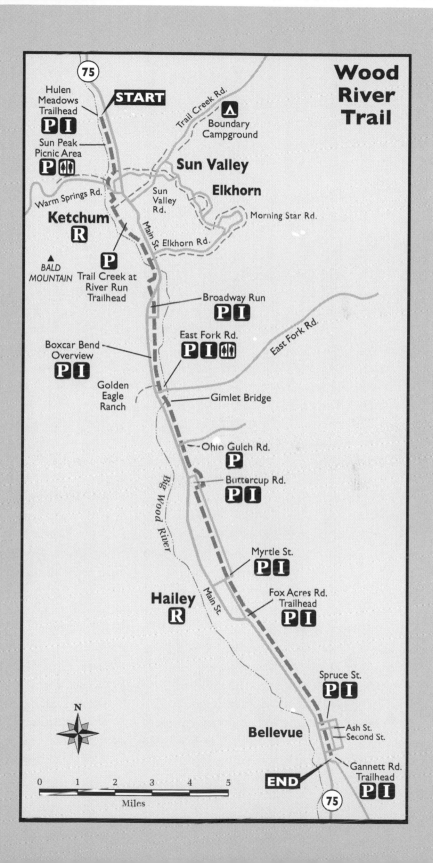

possible between November and April. In spring, summer, and autumn the trail is enjoyed by both local residents and visitors to this popular outdoor recreation destination.

Mining was once integral to this area, beginning with the rush of 1879. The Wood River mining district was once Idaho's major mining area, producing lead and silver. Cattle-and sheep-raising also gained momentum here. The Union Pacific served the mines and livestock industries via a spur line that ran from Shoshone to Ketchum, with the Wood River Branch–Oregon Short Line Railroad reaching the Ketchum Depot in 1884.

Further contributing to the growth of the area was the development of the first destination ski resort in the United States. Averell Harriman, a chairman of the Union Pacific, envisioned and helped develop the prominent Sun Valley Resort, which still stands today as a world-renowned ski and snowboard destination. Railroads played a major role in the resort's success. In the late 1930s the Union Pacific Railroad helped build the ski slopes and ski lifts. The railroad owned and managed the Sun Valley Resort between 1936 and 1968.

In 1987 the Idaho Department of Transportation bought the spur line, known as the Oregon Short Line, and in turn the Blaine County Recreation District picked it up. The original railroad right-of-way was developed into a multiuse nonmotorized rail trail that is part of an extensive trail system. This trail network includes the paved trail on the railbed, known as the Wood River Trail, as well as the Nordic ski trail system in the North Valley Trails. It also includes the pathway called the Harriman Trail, which travels between the Sawtooth National Recreation Area headquarters and Galena Lodge to the north. As you drive ID 75 between the towns of Ketchum and Bellevue, the Wood River rail trail is visible along the highway.

Starting at the northern terminus at Hulen Meadows, at mile 0, the paved trail runs downstream from north to south along the Wood River. Be sure to glance back frequently for stellar views of the mountains up the valley, which hold a snowpack on the summits into midsummer.

Shortly, at mile 0.5, you encounter the Sun Peak Picnic Area on your right. This is one of the few trailside restrooms, so consider using it. In addition to the water source here, there are a number of water fountains along the trail. Bald Mountain, with a height of 9,150 feet, pops into view and will remain along your right side for the upper reaches of the trail. Nicknamed "Baldy," it even looks like a bald head.

The Wood River Trail starts beside the Big Wood River at the Hulen Meadows Trailhead north of Ketchum.

As you leave this area, the trail has a few slight hills and bends as it goes by aspen trees and purple lupine wildflowers. At mile 1.0 the woods open up and you get a full view of Baldy. The Sun Valley Resort, of which Baldy is a part, has a large snow-making system.

Continue south past residences on the west side of the trail. Between miles 2.0 and 3.0, the trail crosses a number of intersections and winds its way through the western edges of Ketchum and back to the Wood River. Watch for the tall wooden trail signs that mark every road crossing, and keep Baldy on your right. Consider a side trip into town for refreshments at one of the many fine eateries located just a few blocks from the trail.

Through this section, Baldy looms large to your right, then the Ketchum Skate Park. Just before Rotary Park, turn left at the intersection and cross the road, picking up the trail as it runs on the east side of the road. Shortly you turn right and cross Warm Springs Road and reenter the trail. Next you weave through the parking lots of the Ernest Hemingway Elementary School, then along Hemingway Lane. Turn right onto 8th Street toward Baldy. At 2.8 miles you will see the trail marker at Atkinson Park. Turn left and continue on the marked trail on 2nd Avenue over the back roads of Ketchum, passing condominiums and arriving at 6th Avenue. Cross over 6th Avenue, continue to the right on the trail, then curve left to trail mile marker 3.0.

At this point the trail returns to the river and becomes peaceful, away from the hustle of Ketchum. Pass condominiums between miles 3.0 and 3.4. Soon you will come to a trail information sign, with water at the site. Continue past the Trail Creek at River Run trailhead. The large parking area on the left serves as part of the lodge and ski lift parking areas in winter.

Shortly after, you cross over a bridge trestle at 3.7 miles. In-line skaters need to be careful on the crossing. The wood is roughly cut and generates a rugged ride. Built in 1883, this bridge is one of the oldest of its type in Idaho. It is the last link of the Wood River Branch of the Oregon Short Line.

After leaving the bridge, the trail goes along wooded areas near the river, where you might see a red or gray fox or even deer. Take a glance north for views of the distant mountain peaks. After 4.0 miles the trail moves left off the railbed. You can see the rails of the original line as the trail quickly returns to the railbed.

Just beyond 5.0 miles is a famous bridge trestle named Cold Springs Pegram Bridge. This frequently photographed icon is one of only ten

Trail users cross trestles over the Big Wood River.

known Pegram bridges still standing in the United States. Idaho is fortunate to have seven of the bridges, with two on the Wood River Trail. This one is a 208-foot single span that was first used by the Oregon Short Line to transport lead and zinc. Between 1936 and 1981, trains crossed this bridge as they shuttled skiers from California to Ketchum.

Rail bridges vary based on their unique truss designs, of which there are more than thirty variations. A truss is composed of structural triangles placed together with riveted or pinned connections. The Pegram truss is a blend between the Warren and Parker trusses.

Shortly after passing over the bridge, the trail goes through a tunnel under a road at the St. Luke's Wood River Medical Center, near 5.6 miles. Continue on the trail through another tunnel beneath ID 75.

From this point you will travel between the highway and residential areas, though the route has open views of the widening valley. Many side canyons enter from the east and west as you head toward the towns of Hailey and Bellevue beyond. Assortments of neighborhood and road access points present themselves, and you can use them to exit the trail

Nearby Attractions

Hiking, bicycling, fishing, camping, and skiing are but a few of the popular outdoor activities in this famous region. Spend some additional time enjoying the mountains.

• Sawtooth National Recreation Area (SNRA): This recreation area contains 756,000 acres of forested, mountainous terrain. The headquarters is located 8 miles north of Ketchum on ID 75. Call (208) 727-5013, or visit www. fs.usda.gov/sawtooth.

• Wood River Trail: Auxiliary to the 20-mile right-of-way paved trail are paved spurs linking to Sun Valley, Elkhorn, and East Fork, adding over 12 miles to the system. Harriman Trail: This trail features an 18-mile pathway between the Sawtooth National Recreation Area and the Galena Lodge Trail System.

• North Valley Trails Nordic Ski Trail System (Blaine County Recreation District Nordic Trail System): Comprising over 100 miles of moderate to difficult singletrack trails, the system includes Galena Lodge Trails and other trails in the Sawtooth National Recreation Area.

• Sun Valley Resort: This four-season destination offers easy access to area attractions including summer gondola rides and lift-assisted access to Baldy Mountain's designated downhill trails. Call (800) 786-8259, or visit www. sunvalley.com.

if you choose to. Avoid private roads if using informal parking for your vehicle.

Just past 7.0 miles you arrive at Gimlet Road. Consider stopping for a visit at the Sawtooth Botanical Garden, located on the west side of the trail. There's another bridge crossing at 7.6 miles. Along the way you will pass cottonwood trees and chokecherry bushes, and large homes set away from the trail. Shortly the Wood River comes into view at 7.7 miles, with the Boxcar Bend Overview just ahead.

Situated above the river, the overlook features interpretive signs describing local fishing regulations and how the area earned the name "Boxcar." Old railroad cars, vehicles, and ski gondolas were once used to prevent erosion of the river's bank; now modern techniques are used. Take the established path to the river's edge to enjoy a closer look at this water-way, or try some fishing.

As the trail approaches 8.0 miles, the valley spreads out as you travel between the river and the highway. To continue toward Hailey, take a left at about 8.5 miles when you come to a Y intersection in the trail. Go over the East Fork Road, and before you head south, read about the East Fork mines on the information sign. Neighborhood spur trails enter at the East Fork Road Trailhead.

Near 8.7 miles the trail runs beside a gravel portion of the original railbed, parallel to the 217-foot Gimlet Bridge, another Pegram-style trestle bridge. Trail users should stay on the paved trail and cross on the modern Anderson Bridge. Between the two bridges sits a little park with a shaded picnic table and an old-fashioned water pump with potable water. This area is also a fishing access trailhead.

After crossing the Anderson Bridge, start up the biggest hill on the trail, which shortly rejoins the railbed after the detour. At about 9.3 miles the route flattens and the trail moves away from the noise of the road. The valley widens, which results in the wind velocity increasing and moving up the valley during the afternoons.

Cross over Ohio Gulch Road after 10.0 miles. You can see the old railbed to your right. Between 10.0 and 13.0 miles the trail alternates between small road crossings, tiny ranches, vegetated areas, large homes, and the Valley Club private golf course.

By 13.0 miles you begin to enter the outskirts of the town of Hailey, passing a City of Hailey sign trailside at about 14.2 miles. While passing through residential areas, you may get whiffs of barbecues or laundry soap as the locals go about their daily lives.

The downtown area is only 4 blocks to your right if you want to stop for food and beverages. International cuisines greet the hungry traveler. Try Mexican, Thai, or fast food if you desire.

An established trailhead comes into view on the south side of Hailey at about 15.4 miles. The corner of Fox Acres Road and ID 75 serve as the location of the Blaine County Native Plant Arboretum. Take time to walk the short path and view native pine trees, fir trees, and berry plants. The site is the result of local students' efforts.

Continue south to Bellevue, passing the Friedman Memorial Airport, to the right. Travel by open fields and housing construction projects. The original railbed lies to your right, serving as a buffer between the trail and highway. Mourning doves and other birds can be seen along this rural stretch.

At about 17.7 miles you enter the north edge of Bellevue, and by 18.2 miles you are in Bellevue. If you go 1 block west from the trail, you can get on Main Street and find food and beverages nearby.

Numerous road crossings may slow your travel. No worries; it is a small town with an easy pace. At the south end of town you pass ranches with horses, and at 20.0 miles, the paved trail ends at Gannett Road. You will see the gravel path that is the railroad right-of-way that continues to US 20. It is used by runners, equestrians, motorized vehicles, ranch machinery, and snowmobiles.

More Rail Trails

 ## OLD BOISE, NAMPA, AND OWYHEE RAILBED TRAIL

Located at the fringe of the Morley Nelson Snake River Birds of Prey National Conservation Area, the 500-foot-long Guffey rail bridge at Celebration Park serves as a gateway to 475,000 acres of open sagebrush desert. Start by crossing the renovated rail bridge and continue upstream on dirt trails along the south side of the Snake River. The Union Pacific as well as other rail companies once owned the original railbed, known as the Stoddard Line. The old rail bridge was abandoned in 1948, and Celebration Park purchased it in 1989. The park renovated the bridge for foot traffic. This historic icon, built in 1897, is used by recreationists to access motorized and nonmotorized trails in the conservation area. Bridge Trail, located along the river's north side, links to the visitor center parking area. Be sure to stop at the education center at Celebration Park, Idaho's only archaeological park. Consider refreshing yourself after your park visit at the tasting rooms of local wineries off ID 44.

Activities:

Location: Near Melba, in Canyon County

Length: A 500-foot-long rail bridge accesses the trail system in the Morley Nelson Snake River Birds of Prey National Conservation Area.

Surface: Wooden boards on bridge, dirt trails in conservation area

Wheelchair access: The decked bridge is wheelchair-accessible.

Difficulty: The bridge crossing is easy. Trails in the conservation area are easy to moderate.

Food: Food services in the town of Melba include a cafe at the supermarket and a bar that serves hot cooked food.

Restrooms: There are restrooms at the main parking lot at Celebration Park.

Seasons: The trail can be used year-round.

Rentals: See appendix A for bicycle rentals in the Treasure Valley.

Contacts: Celebration Park, (208) 495-2745, https://www.canyonco.org/elected-officials/commissioners/parks-cultural-natural-resources/

Bus routes: None

Access and parking: To get to the Guffey Bridge at Celebration Park, take exit 35 off I 84 in Nampa. Reset trip meter and turn south onto North-side Boulevard. Travel approximately 0.9 mile to the intersection with 3rd Street South and stay in the middle lane. Continue through intersection as Northside Boulevard becomes North Yale Street. Continue 1.3 cumulative miles on North Yale Street to the T intersection with High Street. Veer left as North Yale Street becomes 7th Street South. Continue on 7th Street South a total of 1.9 miles from the interstate exit and turn right onto 12th Avenue South / ID 45. Drive south from Nampa for approximately 16 miles to Ferry Road. Turn left on Ferry Road (Western Heritage Historic Byway) and drive about 2 miles to a T intersection in the road. Turn right at the T onto Hill Road, which becomes Warren Spur Road. Continue following the byway signs. From the T, continue 2.1 miles to the cattle feedlot. There is a sign for Celebration Park. Turn right onto Sinker Road and drive about 2.7 miles to the Guffey Bridge, where there is a small pullover to the right. Begin your adventure at the bridge. GPS: N43 17.98' / W116 31.76'

To get to the large paved parking lot at Celebration Park, turn left at the bridge onto Hot Spot Lane and drive on the paved road into the parking lot.

R NORTHERN PACIFIC TRAIL

Traveling through deep forests and up a steady incline to Lookout Pass on the Idaho–Montana border, this trail on a dirt road is known for its remoteness, scenery, and potential wildlife sightings. It is a continuation of the Union Pacific Railroad that served the Silver Valley in Idaho. During winter it is a popular trail for snowmobiles. The town of Mullan is the start of the multiuse Northern Pacific Trail and the eastern terminus of the nonmotorized Trail of the Coeur d'Alenes.

Activities:

Location: Mullan, in Shoshone County

Length: 11.7 miles

Surface: Asphalt road, dirt, and gravel

Wheelchair access: The trail is wheelchair-accessible for the first 3 miles, where it is an asphalt rural road.

Difficulty: Moderate to difficult. There is a steep climb as the trail progresses to Lookout Pass.

Food: There is a restaurant in Mullan and food services at Lookout Pass Ski and Recreation Area.

Restrooms: There are restrooms at the Mullan Trailhead parking area, East Shoshone Park, and Lookout Pass Ski and Recreation Area.

Seasons: The trail can be used year-round. Snow may be on the trail late Oct to late May. During winter the trail is heavily used by snowmobiles. During other seasons you'll share the trail with occasional motorized vehicles.

Rentals: Mountain bike rentals available at the eastern terminus at Lookout Pass Ski and Recreation Area, (208) 744-1301, www.ridethehiawatha. com. See appendix A for additional rental options in northern Idaho.

Contacts: For trail information visit the Friends of the Coeur d'Alene Trails—Idaho Panhandle website, www.friendsofcdatrails.org.

Bus routes: None

Access and parking: To reach the western terminus in Mullan coming from western Idaho, take exit 68 off I-90. The off-ramp becomes River Street and practically puts you at the trailhead. Travel on River Street, driving toward the town of Mullan, which is visible from the exit. Take a left off River Street onto 2nd Street and turn right immediately into the parking lot. GPS: N47 28.14' / W115 48.03'

The trail begins at the eastern end of the parking area and starts as an asphalt road, which runs for about 3 miles, until just before East Shoshone Park. Follow the signs at each intersection to stay on the road/trail, which turns into a dirt and gravel road.

To reach the eastern terminus, head east on I-90 and take exit 0 at the Idaho–Montana border. Turn right off the ramp and right again into the Lookout Pass Ski and Recreation Area. Park in the large lot and look for the signs directing you onto the trail.

S YELLOWSTONE BRANCH LINE RAILROAD ROW TRAIL

Known for scenic views of rivers, wildlife, and mountain ranges, this trail runs on a railroad right-of-way through the Caribou-Targhee National Forest. It runs near the Mesa Falls Scenic Byway near the town of Ashton to Reas Pass at the Montana border. Visitors travel more than 5 miles along the Warm River, pass around a long tunnel, and cross the Henry's Fork of the Snake River. The Teton and Centennial Mountain Ranges are visible from the trail.

Activities:

Location: Ashton and Island Park, in Fremont County

Length: 38.2 miles, of which 3.0 miles are designated for nonmotorized trail use at the southern end between Warm River Campground and the Bear Gulch Trailhead

Surface: Gravel, except for a couple hundred yards of asphalt at the southern end initiating from the campground

Wheelchair access: There's a paved section a few hundred yards along the river, accessed from the Warm River Campground.

Difficulty: Easy

Food: Eateries can be found in Ashton and Island Park.

Restrooms: There are restrooms at the Bear Gulch Trailhead and the Warm River Campground.

Seasons: The trail can be used year-round. Beyond the 3.0-mile nonmotorized section, the trail is used by off-road vehicles in summer and snowmobiles in winter.

Rentals: None

Contacts: Caribou-Targhee National Forest, Ashton Ranger District, (208) 652-7442; Island Park Ranger District, (208) 558-7301; www.fs.usda.gov/ctnf

Bus routes: None

Access and parking: The southern nonmotorized segment is accessed at Warm River Campground by taking ID 47, the Mesa Falls Scenic Byway, 10 miles east out of Ashton. Turn right into the campground and go to the large parking area at the end of the road. GPS: N44 07.24' / W111 18.63'

To get to the trailhead at Bear Gulch, continue east on ID 47 for about 3 miles to the Bear Gulch pullout on the left side of the highway. This lot is plowed in winter and serves as the only access point during snow season. Many forest service roads pass over the trail; procure USDA Forest Service maps.

T VICTOR TO DRIGGS PATHWAY

Traveling beside the Teton Scenic Byway through a valley that measures 6,000 feet in elevation, the trail serves as a bicycle commuter route between the rural towns of Victor and Driggs. Located in eastern Idaho, this retired Union Pacific railbed offers a refreshing rural exercise option for residents and for visitors heading to Wyoming's Grand Targhee Resort. For the most awe-inspiring views of mountain ranges in the Caribou-Targhee National Forest, Jedediah Smith Wilderness Area, and Grand Teton range, head north to south. Future plans include connecting a 45-mile pathway between Victor and Ashton.

Activities:

Location: Victor to Driggs in Teton County

Length: 7.0 miles

Surface: Paved

Wheelchair access: At southern end in Victor

Difficulty: Easy

Food: In Victor and Driggs

Restrooms: Try at fuel stations and eateries.

Seasons: Trail is usable year-round.

Rentals: Bicycle rentals are found at Habitat, 18 North Main Street, Driggs, (208) 354-7669, www.ridethetetons.com.

Contacts: Teton County, www.tetoncountyidaho.gov; City of Victor, www.victorcityidaho.com; Caribou-Targhee National Forest, Teton Basin District Office, (208) 354-2312; Ashton Ranger District, (208) 652-7442; www.fs.usda.gov/ctnf.

Bus routes: Winter bus service between Driggs and Victor, https://www.grandtarghee.com/vacation-planning/teton-travel-options/shuttle-2/

Access and parking: Find the southern trailhead in Victor by taking US 26 east from Idaho Falls for approximately 46 miles to the intersection with ID 31 in Swan Valley, then turn left (northeast) onto ID 31. Travel 20.7 miles toward Victor to the junction of ID 31 and ID 33 in Victor, then turn left (north) onto ID 33. Travel 0.2 mile to Cedron Road / 8000 S. and turn left, then immediately right on S. 500 W. The trailhead parking lot is on the right, clearly visible from ID 33. GPS: N43 36.42' / W111 06.68'

Start from the parking lot near the kiosk and continue north to the Moose Creek trailhead near Driggs, crossing several access roads en route. Use caution when crossing intersections.

Access the northern trailhead at Moose Creek near Driggs by driving 6.7 miles northward from the Victor trailhead on ID 33 toward Driggs. Turn left (west) into the large gravel lot next to Teton Creek just before the "Entering Driggs" sign and bridge crossing on ID 33. Take the wooden stairs onto the trail and turn left (south) onto the trail.

U ASHTON-TETONIA TRAIL

Gain a sense of a railroad used for agriculture transport and for passenger trains on this rural, open-range route. Views of distant peaks in the Teton Range, ranch land, and retired Pillsbury and General

Mills grain elevators dot this rugged gravel trail. Remoteness sets the tone for a Western-style adventure near the Teton Scenic Byway. Travel on the retired Teton Valley Branch of the Union Pacific Railroad, passing through defunct towns including Felt, Judkins, Lamont, France, Drummond, and Grainville. Identify the towns by the old buildings scattered along the trail. Follow the trail from one retired grain elevator to another, descending 790 feet in elevation from south to north. Cross trestles at Bitch Creek, Conant Creek, and Fall River. The Ashton-Tetonia Trail ultimately will connect with the Greater Yellowstone Trail regional network.

Activities:,

Location: Tetonia and Ashton, in Teton and Fremont Counties

Length: 29.6 miles

Surface: Gravel/dirt

Wheelchair access: No

Difficulty: Moderate to difficult, with loose thick gravel in places and possible detour onto dirt road and highway

Food: In Tetonia and Ashton

Restrooms: Flush toilets are at Ruby Carson Memorial Park, just north of the Ashton-Tetonia Trailhead on Egbert Avenue. There is a vault toilet at Judkins Trailhead and at Marysville Trailhead near Ashton.

Seasons: Year-round, though you may share the trail with snowmobiles in the winter and ATVs in summer.

Rentals: Bicycle rentals are found at Habitat, 18 North Main Street, Driggs, (208) 354-7669, www.ridethetetons.com.

Contacts: Idaho Department of Parks and Recreation–Harriman State Park, (208) 558-7368, www.parksandrecreation.idaho.gov; Ashton Chamber of Commerce, https://ashtonidaho.com; Fremont County, https://www.co.fremont.id.us/departments/parks_rec/biking.htm; Caribou-Targhee National Forest, Teton Basin Ranger District, (208) 354-2312; Ashton Ranger District, (208) 652-7442; www.fs.usda.gov/ctnf.

Bus routes: None

Access and parking: Trailheads are marked with "Ashton-Tetonia Trail" and "Idaho State Parks and Recreation" signs. To start on the trail's official southern terminus at 6,064 feet elevation at the Ashton-Tetonia Trailhead, take ID 33 east from Rexburg. Go approximately 40 miles, passing through the town of Tetonia (Gateway to the Tetons) to the intersection south of town at N. 3000 W. / W. 3000 N., south of the gasoline station. Turn right and go 0.1 mile to Egbert Avenue. Turn right on Egbert Avenue and continue 0.2 mile to the right turn into the Ashton-Tetonia Trailhead parking area. GPS: N43 48.67' / W111 09.91'

The trailhead starts at the north end of the parking area. From there, you'll head north toward the Marysville trailhead. (**Note:** In Tetonia near the southern terminus, you will see road signs indicating "Ruby Carson Memorial Park" and "Ashton-Tetonia Trail," indicating another trailhead located on the west side of ID 33 with restroom access.)

Access the northern terminus at Marysville near Ashton by heading west from Tetonia on ID 33. Turn right onto ID 32. Follow ID 32 north to the intersection of ID 47, passing the Felt, Judkins, Lamont, France, and Grainville trailheads on the east side of ID 32. Turn right onto ID 47 and continue 0.6 miles to the Marysville trailhead located on your left at 5,277 feet elevation, indicated by the red train boxcar and a vault toilet.

APPENDIX A: RENTAL INFORMATION

WASHINGTON

Western Washington

Bicycles

Electric & Folding Bikes Northwest
4810 17th Ave. NW
Seattle, WA 98107
(206) 547-4621
www.electricvehiclesnw.com

Evo Seattle
3500 Stone Way N.
Seattle, WA 98103
(206) 973-4470
www.evo.com

Recycled Cycles
1007 NE Boat St.
Seattle, WA 98105
(206) 547-4491
www.recycledcycles.com

Ride Bicycles Bike Shop
160 NW Gilman Blvd. #102
Issaquah, WA 98027
(425) 961-9061
www.ridebicycles.com

Bothell Ski & Bike
8020 NE Bothell Way
Kenmore, WA 98028
(425) 486-3747
www.bikesale.com

Bicycles and Kayaks

Adventures through Kayaking
2358 West Highway 101
Port Angeles, WA
(360) 417-3051
www.atkayaking.com

Snowshoes

REI
222 Yale Ave. N.
Seattle, WA 98109
(206) 470-4020
https://www.rei.com/stores/rentals

Eastern Washington

Bicycles

B & L Bicycles
219 East Main St.
Pullman, WA 99163
(509) 332-1703
http://bandlbicycles.com

Spoke 'N Sport
212 N. Division St.
Spokane, WA 99202
(509) 838-8842
http://spokensportinc.net

OREGON

Bicycles

Banks Bike Repairs and Rentals
14175 NW Sellers Rd.
Banks, OR 97106
(503) 680-3269
https://www.banksbikes.com/

Bikes and Beyond
125 9th St.
Astoria, OR 97103
(503) 325-2961
www.bikesandbeyond.com

Zack's Bikes
831 Main St.
Klamath Falls, OR 97601
(541) 851-9200
www.zacksbikes.com

Everybody's Bike Rentals and Tours
305 NE Wygant St.
Portland, OR 97211
(503) 358-0152
www.pdxbikerentals.com

IDAHO

Northern Idaho

Bicycles

Coeur d'Alene Bike Company–Kellogg
21 Railroad Ave.
Kellogg, ID 83837
(208) 786-3751
www.cdabikeco.com

Coeur d'Alene Bike Company–Coeur
d'Alene
314 N. 3rd St.
Coeur d'Alene, ID 83814
(208) 966-4022
www.cdabikeco.com

The Cycle Haus
100 N. Coeur d'Alene Ave.
Harrison, ID 83833
(208) 689-3436
www.thecyclehaus.com

Lookout Pass Ski and Recreation Area
I-90, exit 0
Mullan, ID 83843
(208) 744-1301
www.ridethehiawatha.com

Silver Mountain Sports Shop
Silver Mountain Resort
110 Morningstar Dr.
Kellogg, ID 83837
(866) 344-2675
www.silvermt.com

Bicycles, Cross-Country Skis, and
Snowshoes

Vertical Earth
1323 East Sherman Ave.
Coeur d'Alene, ID 83814
(208) 667-5503
www.verticalearth.com

Latah County

Bicycles

Paradise Creek Bicycles
513 South Main St.
Moscow, ID 83843
(208) 882-0703
https://paradisecreekbicycles.com/

Cross-Country Skis and Snowshoes

University of Idaho Outdoor Program
Outdoor Rental Center
Student Recreation Center
1000 Paradise Creek St.
Moscow, ID 83844-1230
(208) 885-6170
https://www.uidaho.edu/current-
students/recwell/outdoor-program/
rental-center

Valley County

Bicycles, Cross-Country Skis, and
Snowshoes

Gravity Sports
503 Pine St.
McCall, ID 83638
(208) 634-8530
www.gravitysportsidaho.com

Home Town Sports
300 E. Lenora St.
McCall, ID 83638
(208) 634-2302
www.hometownsportsmccall.com

Boise

Bicycles

Eastside Cycles
3072 S. Bown Way
Boise, ID 83706
(208) 344-3005
www.rideeastside.com

McU Sports
822 W. Jefferson St.
Boise, ID 83702
(208) 342-7734
www.mcusports.com

Bicycles, Cross-Country Skis, and
Snowshoes

Idaho Mountain Touring
1310 W. Main St.
Boise, ID 83702
(208) 336-3854
www.idahomountaintouring.com

Blaine County

Bicycles

Peter Lane's Mountain Sports at River
Run Plaza
Sun Valley Resort
520 Serenade Ln.
Ketchum, ID 83340
(208) 622-6123
www.sunvalley.com

Peter Lane's Mountain Sports at Sun
Valley Village
Sun Valley Resort
1 Sun Valley Rd.
Sun Valley, ID 83353
(208) 622-2279
www.sunvalley.com

Bicycles, Cross-Country Skis, and
Snowshoes

The Elephant's Perch
280 East Ave.
Ketchum, ID 83340
(208) 726-3497
http://elephantsperch.com

Sturtevants
340 N. Main St.
Ketchum, ID 83340
(208) 726-4512
http://sturtevants-sv.com

Sturtevants–Limelight Hotel
151 S. Main St.
Ketchum, ID 83340
(208) 726-0898
http://sturtevants-sv.com

Sturtevants
1 W. Carbonate St.
Hailey, ID 83333
(208) 788-7847
http://sturtevants-sv.com

Cross-Country Skis and Snowshoes

Backwoods Mountain Sports
711 N. Main St.
Ketchum, ID 83340

(208) 726-8818
www.backwoodsmountainsports.com

Eastern Idaho

Bicycles

Habitat High Altitude Provisions
18 N. Main St.
Driggs, ID 83422
(208) 354-7669
www.ridethetetons.com

APPENDIX B: ORGANIZATIONS FOR ADVOCACY, EDUCATION, AND INFORMATION

Adventure Cycling Association
PO Box 8308
MIssoula, MT 59807
(800) 755-2453
www.adventurecycling.org

Bike Works
3709 S. Ferdinand St.
Seattle, WA 98118
(206) 725-8867
http://bikeworks.org

Cascade Bicycle Club and Washington Bikes
7787 62nd Ave. NE
Seattle, WA 98115
(206) 522-3222
www.cascade.org

Cycle University
www.cycleu.com

Evergreen Mountain Bike Alliance
249 Main Ave. S., Ste. 107-188
North Bend, WA 98045
(206) 524-2900
www.evergreenmtb.org

Friends of the Coeur d'Alene Trails
www.friendsofcdatrails.org

Friends of the Weiser River Trail
https://weiserrivertrail.org

Great American Rail-Trail
www.greatamericanrailtrail.org

International Mountain Bicycling Association (IMBA)
www.imba.com

The Intertwine Alliance
PO Box 14039
Portland, OR 97293
(503) 445-0991
http://theintertwine.org

Latah Trail Foundation
www.latahtrail.org

The League of American Bicyclists
1612 K St. NW, Ste. 1102
Washington, D.C. 20006
(202) 822-1333
www.bikeleague.org

Moscow Area Mountain Bike Association
www.mambatrails.org

Mountain Bike the Tetons
www.mountainbiketetons.org

North Idaho Centennial Trail Foundation
www.northidahocentennialtrail.org

Pullman Civic Trust—Bill Chipman Palouse Trail
https://www.pullmancivictrust.org/trails

Rails-to-Trails Conservancy
The Duke Ellington Building
2121 Ward Ct. NW, 5th Floor
Washington, DC 20037
(202) 331-9696
www.railstotrails.org
www.traillink.com

Skate Northwest

www.skatenw.com

Southwest Idaho Mountain Biking
Association
www.swimba.org

Valley County Pathways
www.valleycountypathways.org

Washington Bikes
(206) 522-3222
http://wabikes.org

Washington Trails Association
www.wta.org

ABOUT THE AUTHOR

Natalie L. Bartley has resided in this region since the early 1980s. She landed in Idaho for an outdoor program manager job after completing her doctorate in parks, recreation, and leisure services at the University of Utah. She has more than 900 magazine and newspaper articles to her credit, and is author of the FalconGuide *Best Easy Day Hikes Boise*. Natalie is a certified ski instructor, registered yoga teacher, and a member of the Outdoor Writers Association of America and the Northwest Outdoor Writers Association. When not working as a freelance writer, she hikes, mountain-bikes, white-water kayaks, skate-skis, and explores the outdoors with her human and canine friends.

Photo Courtesy of Donald E. Pribble